Critical Essays on
Sylvia Plath

Critical Essays on Sylvia Plath

Linda W. Wagner

G. K. Hall & Company • Boston, Massachusetts

Copyright © 1984 by Linda W. Wanger
All Rights Reserved

Library of Congress Cataloging in Publication Data
Main entry under title:

Critical essays on Sylvia Plath

 (Critical essays on American literature)
 Includes index.
 1. Plath, Sylvia — Criticism and interpretation —
Collected works.   I. Wagner, Linda Welshimer.   II. Series.
PS3566.L27Z631984   811'.54   83-26562
ISBN 0-8161-8682-0

CRITICAL ESSAYS ON AMERICAN LITERATURE

This series seeks to anthologize the most important criticism on a wide variety of topics and writers in American literature. Our readers will find in various volumes not only a generous selection of reprinted articles and reviews but original essays, bibliographies, manuscript sections, and other materials brought to public attention for the first time. Linda Wagner's volume on Sylvia Plath is a welcome addition to our list in that it is the most substantial collection of scholarship yet assembled on this important writer. Among the selections are reprinted articles and reviews by M.L. Rosenthal, Peter Davison, Peter Porter, Laurence Lerner, Nancy Milford, and Marjorie Perloff. In addition, there is an important new introduction by Linda Wagner that provides a history of Plath scholarship as well as original essays by Sandra M. Gilbert, Melody Zajdel, and Roberta Mazzanti. We are confident that this collection will make a permanent and significant contribution to American literary study.

Northeastern University   JAMES NAGEL, GENERAL EDITOR

To Doug, Tom, and Andrea

*My life has been in my poems. To make them
I have broken my life in a mortar, as it were. . .*

William Butler Yeats
(*Letters*, p. 84, 1888)

CONTENTS

INTRODUCTION

With the awarding of the 1982 Pulitzer Prize for Poetry to Sylvia Plath's *The Collected Poems*, the proof of the power of Plath's art finally won out — over all the detractors, the enviers, the death-mongers. Had Plath been only a suicidal poet, writing in a narrow and obsessively limited voice, the poems in *The Collected Poems* would have been correspondingly limited. Instead, the book is a remarkably varied collection, filled with poems comparable to other poetic landmarks of the 1950s — work by Eberhart, Wilbur, Hoffman, Simpson — as well as with Plath's own brilliant 1960s poems that broke through her tendency to imitate and allowed her to explore new directions for the continuing development of an already proficient and cunning craft.

The 274 poems in the collected volume show *why* Plath changed the direction of contemporary poetry — all poetry, not just poems written by women. They prove repeatedly that a versatile structure — the poet's ability to reflect mood in every nuance of the poem, from focusing image to single line formation to patterns of sound repetition — is more important than any prescriptive technique. And they show with even more surprising consistency how successful Plath was in shifting those structures, molding tone and pace and language to reflect the poem in its unique form — both tragic and comic — from the early "Resolve" and "Sow" to "Tulips," "Lady Lazarus," "The Jailer," and "The Edge." Called by a wide range of distinguished reviewers "the most important collected volume of the last twenty years," "a triumph of hard work and artifice," and "the most important book of poetry this year," *The Collected Poems* showed clearly that Plath was, indeed, "one of the most remarkable poets of her time."[1]

As Katha Pollitt concluded in a 1982 *Nation* review, "by the time she came to write her last seventy or eighty poems, there was no other voice like hers on earth."[2] The hallmark of the important modern poet is the distinctiveness of voice, the poet's full identity surging forth in all phases of the poem's expression. Pollitt's praise is, therefore, extraordinary. But, then, so is Plath's accomplishment. As George Steiner explained when he labeled Plath's poem "Daddy" "the Guernica of modern poetry": "It achieves the classic art of generalization, translating a private, obviously intolerable

1

hurt into a code of plain statement, of instantaneously public images which
concern us all." It is this move beyond the intimate, this ability to reach
others through the apparent recounting of the real, that makes Plath's late
poems so provocative. Steiner had written in his 1966 review of *Ariel*, "She
does the job of the poet as few today have done it—she makes her readers
feel the amplified sense of their humanity, which for our time involves shock
and loss and the flexible armors of frustration."[3]

Steiner's accurate assessment of Plath's powerful late work was not the
accepted critical view, however. Critics writing as recently as the 1980s
echoed the convenient term, "confessional," whenever they discussed
Plath's writing. In fact, partly because of its close association with the poetry of Plath, Sexton, Berryman and Lowell and with the suicides of the
first three poets, by the end of the 1970s the term had become almost completely pejorative.

In 1967, M. L. Rosenthal first used "confessional poetry" to describe
Robert Lowell's later poems, and what he saw as a turning inward in a
particularly self-revealing way. According to Rosenthal, Lowell was using
the *I* persona to designate the literal poet, not a mask or a voice for that poet
figure. Rosenthal paired Plath with Lowell, again because of what he saw
as her tactic of revealing in her poems the psychological vulnerability of the
poet persona, the poet self.[4] Rosenthal certainly meant to direct readers to a
crucial new direction in poetry; he did not intend to open the way for quick
dismissals of Plath's or Lowell's work. The quantity of criticism that appeared during the late 1960s and the 1970s about the "dangers" of the confessional mode, however, tended to subvert Rosenthal's sane intention.[5]

The best correctives to the view that Plath's poetry is so autobiographical as to somehow cross the line between art and self-indulgence (and, implicitly, between life and death / suicide) were essays by Ted Hughes,
Marjorie Perloff, Jon Rosenblatt, Sandra Gilbert, and—most completely—
M. D. Uroff (Margaret Dickie).[6] The crux of the re-definition lay in the
identity of Plath's *I* persona, and Uroff argues convincingly that Plath's
characters—though they may be real psychologically—consistently lack
though they may be real psychologically—consistently lack "particularity."

> They are generalized figures, not real-life people, types that Plath manip-
> ulates dramatically in order to reveal their limitations. . . . From her
> earliest madwomen and hysterical virgins to the late suicides and father-
> killers, Plath portrays characters whose stagey performances are subver-
> sions of the creative act. Absorbed in their rituals, they confess nothing.
> They are not anxious to make a breakthrough back into life.

Uroff concludes that Plath's characters—although not the poet-self—
are real enough to be credible because of Plath's understanding of the human psyche in extremis, and because of her skill in creating poems that
convince the reader:

Plath controlled her own terrifying experiences in her poetry . . . by creating characters and later speakers who demonstrate the way in which the embattled mind operates. Far from speaking for the poet, they stage crazy performances which are parodic versions of the imaginative act. . . . [Plath] chose to deal with her experience by creating characters who could not deal with theirs and through their rituals demonstrate their failure. These poems, like the speakers in them, are superbly controlled; but the poet behind the poem uses her immense technical control to manipulate the tone, the rhythm, the rhyme, the pace of the speakers' language in order to reveal truths about the speakers that their obsessive assertions deny.[7]

John Romano, in a 1974 *Commentary* essay, had made somewhat the same point when he insisted "The poem 'Lady Lazarus' is, in the end, not autobiographical enough: it tells us something about how much she suffers, and less about how, and nothing about why."[8] For Barbara Hardy, Plath's work is best understood using the terms *derangement* and *enlargement*: "The poetry constantly breaks beyond its own personal cries of pain and horror, in ways more sane than mad, enlarging and generalizing the particulars, attaching its maladies to a profoundly moved and moving sense of human ills." When Hardy considers the poems that have usually been thought to be revealing of Plath's own mental state, she finds even those well within the bounds of artistic control.[9] And for Judith Kroll, whose important book *Chapters in a Mythology, The Poetry of Sylvia Plath* appeared in 1976, Plath's seemingly personal poetry is really just part of "a timeless mythic system." Her reliance on myth — in its varieties and richness — tends to transmute her personal concerns into something impersonal. Kroll sees Plath's interest in death and rebirth as part of her larger fascination with the mythic problem of rebirth or transcendence: "nearly everything in her poetry contributes either to the statement or to the envisioned resolution of this problem."[10]

Whether these critics approach Plath's poems from a structural perspective, a mythic, or that of characterization, they agree that Plath's art, as expressed in her poetry, should be the focus of the reader's attention and of the critic's exploration. Any survey of the history of the criticism of Plath's writing shows repeatedly this dichotomy between such critics — structuralist, mythic, linguistic — and those readers who employ the confessional, art-equated-with-madness perspective.

This range of critical reaction — and the heat that reaction has generated — suggests that Plath's poetry is more important to contemporary poetics than some critics would have us believe. I have been reminded — during these past twenty years that the critical battle about Plath has been waged — of the similar tone of opinion that existed about the writing of William Carlos Williams (at least from the 1920s into the 1950s).

The poems of both Williams and Plath strike readers as being different — perhaps threateningly different — from existing, accepted poetry. Williams cast off a great many poetic conventions as he tried to reach the center of the commonplace American experience — which was also his personal experience. In Williams' phrase "No ideas but in things," he echoed John Dewey's aesthetic, that the artist could reach the universal only through the particular. Again and again, Williams as persona — the doctor-poet of New Jersey — appeared at the center of his poems. And the Williams persona spoke a language (the "American idiom") that readers found either disarming or insulting. Unsympathetic critics noted repeatedly that Williams' language was not "poetic"; and the same critics would often ask, in fact, were Williams' "poems" even poems?

Critical reaction to Plath's work has taken some of these same paths. She has been criticized for abandoning techniques, only to prove that she was inventing new — but equally effective — poetic tactics. For Plath, the creation of commonplace experience had, of necessity, to be a female experience; but it was no less authentic in its gender-based domesticity. In fact, Plath the housewife shares much experience with Williams the physician — and the very non-intellectual base of their common experiences may be one of the reasons for the lack of academic enthusiasm about both writers.

The sense of a human being, a speaker, dominates Plath's work as well as Williams'; and calls attention to the marvels of characterizing idiom she was able to wrench into most of her late poems. For each writer, the poem was the only means of raising the objects and emotions of life to art. But Plath and Williams would also have agreed on the premise that the materials of that art *had* to come from one's real life — and that the poet had the responsibility of choosing which details and emotions would transform into effective art. The "eye" that Plath developed during her last months was very similar to Williams' sense of focus and timing — what Ezra Pound called his "perfect pitch." They are both poets readers have come to stand in awe of.

There is one distinction that should be made, however. Plath had learned a great deal from the modernists, especially from Eliot, Roethke, Stevens, Yeats, and Dylan Thomas,[11] so that the concrete imagist method was one of her poetic bases. But while these poets, and Williams in particular, had moved beyond the didactic to the catalyzing of pure experience through a concentration on the objective, the catching of the thing, pure, removed from the rationalizations of life, Plath did more: she infused those objects with a sense of her own life and emotion. The object that was so important to some strands of modernist art was in the Plath canon not, by itself, enough. Alone, it could not convey the whole. There are no red wheelbarrows in Plath's writing. There are balloons, bees, gardens — but they exist in peopled surroundings. The modernist object has become an artifact of a culture, an artifact rather than an object because we as readers are more interested in what is being done with the object than just the fact that the object exists. Our complete attention falls on the characterization within the poem, on what the character is able to do with the object in question. Plath has, then, succeeded in removing the sterility inherent in Williams' "No ideas but in things" as she has shifted the reader's focus from object to persona.

Luckily for Williams, he outlived most of his detractors. (He lived to be nearly eighty, writing and publishing more than forty books before his death.) The situation with Plath's reception is more precarious, however, partly because there will be no more writing to evaluate—giving hostile critics the opportunity to change their minds; and partly because the reasons her poems threaten readers are less easily acknowledged. When Ellen Moers wrote in *Literary Women* that "No writer has meant more to the current feminist movement,"[12] that paean was a mixed blessing. Plath as feminist, Plath as woman writer, Plath as suicide—the designations that are accurate in a number of contexts are also threatening to readers and critics from established, usually male and often traditional, backgrounds. Given these difficulties with polarizations of readers, Plath's reputation has still continued to grow and to be enhanced by critical opinion. And one of the most important reasons for this enhancement has been the consistent praise of her work by other writers. Regardless of gender, race, or position, fellow poets have been the chief supporters of Plath's work.

Louis Simpson in 1978, *A Revolution in Taste*: "This was how Sylvia Plath began—the wonder is that she changed into a true poet. The poet of *Ariel* seems to mean what she says. 'Seems,' because she is writing poetry—the meaning of a poem is never literal, it is always a fiction of some kind. The 'seeming' consists of a passion for words. The poet of *Ariel* is filled with a passion for words. . . . Writing of this kind does not depend on mythology—it is original. This is why Sylvia Plath is such an important poet: she 'transcends' *The Golden Bough* and *The White Goddess* just as she transcends her personal history."[13]

And this is Anne Sexton: "not that her lines reminded me of Roethke—but the openness to metaphor, the way they both have (and Sylvia even more so in her last work) of jumping straight into their own image and then believing it. No doubt of it—at the end, Sylvia burst from her cage and came riding straight out with the image-ridden-darer, Roethke. . . . Her poems do their own work. . . . What matters is her poems. These last poems stun me. They eat time."[14]

This, Ted Hughes: "In a poet whose development was as phenomenal as hers, the chronological order of the poems is an important help to understanding them. Most readers will perceive pretty readily the single centre of power and light which her poems all share, but I think it will be a service if I point out just how little of her poetry is 'occasional,' and how faithfully her separate poems build up into one long poem. . . . In her, as with perhaps few poets ever, the nature, the poetic genius and the active self, were the same."[15]

This, Rochelle Ratner: "By the time she began writing the poems that later formed *Ariel*, Plath had craft at her fingertips. . . . Her observations are precise; from the specific to the imaginative is just one giant step. As always, Plath takes that step so smoothly that her images startle the reader who hasn't been paying close attention."[16]

And this, Dave Smith:

> Poetry kept Sylvia Plath alive; her poems are ectoplasmic with the will to live, to be as right as poetry can be, to be unequivocally, seriously, perfectly the voice of the poem as magical as a heartbeat. That is a burden no poet can bear forever, and it surprises any poet who bears it at all. . . . During those six years Plath had learned to write what would be her poem, the poem which was unlike any other, the poem Ted Hughes and others call the Ariel poem. . . . it is not suicide that interests her but the ebb and surge of passion. It has to be sexual and has to feel total.
>
> Plath did not, of course, come to the Ariel poem without labor. *The Collected Poems* shows as none of her single volumes do the chorus of voices she had been hearing: Stevens, Ransom, Roethke, Eliot, Hardy, Hopkins, some Frost and Robinson, of course Shakespeare, even a little William Carlos Williams and not a little Emily Dickinson. They were mostly the hard chargers, the stress makers with swift, clattering boots. Ted Hughes may have been responsible for reinforcing this direction but Plath's pre-Hughes juvenilia proves she was no sweet singer ever. Evanescence wasn't enough for her; she had to be the flame and the radiance. . . .[17]

Luckily for Plath, many of the reviews of her collections were written by poets. Partly for that reason, a critical profile of Plath as writer is generally positive. From her first collection of poems, *The Colossus* in 1960, through the 1982 publication of Plath's journals, critical response was, at the worst, mixed. Comments made about *The Colossus*, for example, include high praise from Geoffrey Dearmer ("The book is a revelation suitcase, bulging, always accurate, humour completely unforced . . .") and John Wain, who also finds humor in the collection ("Sylvia Plath writes clever, vivacious poetry, which will be enjoyed most by intelligent people capable of having fun with poetry and not just being holy about it. Miss Plath writes from phrase to phrase as well as with an eye on the larger architecture of the poem"); and more tempered enthusiasm from Ian Hamilton, Richard Howard, and Roy Fuller.

Hamilton's chief reservation about what he calls her "clever, remarkably sophisticated first volume" is that there are very few fully realized poems, partly because the traces of Plath's borrowings (from Stevens, Roethke, and Marianne Moore) are clearly present. Howard finds her work witty and skillful, but not yet her own; and Fuller — while he enjoys her cleverness — also wonders about her eventual originality. "How excited we would be about Miss Plath if we — and she — had never read Mr. Ransom and Miss Moore. Or if she were 23 and not 28. No experience seems, as yet, to have drawn out other than this controlled and rather ventriloquial voice: too many poems have no other point than their own skill."[18]

Other critics were less approving, but they remained in the minority. William Dickey objected to Plath's narrow range of tone, as did Reed Whittemore, who began his review by identifying Plath as "Mrs. Ted Hughes." Thomas Blackburn did more than identify her; he begins his comments with "It is difficult not to think of Ted Hughes" when reading a Plath poem like "Sow." He continues to make the comparison even more derogatory by qualifying: "Not that her work is in any sense derivative, but that these two poets often share the same vision." Vision may be similar, but Blackburn objects, in the case of Plath's poems, to her "rather baffling obliqueness" and imagery which "tends to get out of hand."[19]

When M. L. Rosenthal writes his retrospective review about the earlier publications of this collection, in 1967, he summarizes the reviews contemporary with the 1960 appearance of *The Colossus* as having emphasized her "academic precisionism. Except for a few poems whose bitter, concentrated force made them unlike the rest, her work seemed 'craft-centered' and a bit derivative."[20] Such a summary may be accurate, but for a beginning poet, faced with such reviews as these on the publication of a first collection, such general approbation was most likely heady. Plath was well reviewed on both sides of the Atlantic, and had she stayed alive to see the reviews of her second book, *The Bell Jar*, published under the pseudonym of Victoria Lucas (and only in England) in January of 1963, she would have been even more pleased.

Three of the novel's earliest reviews (January of 1963) were surprisingly positive. Robert Taubman called *The Bell Jar* a "clever first novel," "the first feminine novel . . . in the Salinger mood" (the comparison with Salinger's *Catcher in the Rye* occurred frequently, both in the British reviews of the 1960s and the American reviews of the early 1970s, when the novel finally appeared, under Plath's name, in an American edition). Laurence Lerner made no comparisons and, seemingly, had no reservations. He called the novel "a brilliant and moving book," triumphing in both language and characterization. Rupert Butler too found the novel "astonishingly skillful," "honest," "intensely interesting," "brave," and "terribly likeable."[21]

Later reviews were written about the novel as *Plath*'s work, not Victoria Lucas's; and were shadowed with the facts of both Plath's suicide (February 11, 1963) and the posthumous publication, in 1965, of *Ariel*, the first collection of the late poems. Most reviewers saw parallels between the novel and the later poems, and many thought the fiction inferior to the poetry. In his 1966 editorial, C. B. Cox praised *The Bell Jar* as an "extremely disturbing narrative" which made "compulsive reading," and then connected it with the poetry: "The novel seems a first attempt to express mental states which eventually found a more appropriate form in the poetry. But throughout there is a notable honesty," and the same "fierce clarity so terrifying in the great poems in *Ariel*."[22]

Rosenthal, too, writing in the *Spectator*, spoke of the novel's "magnificent sections whose candour and revealed suffering will haunt anyone's memory." He then continued into a vein which has become a touchstone for criticism about much of Plath's work, the cultural alienation — and resulting frustration — of the talented young woman. Rosenthal speaks of "the sense of having been judged and found wanting for no externally discernible reason, and the equally terrifying sense of great power gone to waste or turned against oneself."[23] Patricia Meyer Spacks takes that tactic in her 1972 *Hudson Review* essay, when she calls the novel a good survey of the limited possibilities for women:

> the sensibility expressed is not dismissable. The experience of the book is that of electrocution. . . . Female sexuality is the center of horror: babies in glass jars, women bleeding in childbirth, Esther herself thrown in the mud by a sadist, hemorrhaging after her single sexual experience. To be a woman is to bleed and burn. . . . Womanhood is entrapment, escaped from previously by artistic activity, escaped from surely only by death.[24]

Lucy Rosenthal, writing in the *Saturday Review*, compares *The Bell Jar* to Joan Didion's *Play It As It Lays*, but points out that "the Plath mode is gentler." She praises the novel as "a deceptively modest, uncommonly fine piece of work . . . in its own right a considerable achievement. It is written to a small scale, but flawlessly — an artistically uncompromising, witty account."[25] Juxtaposed to these reviews should come Melvin Maddocks' caustic note that he finds the first half of the novel "Bobbsey Twins on Madison Avenue, gradually being disenchanted"; and the second half, hardly related to the first, "less a contrast than a discontinuity." Martha Duffy, however, reviewing for *Time*, points out that the novel, eight years after its initial publication in England, is an American best seller; and refers to its "astonishing immediacy." Simultaneous with these American reviews in the early 1970s came Tony Tanner's opinion in his 1971 *City of Words, American Fiction 1950–1970* that *The Bell Jar* was "perhaps the most compelling and controlled account of a mental breakdown to have appeared in American fiction," "a very distinguished American novel."[26]

While criticism about the novel has continued, and discussion of Plath's work seldom omits *The Bell Jar*, most of her reviewers and critics continue to think of her as primarily a poet. (That such an assessment may be erroneous will be discussed later.) The reviews of her major collection, *Ariel*, accordingly marked the beginning of her present critical reputation. John Malcolm Brinnin set the tone of American reviewers when he claimed that she was "a marvel. . . . what we have here is not, as some bewildered critics have claimed, the death rattle of a sick girl, but the defiantly fulfilling measures of a poet. . . . If Sylvia Plath's performance were not so securely knowledgeable, so cannily devised, so richly inventive and so meticulously reined, it would be intolerable. Many of these poems are magnificent. . . ." Samuel F. Morse, too, in *Contemporary Literature* calls *Ariel* "an absolute achievement," and Derek Parker, in the English *Poetry Review*, admits "Criticism is disarmed, finally, by these poems . . . remarkable poems . . . immensely varied in tone." Parker points to Plath's ability to celebrate "life and her children, in some tender, loving and laughing poems," and notes that "one has the impression of a control so complete and natural that it never inhibits."

Praise came from even comparatively staid reviewers. Richard Tillinghast called *Ariel* "the most interesting new poetic development of recent years. . . . here nothing is wasted, everything is a diamond." He is particularly pleased with "the intensity, the economy, the emphasis on originality, the ability to combine seemingly unrelated things and to separate the expected combinations" — again, with Plath's craft as poet.[27]

So great was the response to the *Ariel* poems that critics writing even a few months later were quick to give warning about the confusion between art and myth. Hugh Kenner, writing in the first issue of *Triumph*, wondered at evidence of what he called "the strange need to play down the poems' art and mix up their nature with a tasteless Plath Legend to which readers can respond not as celebrants of a rhetoric but with the voyeur's intimate purity of participation." He emphasized the sheer talent, the poetic skill, the poems reveal ("Obviously no one is meant to wonder how much work-over the poems in *Ariel* received. My guess would be, a good deal"). Kenner finds Plath's ability to muster such consummate craft during such stressful, anguished times "the victory for which she deserves to be celebrated."[28]

Before the publications of the two later posthumous collections, *Crossing the Water* (1971) and *Winter Trees* (1972), what Kenner calls the Plath Cult was fully developed. Various publications since his epitaph for Plath's death (in the *Observer*, February 17, 1963) had given A. Alvarez a position of almost oracular importance concerning Plath's work and life. His many essays culminated in his often-quoted and excerpted book *The Savage God: A Study of Suicide*, published in 1971 in England and the following year in the States. Despite objections by the Hughes family, Alvarez continued his pronouncements about the destructive nature of such intense personal psychic explorations as he felt Plath had undertaken in her later writing. Many of the reviews of the later collections of poems, as well as of the American edition of *The Bell Jar*, try to balance the invidious image of Plath the suicidal, destructive and destroying woman with that of Plath as artist, mother, friend.

Helen Vendler, for example, in a *New York Times Book Review* essay on *Crossing the Water*, denies that Plath is "schizophrenic," claiming that "her sense of being several people at once never here goes beyond what everyone must at some time feel." She also deals with the issue of Plath's confessional tendencies, pointing out that Plath is seldom out of control. Plath never rages, Vendler contends:

> an undeniable intellect allegorizes the issues before they are allowed expression. Even in the famous "Daddy," the elaborate scheme of Prussian-

and-Jew has been constructed to contain the feelings of victimization, and the decade-by-decade deaths in "Lady Lazarus" are as neat a form of incremental repetition as any metaphysical poet could have wanted.[29]

With the perspicuity of hindsight, Robin Skelton finds the poems in *Crossing the Water* "perturbing" for their evidence of "neurotic self-absorption." Such sophistry leads to flawed structures, Skelton finds, and to "dangerous distortions" of philosophy. He does admit that she writes a "poetry of extreme verbal brilliance," using "imagery that is more vital and surprising than that of any other poet of her generation. . . . *Crossing the Water* goes some way towards beginning to justify the high reputation her work has already been given."[30]

Both Victor Kramer and Linda Ray Pratt stress the "transitional" nature of the poems in this collection, a label more misleading — now that Plath's poems have been arranged in *The Collected Poems* according to her dating of them — than was guessed at the time.[31] In reviews of both *Crossing the Water* and *Winter Trees*, critics attempt to sort out the patterns, and pieces, of the Plath career. Joyce Carol Oates, for example, notes that "it is evident that the bulk of *Winter Trees* does not constitute so finished a work as *Ariel* or *The Colossus*. Nevertheless," Oates continues, "the volume is fascinating in its preoccupation with formlessness, with dissolving, with a kind of premature posthumous disappearance of the poet's personality." Both Oates and Raymond Smith emphasize the importance of the radio play "Three Women," partly as a long coherent piece and partly for its subject matter, the views of three women in a maternity ward. Oates closes her brief review with the affirmation that Plath's poems maintain their "existential authority": "it seems incontestable to me that her poems, line by line, image by image, are brilliant."[32]

James Finn Cotter, writing in *America* about the neglect given most women poets, notices Plath's "spiritual dimension" in such poems as "Mystic," "Brasilia," and "Winter Trees." He finds her to be "a reflective poet," searching for answers that do not depend on clichés and easy definitions. For Jill Baumgaertner, *Winter Trees* is more distinctive because of its tone, "peppered with black humor and bitterness," although she too admires the complexity of "Three Women." What negative criticism exists of these latter collections seems to build on the premise of Plath as possessed poet, as when Roger Scruton remarks that, "In the later poetry we find no attempt to *say* anything. Images enter these later poems as particulars only, without symbolic significance, and however much the poet may borrow the emotional charge from distant and surprising sources . . . it is never with any hint of an intellectual aim. . . . we can feel moved by Sylvia Plath's obsessions without feeling any need to share in them."[33]

If criticism of Plath's later poems during the early 1970s could be characterized by a sense of dutifulness — critics having to take one side of the "possessed poet" argument, having to respond to the brilliance and energy of the poems themselves, the response that greeted *Letters Home, Corre-*

spondence 1950–1963, selected and edited with commentary by Aurelia Schober Plath (1975) was revitalized by firm convictions. Critics maligned Plath's mother for her role as editor (omitting sections, tempering the poet's evident anger, trying to disguise the real psychological problems). In fact, they seemed to disbelieve the Plath persona as it appeared in these hundreds of letters written from Smith College and the subsequent locations in England back to Mrs. Plath; and were ready to blame their own disbelief on any likely explanation.

Jo Brans' remarks are typical of many of the reviews: "we can learn very little of the Sylvia of the poetry, the only Sylvia in whom we can take a legitimate interest, from these letters. . . . the most consistent tone of the letters is bright insincerity, indicated by all kinds of giveaways to anyone conscious of style."[34] Brans also criticizes Aurelia Plath for her editing, although it later became clear that there were certain passages and letters that Ted Hughes would not give permission to reprint.

Other reviews were more solicitous of Mrs. Plath. Martha Duffy wrote with sympathy of the life of this truly sacrificing mother, and even attributed Plath's suicide to her distance from Mrs. Plath. Marjorie Perloff also defends the mother figure in *The Bell Jar*, saying "It will not do to think of Aurelia Plath as the 'Mrs. Greenwood' of *The Bell Jar*, that hopeless Polly-anna-Mother." Perloff makes some striking points in her review of *Letters Home*, among them that Plath "seems to be on an eternal treadmill: she *must* excel, she *must* be popular, she *must* decide. . . ." Perloff's conclusion, after reading the 400-odd letters of the collection, is that "Sylvia Plath had, in Laingian terms, no sense of identity at all." That, for Perloff, is the reason *Letters Home* traces "the American Dream Gone Sour," the bright, promising person, aimed at ostensible success, who fails in the most visible, futile way possible.[35]

The publication of these letters seemed to clarify many of the lines of argument about Plath and the Plath persona, even while reviewers were arguing about "the real Plath." Subsequent books of criticism, and even many essays, made use of the letters; and the relative merits of studies by Mary Lynn Broe and Jon Rosenblatt (published in 1980 and 1979, respectively) when compared with those by Eileen Aird (1973), Edward Butscher (1975), and David Holbrook (1976), seem to bear out the sense that something valuable was implicit in the process of reading Plath's letters.[36]

Publication of the more recent Plath work—*Johnny Panic and the Bible of Dreams, Short Stories, Prose and Diary Excerpts* (1979); *The Collected Poems* (1981); and *The Journals of Sylvia Plath* (1982) — has brought new perspectives and a new sense of culmination to critical response. Even before any of this publication, however, Plath held a position in contemporary poetry that seemed unassailable. As Michael Atkinson wrote in 1979, "she has passed into the pantheon of modern poetry; she exercises a strong and particular power over our contemporary imagination."[37]

From this given, reviewers approached even a mildly interesting collection like *Johnny Panic and the Bible of Dreams* with awe — or at least apprehension. It takes an established writer of both fiction and poetry like Margaret Atwood to speak candidly:

> It was a shock akin to seeing the Queen in a bikini to learn that Sylvia Plath, an incandescent poet of drastic seriousness, had two burning ambitions: to be a highly paid travel journalist and to be a widely published writer of magazine fiction. . . . To this end she slogged away in the utmost self-doubt and agony, composing more than 70 stories, most of which were never published, and filling notebooks with the details of what she thought of as real life. . . .
>
> On one level "Johnny Panic" is the record of an apprenticeship. It should bury forever the romantic notion of genius blossoming forth like flowers. Few writers of major stature can have worked so hard, for so long, with so little visible result. The breakthrough, when it came, had been laboriously earned many times over.[38]

Most reviewers tended to criticize the fiction, as does Lorna Sage, for its failure as fiction: "She is surprisingly inept at inventing structures, even ordinary plots, taking refuge instead in archaic, would-be wry, O. Henry 'twists' to rescue directionless narratives. Only four or five of the stories take on a full fictional identity." And for William Dowie, "There is a fastidious choice of vocabulary, a distinguished use of language conveying the moods that hang heavily over all her writing . . . there is remarkable control which is almost too tense."[39] The most positive criticism came from those critics who knew the Plath canon well, and could see the connections and interrelationships with her poems and with *The Bell Jar*. Douglas Hill calls the best of the work here "as indelibly distinctive" as Plath's best writing, and asks that readers appreciate the "flashes of intense vision" available in even the less successful stories. G. S. Fraser also writes an important review, praising Ted Hughes for his editing skills. Douglas Hill, in contrast, takes issue with Hughes (and with Aurelia Plath) for their monopoly with the Plath estate. His complaint will surface repeatedly in reviews of *The Collected Poems* and *The Journals of Sylvia Plath*:

> the question of when, how, and by whom Plath's works are to be edited and presented is now — as it has been for fifteen years — absolutely crucial. Even granted an inhuman amount of tact, taste, and impartiality, Sylvia Plath's mother and husband . . . ought not to have the exclusive responsibility of deciding what the world is to know of her. No wonder we have a legend on our hands.[40]

Aside from the issue of Plath's primary talent, and the quandary over editing and its various responsibilities, the publication of *Johnny Panic and the Bible of Dreams* created a nexus of useful criticism, for readers were once more invited to consider Plath as fiction writer. *The Bell Jar* gained

importance, viewed in the context of these countless other fictions: it became clear that Plath did, indeed, consider herself a prose writer as well as a
poet, even perhaps, a prose writer first.[41] As with any accomplished artist,
the insights gained from considering the oeuvre are incrementally valuable.
Part of the impetus for the excellent criticism of *The Collected Poems* in
1980 and 1981 may have been the new perspectives available from the consideration of Plath as short story writer.

Whatever the reason — whether it was the sheer excellence of the collection, as many critics have suggested; or the apprenticeship of critics who
had worked their ways through the earlier, separate publications of her
work — criticism of *The Collected Poems* was uniformly perspicacious. Seeing the poems in their chronological order brought many insights which had
been unavailable before, as when Philip Larkin emphasizes the change
from "poems of a prize pupil, crammed with invention" — as he characterizes Plath's early work — to the work in 1959. There, in such poems as "Suicide Off Egg Rock" and "The Ravaged Face," Larkin recognizes Plath's
distinctiveness, in both style and theme. These were the poems Plath referred to as "forthright." Once again, Larkin stresses the "jauntily impersonal" tone of Plath's best poems, and adds as coda to his review, "it is hard
to see how she was labelled confessional."[42]

Larkin's reading of Plath, however, remains that of her as neurotic, dis-
placed poet; and his ultimate reservations about her art hinge on whether or
not coming to know insanity is an appropriate theme for poetry. For Emily
Grosholz, writing in the *Hudson Review*, Plath's body of work ties repeatedly into the conflict between purity and debasement, and that conflict is
imaged in the roles of women and men. "Women, as the debased and subor-
dinate half of humanity, are typically branded as impure. . . . If men are
the proper version of humanity, then women are anomalous, something un-
clean and threatening which falls outside the norm. Plath grants her own
impurity. . . . Her poetic project, then, is to change somehow to a state of
purity." Grosholz points out, in conclusion, that Plath's various "strategies
of purification are inadequate taken alone, and, together, irreconcilable."[43]

Most reviewers concentrated on the power of the collected poems,
choosing work less frequently discussed to prove the real strength of Plath's
output. The previously-held notion that she was an "uneven" poet fell before the weight of the nearly 300 poems, many of them as fine as any work
published in this century. Realization grew that the somewhat sporadic
sense of her poems had probably been due to the piecemeal publication:
poems written within days of each other, tied together through repeated
images or themes, had been published in *Ariel* and *Winter Trees* and *Crossing the Water*, separated not only by text but by time. *The Collected Poems*
remedied many crucial difficulties.

Several of the reviews followed the pattern of William H. Pritchard's
New Republic comment, entitled, ironically, "An Interesting Minor Poet?"
Pritchard acknowledges that his assessment of Plath's work — until the

publication of the collected volume—had been an endorsement of Irving Howe's belittling "interesting but minor" categorization. He now considers her truly central, "an altogether larger and more satisfying poet" than he had thought previously; a poet to be studied and learned from, poem by poem, repeatedly.[44]

Just as Pritchard, echoing John Frederick Nims, stresses the lessons to be learned from all Plath's poems, not just the later ones, so Laurence Lerner sees the work as a continuum. He points out that poems in *The Colossus* might well have been included in *Ariel* (discounting the sense of rigid separation most critics believed existed between the two books), and that many of the *Ariel* poems are not the "wild" best-known pieces, but rather poems that "stand back a little," that work through "greater formality . . . half-rhymes and regular stanzas. . . . It undercuts at least one popular view of Sylvia Plath, that her early work is controlled, formal, even superficial, and the later poems make true contact with her anxieties, and so are imbued with a new power. There is some truth in this, but it should not be taken too rigidly."[45] Michael Hulse repeats this injunction, that *The Collected Poems* "is a corrective to many myths and misunderstandings." Hulse, writing one of the earliest reviews, in the *Spectator*, finds the characteristic Plath power in her best poems, and describes the origin of that power succinctly:

> Simplicity of language wedded to complexity of emotional perception: it is this that constitutes the origin of everything that is typical of Plath, from the shredded syntax to the startling, beautiful images.
>
> And it is this synthesis that has proved Plath's most inimitable asset. Hundreds of magazine poets have been ruined by too shallow an understanding of Plath, and the reason why so much post-Confessional poetry is bad is that probing of personal problems seems to so many the easy way to write an instant poem. Plath knew better. Her distinctive authority derives from her stern, almost harsh insistence on submitting the responses of the emotions to the scrutiny of the intellect. . . .[46]

The 1982 publication of the excerpted *Journals* preceded by only a few weeks her being awarded the Pulitzer Prize for Poetry, for *The Collected Poems*. Many reviews of the *Journals* include mention of that major prize; most of those reviews were colored with a sense of the waste of Plath's life, and a recognition of the anguish evident throughout her mature life, not only the last year.

For Marni Jackson, the journals express Plath's "vulnerability. Not only is the writer's love of the world here, but so is the fearful '50s woman driven to be everything to everyone. . . . She managed . . . but in her own mind she was always falling short. Her private writing is one long ache of self-recrimination." Jackson points out, too, the bursts of "radiant well-being," the thirst for life and experience. But as Nancy Milford notes in her review, full self-expression as a woman is at odds with being someone's wife, and

Plath's journals chart long years of that dilemma. As Milford describes the pervasive themes: "the twin thrusts of sex and vocation, which are, unfortunately for her, linked to idealized domesticity and female dependence." And in the words of Le Anne Schreiber, in another *New York Times* review, Plath's "pagan relish for life" was all but subsumed in her fears that her "true deep voice" will never speak. Schreiber finds that late-poem voice intermittently in the journal entries, and notes,

> The irony is that the voice she was looking for . . . is present in these diaries from the beginning. In a raw state, to be sure. And only fitfully. But while she was looking to D. H. Lawrence, Dylan Thomas, Theodore Roethke and, of course, Mr. Hughes, and practicing a kind of ventriloquism that made her doubt her talent and even her existence, her own voice was pouring itself out in these journals. [47]

Several reviewers also stress the record of the apprenticeship Plath served as writer, and Walter Clemons finds that emphasis one of the most important of the collection. "The revelation of how unremittingly she works makes this a book I recommend to any aspiring writer, particularly to a novice who thinks of Plath as a special case — a star clothed in the glamour of suicide . . . the journals help us appreciate the protracted, hard-working apprenticeship that led to her final blazing utterance." [48]

In 1946, when Plath had just turned fourteen and was in the ninth grade, her diary entries include several poems copied out entire — among them, Sandburg's "Fog" and Sara Teasdale's "Late October." Following the Teasdale poem, Plath writes in her then characteristic, exclaiming style: "What I wouldn't give to be able to write like this!"[49] Throughout her diaries, which begin with the year 1944 and continue through high school and to the period the now-published *Journals* cover, she consistently mentions either her own writing or what she has been reading ("   lost myself in the thrilling book 'The Three Musketeers' by Dumas! I cannot put into proper words the way I feel about this enthralling masterpiece . . ."[50]). It is increasingly clear from her diaries that Plath devoted much of her adolescent energy to her "work" as a would-be writer: she sometimes includes her own poems; she often writes about what she has read; and she frequently worries over what she sees even then as the inherent conflict between being a talented, achieving woman and being a sexually desirable one. On October 10, 1947, when she is in the tenth grade, she takes some of her poems to Mr. Crockett, the English teacher who helped shape her interest and ability for so many years. She is delighted when he chooses some to read to the class, and she evidently treasures his comment that she has "a lyric gift beyond the ordinary," but she also worries: "I was overjoyed and although I am doubtfully doubtful about poetry's effect on the little strategy of "popularity" that I have been slowly building up, I am confident of admiration from Mr. C.!"[51]

Plath's diaries show even more expressly — and with even more exclamation points — how important a consideration her "popularity" is. Indeed, the short stories she is writing during her early high school years deal almost exclusively with that conflict between academic success and personal social success.[52] Child of the 1940s and 1950s, immured in the notion that the truly smart girl would be able to hide her brains, Plath works indefatigably at disguising her abilities as a writer. (Getting good marks seems to be allowable — probably because many girls are academic achievers — but the talents beyond those involved in just learning, the abilities that set her apart from other women, these are the ones she tries to discount.) Her very late letters to Olive Higgins Prouty (fall, 1962 and early 1963) speak movingly of the self-imposed isolation she has lived through in her years as "woman writer." With good reason she comes to call Prouty her "literary mother," and this late outpouring suggests the reliance Plath felt on the older writer:

> "My study has become a haven, a real sanctuary for me! I have late poppies, bright red, and blue-purple cornflowers on my desk now. . . . *Here* is my hearth, my life, my real self. I have never been so happy anywhere in my life as writing at my huge desk in the blue dawns, all to myself, secret and quiet. I know *you* will understand this — this quiet center at the middle of the storm. . . . I shall forge my writing out of these difficult experiences — to have known the bottom, whether mental or emotional, is a great trial, but also a great gift."[53]

Very near the end of her life, Plath again writes to Prouty, and closes that letter, dated January 22, 1963, with the plea, "Do write me again! Your letters are like balm, you understand the writer in me, and that is where I must live."[54]

Late in 1962, Plath also writes to Stevie Smith, one of the few British poets who was a woman, "I have been having a lovely time this week listening to some recordings of you reading your poems for the British Council, and Peter Orr has been kind enough to give me your address. I better say straight out that I am an addict of your poetry, a desperate Smith-addict." She continues that she hopes to move to London soon (the letter is dated November 19, 1962), and "would be very grateful in advance to hear if you might be able to come to tea or coffee when I manage my move — to cheer me on a bit. I've wanted to meet you for a long time."[55] Such evidence of Plath's trying, hard, to reach other women who had survived what Suzanne Juhasz calls the "double-bind situation," (that of being an aggressive poet simultaneously with being a passive woman),[56] even at a period in her life when she was both emotionally devastated and physically exhausted, shows how crucial Plath's image of herself as writer was.[57]

"I am a genius of a writer; I have it in me. I am writing the best poems of my life; they will make my name. I could finish the novel [the second] in *six weeks* of day-long work."[58] In her October 16, 1962, letter to her mother, Plath writes the now often-quoted affirmation. Two days later, October 18, she writes to Olive Higgins Prouty. "Miraculously, and like some gift, my writing has leapt ahead and not deserted me in this hour of need."[59] *The Collected Poems*, with the apparently accurate dates, shows that since October 1, 1962, Plath had written the two quasi-comic anti-Hughes poems, "The Detective" and "The Courage of Shutting-Up," the bee poems, "A Secret," "The Applicant," "Daddy," "Medusa," "The Jailer," "Lesbos," and — within a few more days — would write "Fever 103°," "Cut" "By Candle-light," "The Tour," "Ariel," "Purdah," "Lady Lazarus," and, early in November, "Getting There." These poems certainly bear out her pride in her "genius," and force us to realize some sense of the worth that probably existed in the second novel, undoubtedly the 130 pages that Hughes reports as being lost, titled *Double Exposure*.[60] The sheer defiance in Plath's statements speaks to the conflicts between her role as wife / mother / woman and her role as artist; as Carol Christ notes, "The simple act of telling a woman's story from a woman's point of view is a revolutionary act."[61] When Ted Hughes says, in celebration of Plath's work, "A real self, as we all know, is a rare thing. The direct speech of a real self is rarer still. . . ."[62] his praise is greater than he knows. For a woman writer to come to such validity is the rarest acheivement of all.

Tillie Olsen's *Silences* has become the comfort of many contemporary women writers, and taken with the important work of feminist critics, and those male critics who are responsive to the need of finding ways to read, and categorize, the work of all "non-traditional" writers, provides a scaffolding of support today.[63] But long before our own critical recognition of the inherent woman-as-writer dilemma, and somewhat before her own explicit description of the conflict, Plath was exploring the problem in her honors thesis at Smith, "The Magic Mirror; A Study of the Double in Two of Dostoevsky's Novels." Reading Otto Rank, Frazer, Jung, Nietzsche, and others, Plath plunged into the study of what she called "all fascinating stuff about the ego as symbolized in reflections (mirror and water), shadows, twins. . . ."[64] Benefiting from recent work by Barbara Hill Rigney, Maurice Beebe, Irving Massey, Peter M. Axthelm, and others, we can attribute much of Plath's interest in Dostoevsky's double to her own understanding of her divided consciousness / role (as writer and as woman); but we must notice, too, the positive emphasis in both the thesis and in Plath's comments about it. As she writes in her conclusion: "Although the figure of the Double has become a harbinger of danger and destruction, taking form as it does from the darkest of human fears and repressions, Dostoevsky implies that recognition of our various mirror images and reconciliation with them will save us from disintegration."[65] Plath's trying to face the conflict — and, by writing about it, both in her fiction and her scholarship, to work her way through it; to explore it instead of dismissing it, and, finally and by that method, to survive it — is the mark of psychological bravery that colors her oeuvre as writer; and makes the last, late poems that incredibly complex and coherent statements they are. Plath's investigation into the self caught in an unquestionable — and perhaps unresolvable — cultural dilemma is probably the quality that led Arthur Oberg, in his own posthumously-published study of the contemporary lyric, to describe Plath as "perhaps a poet who lived and wrote almost before what might have been her time."[66] Oberg's statement reminds us that the mode of the 1950s tended to be denial, not exploration.

Such a view of Plath leads to Anne Cluysenaar's image of Plath as "a typical 'survivor' in the psychiatric sense. Her work shows many traits which are recognized as marking the psychology of those who have, in some bodily or psychic sense, survived an experience of death . . . extreme vulnerability to danger. As an element in this complex of emotions, imagining death has a life-enhancing function. It is an assertion of power, over death but also (less attractive but psychologically authentic) over other human beings." Cluysenaar concludes, "That is the crux of her message—the retention of discrimination and the will to speak, the will to communicate. Her determination not to accept relief from any ready-made dogma is admirable."[67]

Being privy to the unpublished Plath letters, especially those from 1962 and 1963, tends to confirm Cluysenaar's sense of the anguish, not to mention the anger, Plath had survived. But her work itself, and her comments about it, show that instead of "dogma," she had rooted herself in art; and that her own very central sense of herself had sprung from her knowledge of that art, and of her own important role in it.

In 1957, when Plath reviewed *The Stones of Troy*, a collection of poems by C. A. Trypanis, her aesthetic principles for the good poem were already authoritatively in place. The best poems, according to Plath, work through "extended metaphor," a device that provides both the poem's meaning and the consistent tone imperative for any work of art. She praises Trypanis' poem "Chartres" by explaining, "The metaphor-moral is intrinsic to the poem, working back and forth on itself, not expressed prosaically at the close, like a moral in a fable." Her comment also illuminates the endings of many of her own poems, which tends to lift readers into a concluding pace despite the fact that their content is by no means "summary."

As might be expected, Plath is tough about word choice (particularly what she calls "tired adjective-noun combinations which do nothing to recreate experience, but underline it in the old grooves"), and about the unimaginative *use* of words that, in the right context, might be strong.

The most important criterion for the successful poem, however, is the poet's ability to write the poem that is uniquely his or her own. In the case of Trypanis, who uses a great deal of myth in his work, Plath admonishes "There is always the danger that the poet will not transform the material, will not, in some way, make it freshly his own and ours."[68]

In 1960 and 1961, when she edited *American Poetry Now*, a supplement to *Critical Quarterly*, her choice of recent American poems ("by new and / or youngish Americans poets for the most unknown in Britain") seemed to be guided by equally stringent but catholic criteria. Robert Creeley's understated, even fey, "The Way" appeared with work by Edgar Bowers and Richard Wilbur. Barbara Guest's dramatic loss-of-love poem, "The Brown Studio," worked through a restrained extended metaphor of color, shades and tones of color; whereas Denise Levertov's eloquent "The Five-Day Rain" moved through changing rhythms from objective statement to a powerful closing imperative;

> Wear scarlet! Tear the green lemons
> Off the tree! I don't want
> to forget who I am, what has burned in me,
> and hang limp and clean, an empty dress —

Plath included three poems each by William Stafford, Adrienne Rich, and W. S. Merwin (three poets less like each other hardly exist, either now or then), and two by Howard Nemerov, W. D. Snodgrass, and Anne Sexton. The Sexton and Snodgrass poems close the collection, giving them an importance that parallels Plath's comment in her BBC interview about the significance of Sexton, Lowell, and others who write more personally.[69] Louis Simpson, George Starbuck, E. Lucas Myers, Dan Hoffman, Anthony Hecht, and Hyam Plutzik were also represented, and the credits page mentions that Plath wanted to use a poem by Gregory Corso, but could not get permission. The collection is remarkable for the excellence of the poems as well as the poets included, and for the eclectic vision that did not automatically discount poets from different — and often competing — schools.

The profile that emerges — as we read Plath's unpublished letters, journals, and writing as well as the published; as we piece together the aesthetic and motivational operatives of her intense if brief career — is one of impassioned diligence. Less articulate about her aesthetics than about her emotions, Plath relied on an instinctive comprehension (what Ted Hughes describes as "an instant special pass to the center"[70]) of what made great writing, both in her own work and in that of others. Part of Plath's greatness lay in the fact that she not only trusted those insights; she also worked terribly hard to find means of implementing them.

That single-mindedness Plath shares with all known great writers, as Lawrence Lipking stresses in *The Life of the Poet*, because what they have in common is just this "sense of vocation and a destiny." As Lipking describes the inherent artistic dilemma, "A poet so in love with his destiny must face the consequences of ambition: the constant pressure to grow and build; the sacrifice of modest successes and ordinary pleasures; the extraordinary self-consciousness. . . ." Lipking concludes "The life of the poet is achieved at the cost of many other possible lives; it fixes the poet in place like a worm in amber."[71]

LINDA W. WAGNER

East Lansing, Michigan

Notes

1. Reviews of Plath's *The Collected Poems* (New York: Harper & Row, 1981), in sequence, are "Formal Bleeding" by Michael Hulse (*Spectator*, 247 [November 14, 1981], 20); "Games with Death and Co.," by John Bayley (*New Statesman*, 102 [October 2, 1981], 19); and "Sylvia Plath" by Laurence Lerner (*Encounter*, 58 [January, 1982], 53); Lerner makes the last statement as well. As American poet Dave Smith remarked in his long *American Poetry Review* essay, "I have reviewed Sylvia Plath because her book gave me no choice" (p. 36, "Some Recent American Poetry: Come All Ye Fair and Tender Ladies," *APR*, 11 [January, 1982]).

2. Katha Pollitt, "A Note of Triumph," *Nation*, 234 (January 16, 1982), 54.

3. "Russian Roulette," *Newsweek*, 67 (June 20, 1966), 109A–110.

4. M. L. Rosenthal, *The New Poets* (New York: Oxford University Press, 1967), pp. 25–89.

5. Robert Phillips' *The Confessional Poets* (Carbondale: Southern Illinois Univ. Press, 1973) is one culmination of this critical preoccupation ("balanced narrative poems with unbalanced or afflicted protagonists"); other critics who have adopted this stance are Jan B. Gordon (" 'Who Is Sylvia?' The Art of Sylvia Plath," *Modern Poetry Studies*, 1 [1970], 6–34); Irving Howe ("Sylvia Plath, A Partial Disagreement," *Harper's*, January, 1972, pp. 88–91); Alfred Alvarez (*The Savage God: A Study of Suicide*, [New York: Random House, 1972]); David Holbrook (*Sylvia Plath, Poetry and Existence* [London: Athlone Press, 1976]); Murray M. Schwartz and Christopher Bollas ("The Absence of the Center: Sylvia Plath and Suicide," *Criticism*, 18 [1976], 147–72); and Edward Butscher's biography, *Sylvia Plath, Method and Madness* (New York: Seabury Press, 1976).

6. Ted Hughes, "Notes on the Chronological Order of Sylvia Plath's Poems," *Tri-Quarterly*, 7 (Fall, 1966), 81–82; Marjorie Perloff, *The Poetic Art of Robert Lowell* (Ithaca: Cornell Univ. Press, 1973), pp. 181–83; Jon Rosenblatt, "The Limits of the 'Confessional Mode' in Recent American Poetry," *Genre*, 9 [1977], 153–59; Sandra Gilbert, " 'My Name Is Darkness': The Poetry of Self-Definition," *Contemporary Literature*, 18 [1977], 443–57; and M. D. Uroff (Margaret Dickie), "Sylvia Plath and Confessional Poetry: A Reconsideration," *Iowa Review*, 8 (Winter, 1977), 104–15. In 1978, M. L. Rosenthal and Sally M. Gall added helpful commentary to the effect that Plath's poems were "constructs rather than symptoms"; they may use the subjects of explosive psychological states, but they themselves remain art (" 'Pure? What Does It Mean?' Notes on Sylvia Plath's Poetic Art," *APR*, 7 [1978], 37–40).

7. Uroff, pp. 105, 106, 115.

8. "Sylvia Plath Reconsidered," *Commentary*, 57 (April, 1974), 48.

9. Barbara Hardy, "The Poetry of Sylvia Plath: Enlargement or Derangement?" *The Survival of Poetry: A Contemporary Survey*, ed. Martin Dodsworth (London: Faber & Faber, 1970), pp. 164–87; this quote, pp. 164–65.

10. Judith Kroll, *Chapters in a Mythology, The Poetry of Sylvia Plath* (New York: Harper & Row, 1976), pp. 2–3.

11. Among critics who have traced influences on Plath's work are Judith Kroll (above); Charles Newman, "Candor Is the Only Wile," *The Art of Sylvia Plath, A Symposium* (Bloomington: Indiana Univ. Press, 1970), pp. 21–55; Jon Rosenblatt, *Sylvia Plath, The Poetry of Initiation* (Chapel Hill: Univ. of North Carolina Press, 1979); Gary Lane, "Influence and Originality in Plath's Poems," *Sylvia Plath, New Views on the Poetry*, ed. Gary Lane (Baltimore: Johns Hopkins Univ. Press, 1979), pp. 116–37. My essay comparing Plath and W. C. Williams, to some extent, appeared in *Centennial Review*, 21 (Fall, 1977) as "Modern American Literature: The Poetics of the Individual Voice"; and my writing on Williams has appeared in many journals and in *The Poems of William Carlos Williams: A Critical Study* (1964) and *The Prose of William Carlos Williams* (1970, both Wesleyan Univ. Press), as well as "*Speaking*

Straight Ahead": Interviews with William Carlos Williams (Norfolk, Conn.: New Directions Press, 1976).

12. Ellen Moers, *Literary Women* (Garden City, N.Y.: Doubleday, 1976), p. xv.

13. Louis Simpson, *A Revolution in Taste* (New York: Macmillan Publishing Co., 1978), p. 123.

14. Anne Sexton, "The Barfly Ought to Sing," *The Art of Sylvia Plath, A Symposium*, ed. Charles Newman (Bloomington: Indiana Univ. Press, 1970), pp. 178–79.

15. Ted Hughes, "The Chronological Order of Sylvia Plath's Poems," ibid., p. 187.

16. Rochelle Ratner, "Sylvia Plath: Beyond the Biographical," *American Writing Today*, ed. Richard Kostelanetz (New York: America / Forum Editions, 1982), p. 61.

17. Dave Smith, "Sylvia Plath, The Electric Horse," *American Poetry Review*, 11 (January, 1982), 45–46.

18. Geoffrey Dearmer, "Sows' Ears and Silk Purses," *Poetry Review*, 52 (July-September, 1961), 167; John Wain, "Farewell to the World," *Spectator* (January 13, 1961), 50; Ian Hamilton, "Review of *The Colossus*," *London Magazine*, N.S. 3 (July, 1963), 54–57; Richard Howard, "Review of *The Colossus*," *Poetry*, 101 (March, 1963), 412–13; and Roy Fuller, "Review of *The Colossus*," *The London Magazine*, 8 (March, 1961), 69–70.

19. William Dickey, "Responsibilities," *Kenyon Review*, 24 (Autumn, 1962), 762; Reed Whittemore, "The Colossus and Other Poems," *Carleton Miscellany*, 3 (Fall, 1962), 89; Thomas Blackburn, "Poetic Knowledge," *New Statesman*, 60 (December 24, 1960), 1016.

20. M. L. Rosenthal, "Metamorphosis of a Book," *Spectator*, 218 (April 21, 1967), 456.

21. Robert Taubman, "Anti-heroes," *New Statesman*, 65 (January 25, 1963), 127–28; Laurence Lerner, "New Novels," *Listener*, 69 (January 31, 1963), 215; Rupert Butler, "New American Fiction: Three Disappointing Novels—But One Good One," *Time and Tide*, 44 (January 31, 1963), 34.

22. C. B. Cox, "Editorial," *Critical Quarterly*, 8 (Autumn, 1966), 195.

23. M. L. Rosenthal, "Blood and Plunder," *Spectator*, 217 (September 30, 1966), 418.

24. Patricia Meyer Spacks, "A Chronicle of Women," *Hudson Review*, 25 (Spring, 1972), 164.

25. Lucy Rosenthal, "*The Bell Jar*," *Saturday Review*, 54 (April 24, 1971), 42.

26. Melvin Maddocks, "A Vacuum Abhorred," *Christian Science Monitor*, April 15, 1971, 11; Martha Duffy, "Lady Lazarus," *Time*, 97 (June 21, 1971), 87; Tony Tanner, *City of Words* (New York: Harper & Row, 1971), p. 262.

27. John Malcolm Brinnin, "Plath, Jarrell, Kinnell, Smith," *Partisan Review*, 34 (Winter, 1967), 156–57; Samuel F. Morse, "Poetry 1966," *Contemporary Literature*, 9 (Winter, 1968), 127; Derek Parker, "*Ariel*, Indeed," *Poetry Review*, 56 (Summer, 1965), 118–20; Richard Tillinghast, "Worlds of Their Own," *Southern Review*, 5 (Spring, 1969), 582.

28. Hugh Kenner, "Arts and the Age, *Ariel*, by Sylvia Plath," *Triumph*, 1 (September, 1966), 33–34.

29. Helen Vendler, "Sylvia Plath," *Part of Nature, Part of Us, Modern American Poets* (Cambridge: Harvard University Press, 1980), pp. 271, 273.

30. Robin Skelton, "Sylvia Plath, *Crossing the Water*," *Malahat Review*, 20 (October, 1971), 137–38.

31. For the best statement of the misdating of Plath's poems, see Marjorie Perloff, "On the Road to *Ariel*: The 'Transitional' Poetry of Sylvia Plath," *Iowa Review*, 4 (Spring, 1973), 94–110. Victor Kramer, "Life-and-Death Dialectics," *Modern Poetry Studies*, 3 (1972), 40–42; Linda Ray Pratt, " 'The spirit of blackness is in us . . . ,' " *Prairie Schooner*, 67 (Spring, 1973), 87–90.

32. Joyce Carol Oates, *"Winter Trees," Library Journal*, 97 (November 1, 1972), 3595; Raymond Smith, "Late Harvest," *Modern Poetry Studies*, 3 (1972), 91–93.

33. James Finn Cotter, "Women Poets: Malign Neglect?" *America*, 128 (February 17, 1973), 140; Jill Baumgaertner, "Four Poets: Blood Type New," *Cresset*, 36 (April, 1973), 16–19; Roger Scruton, "Sylvia Plath and The Savage God," *Spectator*, 227 (December 18, 1971), 890.

34. Jo Brans, "The Girl Who Wanted To Be God," *Southwest Review*, 61 (Summer, 1976), 325.

35. Martha Duffy, "Two Lives," *Time*, 106 (November 24, 1975), 101–02; Marjorie Perloff," Review of *Letters Home," Resources for American Literary Study*, 7 (Spring, 1977), 77–85. Another good review is Nancy Reed, "Still those ellipses . . ." in *Christian Science Monitor*, January 7, 1976, p. 23: "The letters serve the useful function of reminding us that she was a very human, very approachable young woman. In spite of an almost mind-boggling talent, the personality which becomes more visible through these letters is of a girl with a great need for reassurance, a tremendous will to love and to be loved."

36. Jon Rosenblatt, *Sylvia Plath, The Poetry of Initiation* (Chapel Hill: Univ. of North Carolina Press, 1979); Mary Lynn Broe, *Protean Poetic, The Poetry of Sylvia Plath* (Columbia: Univ. of Missouri Press, 1980); and a third important study from this period, *Sylvia Plath and Ted Hughes* by Margaret Dickie Uroff (Urbana: Univ. of Illinois Press, 1979). Other useful books which should be mentioned are Nancy Hunter Steiner, *A Closer Look at Ariel: A Memory of Sylvia Plath* (New York: Harper Magazine Press, 1973); Judith Kroll's study, 1976; two bibliographies, Thomas P. Walsh and Cameron Northouse, *Sylvia Plath and Anne Sexton: A Reference Guide* (Boston: G.K. Hall, 1974) and Gary Lane and Maria Stevens, *Sylvia Plath: A Bibliography* (Metuchen, N.J.: Scarecrow Press, 1978); and three collections of essays, that from 1970 edited by Charles Newman; another from 1977 edited by Edward Butscher (*Sylvia Plath, The Woman and the Work* [New York: Dodd, Mead & Co.]) and from 1979, Gary Lane, ed. *Sylvia Plath, New Views on the Poetry* (Baltimore: Johns Hopkins Univ. Press). Throughout the 1970s, important essays had been published by Marjorie Perloff, M. D. Uroff, Pamela Smith, Anthony Libby, Arthur Oberg, and many others.

37. Michael Atkinson, "After Twelve Years, Plath Without Tears: A Look Back at 'Lady Lazarus,' " *A Book of Rereadings in Recent American Poetry — 30 Essays*, ed. Greg Kuzma (Lincoln, Neb.: Pebble Press, 1979), p. 301.

38. Margaret Atwood, "Poet's Prose," *New York Times Book Review*, January 28, 1979, pp. 10, 31.

39. Lorna Sage, "Death and Marriage," *Times Literary Supplement* (October 21, 1977), p. 1235; William Dowie, "A Season of Alarums and Excursions: 'Johnny Panic and the Bible of Dreams,' " *America*, 140 (March 3, 1979), 165.

40. Douglas Hill, "Living and Dying," *Canadian Forum*, 58 (June, 1978), 323–24; G. S. Fraser, "Pass to the Centre," *Listener*, 98 (October 27, 1977), 541–52. The chief issue connected with Hughes' editing of Plath's manuscripts is that of repression of her material. When he writes in the Foreword to the *Journals* that he had "destroyed" the last journal — that covering the last "several months" of her life — and that the penultimate book — which traced the (nearly) last three years — had "disappeared," such complacency was difficult for readers to accept (see p. xiii, *The Journals of Sylvia Plath*, New York: Dial Press, 1982). A similar statement appears in the Introduction to *Johnny Panic and the Bible of Dreams* (New York: Harper & Row, 1979), p. 1: "After *The Bell Jar* she wrote some 130 pages of another novel, provisionally titled *Double Exposure*. That manuscript disappeared somewhere around 1970."

41. Hughes recounts in his introduction to the collection the same diligent ambition that her letters and the stories in the Lilly Library Archive (Indiana University) evince. As he writes (pp. 2–4): "Her ambition to write stories was the most visible burden of her life. Successful story-writing, for her, had all the advantages of a top job. She wanted the cash, and the freedom that can go with it. She wanted the professional standing, as a big earner, as the master of a difficult trade, and as a serious investigator into the real world . . . her greatest ambition was

certainly to get a story into *The New Yorker* or the *Ladies Home Journal* — the two alternating according to her mood."

42. Philip Larkin, "Horror Poet," *Poetry Review*, 72 (April, 1982), 51–53.

43. Emily Grosholz, "*The Collected Poems:* Sylvia Plath," *Hudson Review*, 35 (Summer, 1982), 320–22.

44. William H. Pritchard, "An Interesting Minor Poet?" *New Republic*, 185 (December 30, 1981), 32–35.

45. John Frederick Nims, "The Poetry of Sylvia Plath, A Technical Analysis," in Newman, 136–52. Laurence Lerner, "Sylvia Plath," *Encounter*, 58 (January, 1982), 53–54.

46. Michael Hulse, "*Collected Poems,*" *Spectator*, 247 (November 14, 1981), 20.

47. Marni Jackson, "In Search of the Shape Within," *Maclean's Magazine*, 95, (May 17, 1982), 57; Nancy Milford, "*The Journals of Sylvia Plath,*" *New York Times Book Review*, May 2, 1982, pp. 30–32; Le Anne Schreiber, "*The Journals of Sylvia Plath,*" *New York Times*, April 21, 1982.

48. Walter Clemons, "A Poet's Rage for Perfection," *Newsweek*, 99 (May 3, 1982), 77.

49. Box 7, the Plath Archives, The Lilly Library, Indiana University, entry dated October 31 and November 1 in 1946 diary; used by permission of the Archive and Mr. Ted Hughes.

50. Box 7, ibid; entry dated January 3, 1947.

51. Box 7, ibid; entry dated October 10, 1947. Other comments that are typical: "What a life! First I had five boys going out with me — now all of them are strangely silent" (p. 21 of the 1949 diary, Box 7); "my heart was stabbed with pain — These dates are such unsteady things" (from an unpaged 1959, Summer, diary, Box 7). One very interesting set of entries that shows the dramatic importance of male response and Plath's imaginative *use* of her social dilemma occurs in the November 17 and 18, 1948, entries. The November 17 entry is a stark one-liner: "No one called up for the dance." In the context of Plath's usual long, chatty entries, such singleness is emphatic. The following day's entry goes into great length about her anticipation, her days of waiting, her genuine disappointment (although she eventually was asked to the dance): "I've imagined being asked so many times by every reasonable, and sometimes unreasonable, boy in so many varied, fantastic situations. . . ."

52. Such unpublished stories as "The Brink," "Heat," "In This Field We Wander Through," "Among the Shadow Throngs," and "East Wind" are representative of her high school writing that focuses on this theme (Box 8, folios 10, 12, and 14 of the Plath Manuscripts II, The Lilly Library, Indiana University, Bloomington, Indiana).

53. Unpublished letter to Olive Higgins Prouty, October 25, 1962, Box 9, The Lilly Library Plath Manuscripts II Collection.)

54. Unpublished letter to Olive Higgins Prouty, January 22, 1963, ibid.

55. Sylvia Plath to Stevie Smith, November 19, 1962, quoted in "Introduction" to *Me Again, Uncollected Writings of Stevie Smith*, ed. Jack Barbera and William McBrien (London: Virago Press, 1981), p. 6.

56. Suzanne Juhasz, *Naked and Fiery Forms, Modern American Poetry by Women: A New Tradition* (New York: Harper & Row, 1976), p. 1 and first chapter. Juhasz's most important point is that such a conflict changes the nature of the poems women write (see also Sandra Gilbert and Susan Gubar, ed. *Shakespeare's Sisters, Feminist Essays on Women Poets*, [Bloomington: Indiana University Press, 1979], especially their introduction, "Gender, Creativity, and the Woman Poet").

57. Some of the hostility Plath shows toward her mother during the last six months of her life may also stem from her feeling that Aurelia cannot understand this new "center" of her personal, as well as professional, life (see October 21, 1962, letter in *Letters Home*, p. 473). In contrast, her tone in letters to Warren (*LH*, 472) is warm and conspiratorial. She repeatedly announces her gifts as writer ("I am a writer and that is all I want to do"), as she does to Prouty.

58. *LH*, 468.

59. Unpublished letter to Olive Higgins Prouty, October 18, 1962; Box 9, Plath Manuscripts II, The Lilly Library, Indiana University.

60. Ted Hughes, Introduction, *Johnny Panic and the Bible of Dreams* (New York: Harper & Row, 1979), p. 1.

61. Carol Christ, *Diving Deep and Surfacing, Women Writers on Spiritual Quest* (Boston: Beacon Press, 1980), p. 7, See also Sandra Gilbert and Susan Gubar, *Madwoman in the Attic* (New Haven: Yale Univ. Press, 1979) and Elaine Showalter, *A Literature of Their Own* (Princeton, N.J.: Princeton Univ. Press, 1977).

62. Ted Hughes, "Foreword," *The Journals of Sylvia Plath, 1950–1962*, ed. Frances McCullough and Ted Hughes (New York: Dial Press, 1982), p. xii.

63. Tillie Olsen, *Silences* (New York: Delacorte Press / Seymour Laurence, 1978); see also Patricia Meyer Spacks, *The Female Imagination* (New York: Alfred A. Knopf, 1975); Margaret Homans, *Women Writers and Poetic Identity, Dorothy Wordsworth, Emily Bronte, and Emily Dickinson* (Princeton, N.J.: Princeton Univ. Press, 1980); and Anthea Zeman, *Presumptuous Girls, Women and Their World in the Serious Woman's Novel* (London: Weidenfeld and Nicolson, 1977).

64. *LH*, 146.

65. Barbara Hill Rigney, *Madness and Sexual Politics in the Feminist Novel* (Madison: Univ. of Wisconsin Press, 1978); Maurice Beebe, *Ivory Towers and Sacred Founts, The Artist as Hero in Fiction from Goethe to Joyce* (New York: New York Univ. Press, 1964); Grace Stewart, *A New Mythos, The Novel of the Artist as Heroine 1877–1977* (Montreal, Canada: Eden Press Women's Publications, 1981); Annis Pratt, *Archetypal Patterns in Women's Fiction* (Bloomington: Indiana Univ. Press, 1981); Robert Rogers, *The Double in Literature* (Detroit, Mich.: Wayne State Univ. Press, 1970); Peter M. Axthelm, *The Modern Confessional Novel* (New Haven, Conn.: Yale Univ. Press, 1967); and Irving Massey, *The Gaping Pig, Literature and Metamorphosis* (Berkeley: Univ. of California Press, 1976).

66. Arthur Oberg, *Modern American Lyric — Lowell, Berryman, Creeley, and Plath* (New Brunswick, N.J.: Rutgers Univ. Press, 1978), p. 177.

67. Anne Cluysenaar, "Post-culture: Pre-culture?" in *British Poetry Since 1960: A Critical Survey*, ed. Michael Schmidt and Grevel Lindop (Oxford, England: Carcanet Press, 1972), pp. 219–21.

68. Sylvia Plath, "Review of *The Stones of Troy*," *Gemini*, 1, No. 2 (Summer, 1957), 98–103.

69. Sylvia Plath, *The Poet Speaks*, ed. Peter Orr (London: Routledge & Kegan Paul, 1966), pp. 167–72.

70. Ted Hughes, "Introduction," *Johnny Panic*, p. 5.

71. Lawrence Lipking, *The Life of the Poet, Beginning and Ending Poetic Careers* (Chicago: Univ. of Chicago Press, 1981), pp. viii, 183–84.

REVIEWS

[Review of *The Colossus*]

A. E. Dyson*

It is true, but not especially important, to notice that Sylvia Plath is influenced by Theodore Roethke and by Ted Hughes; what is more to the point is that on the evidence of these poems she has to be mentioned in the same breath with them. *The Colossus* is a volume that those who care for literature will wish to buy, and return to from time to time for that deepening acquaintance which is one of the rewards of the truest poetry. It established Miss Plath among the best of the poets now claiming our attention; the most compelling feminine voice certainly, that we have heard for many a day.

The title poem is as significant as we now expect title poems to be; a sense of the huge and the continuing dominates Sylvia Plath's sensibility. But the grandeur of nature oppresses as well as impresses her; apprehensions of lurking menace, more likely to test our endurance than our joy, are seldom far below the surface. In *Hardcastle Crags* the young woman who walks by night through a bleak landscape is offered nothing, unless it be the tion of putting flesh and blood against the iron of the universe itself.

> All the night gave her, in return
> For the paltry gift of her bulk and the beat
> Of her heart was the humped indifferent iron
> Of its hills, and its pastures bordered by black stone set
> On black stone.

In battling with the encroachments of rock, wind, the sea which is "brutal endlessly," a temporary, almost humdrum heroism may be earned, as poems like *Point Shirley* and *The Hermit at Outermost House* suggest; but Nature outlasts man, and wins again in the end.

> A labour of love, and that labour lost.
> Steadily the sea
> Eats at Point Shirley.

When Miss Plath encounters a landscape that has been tamed and reduced by man, she feels it as a type of trifling. Walking in Granchester

*Reprinted with permission from *Critical Quarterly*, 3 (Summer 1961), 183–84.

27

Meadows, the very touchstone of English, and *a fortiori* Cambridge nostalgia, she notes that "Nothing is big or far." The birds are "thumb-size," the cygnets "tame," the Granta "bland," the water rat "droll." Even the students, lost in a "moony indolence of love," are unmenaced and therefore somewhat unreal. "It is a country on a nursery plate," a pretty place, but Sylvia Plath is more at home when she senses behind Nature its naked inhospitality to man.

Wind and sea are only the more natural of the forces she detects waiting to batter and supplant the human race, or patiently take over when it is gone. In *Ouija* there is an eerie evocation of "those unborn, those undone" as they crowd into the seance room, drawn to the living by envy

> Imagine their deep hunger, deep as the dark
> For the blood-heat that would ruddle or reclaim.

In *The Thin People* the threat comes from devitalised humanity itself; from those who in Blake's words "restrain Desire . . . because theirs is weak enough to be restrained," and who having resisted energy, put the "Giants who formed this world into its sensual existence" in chains. Sylvia Plath sees the thin folk as a menace, as Blake does, but she fears too "their talent to perservere / In thinness, to come, later, / Into our bad dreams." In *Mushrooms*, the quality of menace is even more chillingly detected in the sinister, almost cancerous proliferation of fungus. This macabrely ironic vision of a form of life infinitely lower than man simply waiting in endless patience to "Inherit the earth" has the vividness of science fiction at its best, without being in the least sensational. (The associations which the word "mushroom" have for us since Hiroshima may enhance the effectiveness, which is not, however, dependent upon them.) In *Sculptor*, by a further surprising stroke, the forms the sculptor is about to create are felt as bodiless realities waiting to use him for incarnation, after which they will both dwarf and outlast him

> His chisel bequeathes
> Them life livelier than ours.

The theme sounds again in *Frog Autumn*, and in the longer *Mussel Hunter at Rock Harbour*. Perhaps the most remarkable variation, however, is in *All The Dead Dears*, a poem which starts, as a note informs us, from the Archeological Museum in Cambridge, where there is "a stone coffin of the fourth century A.D. containing the skeletons of a woman, a mouse and a shrew. The ankle-bone of the woman has been slightly gnawn." From the stark statement

> These three, unmasked now, bear
> Dry witness
> To the gross eating game

the poet goes on to sense, in the long dead, a host waiting to revisit the living in memories, and later claim them to itself. There is first the suggestion of vampirish affinity between dead and living

> How they grip us through thick and thin,
> These barnacle dead!
> This lady here's no kin
> Of mine, yet kin she is: she'll suck
> Blood and whistle my marrow clean
> To prove it . . .

and then this inexorable community is still more strikingly explored, in a manner that reminds us again of *Ouija* and *Mushrooms*, whilst perhaps reaching even nearer to the heart of the thematic menace

> All the long gone darlings: they
> Get back, though, soon,
> Soon: be it by wakes, weddings,
> Childbirths or a family barbecue:
> Any touch, taste, tang's
> Fit for those outlaws to ride home on,
>
> And to sanctuary: usurping the armchair
> Between tick
> And tack of the clock, until we go,
> Each skulled-and-crossboned Gulliver
> Riddled with ghosts, to lie
> Deadlocked with them, taking root as cradles rock.

The affinity which Sylvia Plath feels with the dead and the alien is not unlike a type of pity; a conviction of kinship with everything that lives or has lived, however inaccessible or sinister. Her feeling for the animal world is similar in kind, not only in *Frog Autumn* and *Mussel Hunter at Rock Harbour*, but in one of the most moving of the poems, *Blue Moles*. And the same may be said of her feeling for human outcasts, in *The Beggars* for instance, a poem published in the *Critical Quarterly*, but unaccountably omitted from this volume.

One further theme running through Sylvia Plath's poems is her occasional sense of being teased by glimpses of better worlds, also lurking just beyond the surfaces of things, but this time in the realm of fantasy rather than fact. Syren voices from under water, at Lorelei,

> sing
> Of a world more full and clear
> Than can be . . .

The "lost otherworld" of dreams presents itself like "hieroglyphics / of some godly utterance," yet the sleeper "merely by waking up" comes to know its lack of substance. In the fine early poem *Black Rook In Rainy Weather* Sylvia Plath reflects, half philosophically, half ironically on the nature of her own poetic gift. She does not expect "miracle," but nonetheless "a certain minor light" might still at times shine out, transfiguring the everyday world in a manner

> to seize my sense, haul
> My eyelids up, and grant
> A brief respite from fear
> Of total neutrality.

Continuing the logic of this she moves, consciously and delicately tentative, to a limited claim for poetry itself

> With luck,
> Trekking stubborn through the seasons
> Of fatigue, I shall
> Patch together a content
>
> Of sorts. Miracles occur,
> If you care to call those spasmodic
> Tricks of radiance miracles.

The differences between this sensibility, and that of Ted Hughes, scarcely need underlining, even after so brief a survey. There are, one admits, similarities — forceful narrative skill; verbal precision of high order; effective use of homely events and observations as taut but unstrained allegory; several poems, about animals, and so on. But the sensibility itself is different. Ted Hughes is heroic and violent in his dominating mood, Sylvia Plath brooding and tentative. Their gods are also different. Ted Hughes's is the god of the tiger, Sylvia Plath's "a chilly god, a god of shades." He is Neptune, the inscrutible Father of the endlessly brutal sea, an alien and useless deity, whom she half believes in, half worships. He defies questions, defies other godhood, yet still she can call him 'Father.' The application of this supremely religious word to a god so far removed from the personal or the approachable, so intermingled with hallucination and conjecture — an application ironic in overtones, yet wholly serious and central to Miss Plath's sense of life — is very profoundly characteristic of this fine body of work.

The Tranquilized Fifties
[*The Colossus*]
E. Lucas Myers*

The poets who first appeared during the fifties have some distinction; the best of them write with technical skill, intelligence, and resourcefulness. Yet a stack of their books, read through, leaves a sense of dissatisfaction, just as living through the decade did, especially in those whose minds were still

*Reprinted with permission from *Sewanee Review*, 70 (January-March, 1962), 212–13, 216.

being formed. What fails to emerge is a statement, in some measure coherent, of the experience of a decade, such as can be made out from the poetry of the twenties or the thirties. (The beat writers essay something like this, of course — it is symptomatic of the temper of the decade that more accomplished ones do not.) The young poets, in fact, share a conceptual framework handed down almost unmodified from the twenties and thirties, which can not serve them as well as it served their predecessors; beyond that, no important relations can be established among the worlds they evoke, and, more often than not, the world of the individual practitioner is itself without substantial unity of thought or attitude. No confluences of new ideas which would sweep things along in one direction appear. It was a time for spinning from the belly, not of cross-fertilization or mutual aid in growth. There are a great many poems (especially from the British) about incidentals of daily life, completed by the metaphysical or psychological observations they occasion, and a great many more (especially from Americans) about Rome, Florence, Granada, etc., seen through expatriates' or tourists' eyes, and similarly completed. Neither topic delivers many of the poems to generally significant ground; they tend to remain private. Many poets seem to feel that further protest against the state of our sensibility is pointless, and aim to write as positively as possible, but the search for renewal of passion too often follows a long cerebral detour and issues in verse with an unmistakable dryness and air of fatigue about it, and a mechanical quality in the motions of its sense. Curiously enough, in some of the most telling performances, one feels that the poet is experientially or psychologically detached from what he or she is writing about. . . .

There is not an imperfectly finished poem in Sylvia Plath's book. She is impressive for control of form and tone, appropriateness of rhythmic variation within the poem, and vocabulary and observation which are often surprising, and always accurate: "The waves' / Spewed relics clicker masses in the wind," or (the place is a laboratory), "In their jars the snail-nosed babies moon and glow." "Poem for a Birthday," in seven parts, concludes the volume, and catalogues the sensation of pregnancy in rich images altogether astonishing to the mere male, even though he may have heard described the parti-colored dreams of pregnant women. In "Metaphors," a shorter (nine-line) but equally engaging poem about pregnancy, she is "a melon strolling on two tendrils," has "boarded the train there's no getting off." I am struck, in reading a lot of her poems together, by her posture *vis-à-vis* her material, which is one of considerable objectivity, even when the material is her childhood, her Muses, her pregnancy. The focus of the emotions, like the visual focus, is sharp and is found at medium distance or more, the perspective in which we see her spinster, her strumpet, her suicide, the perspective which, in the following from "Blue Moles," is characteristically restored from the initial close-up by the words "easy" and "often": "What happens between us / Happens in darkness, vanishes / Easy and often as each breath." Poems should be criticized as they are, not as the critic thinks they might have been, and these poems, as they are, merit anybody's reading; but I can not help wondering what will happen if, in Miss Plath's second volume of poems, the emotional distance is shortened — no melting of the moulds her craftsmanship has created, I think, but a lesser frequency of phrases like, "Now, this particular girl," "Mark, I cry," "gimcrack relics," and more of the pressure of "Lorelei," of the close of "The Colossus," or of "Departure," which is an example of her finest writing.

Metamorphosis of a Book
(*The Colossus*)
M. L. Rosenthal*

Sylvia Plath's *The Colossus* was first published in 1960 by Heinemann, and then was issued two years later in the United States by Knopf in a new edition with ten of the original poems omitted. Miss Plath's promise was quickly recognised, despite a general impression of academic precisionism. Except for a few poems whose bitter, concentrated force made them unlike the rest, her work seemed 'craft'-centred and a bit derivative. In 1963 came the shocking news of her suicide. Soon afterwards we began to read in the *Observer* and elsewhere those extraordinary last poems that went into the 1965 volume *Ariel* and all but swamped the memory of the earlier book.

Now *The Colossus* has been reissued in its original form, though Miss Plath's cuts for the American edition had actually improved the book. For me at least, it has become almost an entirely different organism. After one has experienced *Ariel,* the poet's death-obsession and its deep link with her fear of yielding to the impersonal processes of her body stand out in *The Colossus* with morbid emphasis. The way in which many of the poems are haunted by images of cold terror, and the empathy involved in her poems about dead animals, are more striking now, and the theme of suicide is seen to be more pervasive than was at first evident.

The psychological horror of "Daddy" is revealed to have a less drastic forerunner in the title poem of the earlier book. Familiarity with later poems like "Lady Lazarus" and with the autobiographical novel *The Bell Jar* has sensitised me to the orientation of much of *The Colossus. Ariel* was not a completely new direction for its author, but the realisation and clarification of irresistible motives that were seeking their way to the surface from the start. I do not mean that *The Colossus* is artistically on the same level as *Ariel,* but that it has become far more interesting than it was at first. It has flashes of Sylvia Plath's final, and special, kind of awareness. We see it, for instance, in one macabre line in her "Two Views of a Cadaver Room," with

*Reprinted with permission from the *Spectator*, 218 (April 21, 1967), 456–57.

its grisly echo of "Prufrock:" "In their jars the snail-nosed babies moon and glow."

We see it, in fact, in the whole of this poem. The first of its two sections is about a girl's visit to a dissecting room, where she sees "white-smocked boys" working on four cadavers, "black as burnt turkey," and where her friend (one of these boys) hands her "the cut-out heart like a cracked heirloom" — a gross love-token that seems to foreshadow the morbidity of the lover hinted at in "Lady Lazarus." The second section describes a Brueghel painting of a war scene, but with a romantic love-scene painted in the lower right-hand corner showing two lovers absorbed in one another and "deaf to the fiddle in the hands of the death's head shadowing their song."

Her attempt here to relate by simple juxtaposition her painful private experience in the dissecting room to the general theme of war represented in Brueghel's "panorama of smoke and slaughter" and to Brueghel's other implied themes of love and of the transcendent character of art points to Sylvia Plath's major preoccupations just a short time later. So does her attempt in "Suicide off Egg Rock" to reconstruct exactly how the protagonist of the poem felt at the moment when he drowned himself and how it was with him afterwards when his body was an inert object.

Sylvia Plath was a true "literalist of the imagination." When we use the word "vision" about her poems, it must have a concrete, not a philosophically general, sense. Thus "The Disquieting Muses" gives us a literal account of her "muses." After her death, her husband, Ted Hughes, said in a memorial note that in her later poems "there is a strange muse, bald, white, and wild in her hood of bone, floating over a landscape like that of the primitive painters, a burningly luminous vision of Paradise. A Paradise which is at the same time eerily frightening, an unalterably spotlit vision of death." The evolution of her muse is one sign of the growth and clarification, within a brief span of months, of Sylvia Plath's peculiar awareness of the burden of her sensibility in the whole context of the lifelong "association" with such visions.

The happier side of her poetic character is revealed in poems and passages of entrancement within nature, moments of the subordination of that sensibility to the pure rapture of existence. A marvellous moment of such entrancement comes at the beginning of "The Eye-Mote:"

> Blameless as daylight I stood looking
> At a field of horses, necks bent, manes blown,
> Tails streaming against the green
> Backdrop of sycamores. . . .

It is all turned into merely nostalgic, rueful memory, however, by a splinter that flies into the speaker's eye, as if with the deliberate intention of knocking the Wordsworth out of her — leaving only a doleful, Larkin-like sense of loss behind. Only one poem of this volume, "Flute Notes from a Reedy Pond," ends more joyfully than it began.

More characteristic are "Hardcastle Crags," a poem of absolute alienation from town and landscape both, without an ounce of self-pity or sentimentality, but as concrete and irrefutable as the rocks of which it speaks, and "The Stones." This last poem, with which the book closes, is one of those whose bearing is clearer and more harshly moving now that *Ariel* and *The Bell Jar* have illuminated the mind behind them for us. I feel rebuked not to have sensed all these meanings in the first place, for now they seem to call out from nearly every poem.

The Bell Jar

Mason Harris*

There is a general tendency to view Sylvia Plath's only novel as an immature and artistically flawed piece of catharsis, useful as background to the lyrics but not up to par for the author of *Ariel*. This rating of the novel is supported by the author herself, who, as we learn in the "Biographical Note," explained to her mother that

> What I've done is to throw together events from my own life, fictionalizing to add color — it's a pot boiler really, but I think it will show how isolated a person feels when he is suffering a breakdown. . . . I've tried to picture my world and the people in it as seen through the distorting lens of a bell jar. . . . My second book will show the same world as seen through the eyes of health ("Note," 294–95)".

Her mother thought this admission amply justified blocking publication of the novel in the U.S. on the grounds that it contained unkind caricatures of a number of people "whom Sylvia loved" when she was sane. However, authors' opinions of their own work are notoriously suspect, Sylvia's here in particular. Firstly, it would seem that she is trying to mollify in advance the wounded feelings that her mother would experience when she read the novel and found that she was one of the caricatures. Also the plan for a "healthy" novel smacks of the brisk, determinedly cheerful, efficient woman Sylvia strove to appear in her everyday life, but fortunately not in her writing. Does any of her best work seem healthy, or even tell us what health is?

Perhaps as a poet Sylvia felt some contempt for the limitations of prose. While the novel seems as morbidly self-obsessed as the final poems it can hardly, as straightforward narrative, score *Ariel's* extraordinary breakthrough in language and imagery. However, the novel also achieves something that intense confessional lyrics cannot: the poems dredge a private

*Reprinted with permission from the *West Coast Review*, 8 (October, 1973), 54–56.

sickness which seems to arise only from the personal past while the novel throws open the social dimension of madness, indicating the culture in which the heroine has grown up, or rather which prevents her from doing so. Nowhere have I found so forceful a depiction of what it was like to be an adolescent in the stifling, hermetically-sealed world of the Eisenhower 'Fifties. The "distorted lens" of madness gives an authentic vision of a period which exalted the most oppressive ideal of reason and stability.

Esther Greenwood, narrator and thinly-disguised version of Sylvia, is a brilliant straight-A student at an ivy-league Eastern women's college (Sylvia graduated *summa* from Smith). With the uncertainty attendant on compulsive drives she secretly suspects, despite all evidence to the contrary, that she is really quite stupid and ignorant and will someday be found out. As the novel opens in the summer of her Junior year she is in New York City as prize-winning guest editor of a leading fashion magazine (*Mademoiselle* in real life) experiencing, along with twelve other lucky girls, a publicity-stunt tour of the fashion world at its most superficial (the "Note" gives a sample of some deliciously awful prose Sylvia turned out for the mag). Esther forlornly reflects that this is a great opportunity for a girl of such limited means, and that she is supposed to be having the time of her life. The witty satire of the first half of the novel acquires darker meaning as the heroine (like Sylvia) lapses into madness and makes a most determined suicide attempt (far more thorough and apparently foolproof than the one which succeeded ten years later).

If this novel goes less deeply into psychotic experience than Hannah Green's *I Never Promised You A Rose Garden* or Janet Frame's *Faces in the Water* it also does a much more complete job of relating the heroine's madness to her social world. Esther's collapse is precipitated by the discovery of an inner deathliness concealed under the glossy surface of New York and her own compulsive drive to achievement. Because they are so personal, many of the poems of *Ariel* seem liable to explanation in classic Freudian formulae, but here something more is demanded. Granted that Esther-Sylvia suffered from fixation on her childhood relation to her parents, we also must ask how failure to find any feasible road to maturity contributed to her illness. Her longing to regress permeates the novel, but might not regression be partly the result of the apparent impossibility of further development?

In New York Esther acknowledges the inadequacy of the compulsive achievement which dominated her childhood and adolescence, yet cannot find a mature identity to replace it: "The one thing I was good at was winning scholarships and prizes, and that era was coming to an end. I felt like a racehorse in a world without racetracks. . . ." (84). In a significantly mechanical metaphor she sees her life as a no-thoroughfare: "I saw the years of my life speed along a road in the form of telephone poles, threaded together by wires. I counted one, two, three . . . nineteen telephone poles, and then the wires dangled into space, and try as I would, I couldn't see a single pole beyond the nineteenth" (137). Erik Erikson has described the transition from childhood to maturity as a daring leap across an abyss; the heroine of the *Bell Jar* finds only a cliff edge with nothing beyond.

The relation between regression and stifled development is particularly evident in the narrator's use of baby-images—central also to the poetry but developed with special clarity here. Pleasant baby-images are associated with the joys of regression but the novel is also haunted by the nightmare image of a fetus in a bottle—to which she was first introduced by her medical-student boyfriend. This aspect of the baby becomes a graphic expression of that sense of strangled development which is the other side of her tendency to regression. When after her recovery her mother says, "We'll act as if all this were a bad dream;" Esther thinks "To the person in the bell jar, blank and stopped as a dead baby, the world itself is the bad dream" (267). A particularly striking image links arrested growth to the world of the 'Fifties. From the pages of *Life Magazine* "The face of Eisenhower beamed up at me, bald and blank as the face of a fetus in a bottle" (98). Esther also hates babies because they represent the ideal of total domesticity, but sometimes longs to become a mother as a form of psychic suicide.

Esther's breakdown comes after a series of unfortunate encounters with sex in New York. The ensuing psychosis could partly be explained on the grounds of sexual repression and morbid attachment to her dead father, but it is also true that all the men she has known manifest variations on a consistently sick attitude toward women and marriage; since no remotely acceptable relationship is available her libido has nowhere to go but backwards.

The novel's sexuality is dominated by the American Mom as represented by her boyfriend's mother, Mrs. Willard, "with her heather-mixture tweeds and her sensible shoes and her wise, maternal maxims. Mr. Willard was her little boy, and his voice was high and clear, like a little boy's" (245). The most oft-repeated of these maxims are " 'What a man wants is a mate and what a woman wants is infinite security,' and 'What a man is is an arrow into the future and what a woman is is the place the arrow shoots off from' " (79). Her boyfriend Buddy, a "nice, clean boy" and a magnificent specimen of the male ideal of the 'Fifties in all his sentimental nobility, is particularly devoted to his mother. (When he sexlessly exhibits himself to Esther he explains that he wears net underpants because " 'my mother says they wash easily' " (75).

The Oedipedal split between pure love and degraded sexuality is made explicit by a Southern gentleman who laments to Esther that he can't have sex with a woman he truly loves: "it would be spoiled by thinking this woman too was just an animal like the rest, so if he loved anybody he would never go to bed with her. He'd go to a whore if he had to and keep the woman he loved free of all that dirty business" (87). Esther gives up on him when he writes with incestuous ardor that she has "such a kind face, surprisingly like his older sister's."

In their big date at Yale, Buddy treats her "like a friend or cousin," kissing her only once gently behind the chem. lab—" 'Wow, it makes me feel terrific to kiss you' " (68). Esther has been much impressed with the necessity of remaining pure till her marriage night, and is outraged to find that while dating her the "clean" Buddy has fornicated at least thirty times with "some tarty waitress" who seduced him over the summer. Her more experienced friends explain that "most boys were like that" but Esther can't stand "the idea of a woman having to have a pure life and a man being able to have a double life, one pure and one not" (90). She also begins to suspect that being the object of his "pure life" might become a bit oppressive: "I . . . remembered Buddy Willard saying in a sinister, knowing way that after I had children, I would feel differently. I wouldn't want to write poems any more" (94). Perhaps "infinite security" is only a more painful form of suicide.

The most intense form of Oedipedal passion is demonstrated by Marco, a Latin woman-hater Esther meets at a party on her last evening in New York. He adores his first cousin — about to enter a nunnery — but can't marry her because of South American ideas about incest. When Esther offers the consolation that someday " 'you'll love somebody else' " he responds by throwing her in the mud — " 'Your dress is black and the dirt is black as well' " — spitting in her face, and trying to rape her while repeatedly hissing " 'Slut!' " in her ear. She virtuously fights him off but he still insists. " 'Sluts, all sluts. . . . Yes or no, it is all the same' " (121). It would seem that some violence also lurks in Buddy's love. He contracts T.B. and when Esther visits him at the sanitorium he resents her relative health and freedom. He forces her to ski down a dangerous slope and when she takes the inevitable spill informs her, smiling with a "queer, satisfied expression," that " 'Your leg's broken in two places. You'll be stuck in a cast for months' " (109). These episodes seem so apt that one wonders whether they really happened that way, or were structured by the author to represent the inner truth of her experience — but since they are quite convincing this hardly matters.

Thus personal relationships present no alternative to Esther's pursuit of straight A's. Hysterical and sexless devotion to the performance principal is exemplified by her friend Joan Gilling, a local "big wheel — president of her class and a physics major and the college hockey champion" (65). Joan, who later turns out to be a Lesbian, dates Buddy because she so admires his mother. After learning of Esther's suicide attempt Joan becomes inspired to try it herself and winds up at the same asylum, where Esther sees her as "the beaming double of my old best self" (231). Joan brings along all her schoolbooks, studies Freud, plans to become a psychiatrist, and finally hangs herself. At her funeral Esther finds some consolation in the fact that she herself has escaped this fate, but the reader knows that her apparent recovery is only a reprieve.

This novel is enclosed in many prisons, all expanded forms of the bell jar. The ladies in "Belsize," the "best" ward of Esther's exclusive hospital, put on a good imitation of upper middle class living: "What was there about us, in Belsize, so different from the girls playing bridge and gossiping and studying in the college to which I would return? Those girls, too, sat under bell jars of a sort" (268). During her summer in New York the Rosenbergs are electrocuted and Esther "couldn't help wondering what it would be like, being burnt alive along all your nerves"(1). Later in a seedy private mental hospital she is punished for madness by shock therapy incompetently (or sadistically) administered: "with each flash a great jolt drubbed me till I thought my bones would break and the sap fly out of me like a split plant. I wondered what terrible thing it was that I had done" (161). The parents of Esther's world seem to feel that mental and even physical illness arises from weak moral character. Esther's mother makes her become a volunteer worker in local hospitals because "the cure for thinking too much about yourself was helping somebody who was worse off than you" (182). Buddy's father "simply couldn't stand the sight of sickness and especially his own son's sickness, because he thought all sickness was sickness of the will" (101).

In the end Esther's cure seems to consist more of resignation to prison than escape from it. If madness was precipitated by a demand for something better than the compulsive past, recovered sanity seems a depressing return to her "old best self" because nothing better has been found. Esther's coldly calculated plan to lose her virginity ends in a freak hemorrhage which seems to comment on the fallacy of trying to will an emotional experience. Sylvia once described the *Bell Jar* as "an autobiographical apprentice work which I had to write in order to free myself from the past" ("Note," 293). Though better than this the novel did not grant the self understanding that would free her, nor did the even more brilliant *Ariel*. On the other hand if madness is a form of insight and itself a comment on its causes, then effective expression of it may achieve success in art, if not in life. In its forceful linking of private to public madness the *Bell Jar* not only adds a new dimension to the poetry but deserves to be considered a major work in its own right.

Inhabited by a Cry: The Last
Poetry of Sylvia Plath [*Ariel*]   Peter Davison*

Only rarely, and almost never when still alive, does a poet become the object of a cult. Sylvia Plath, age thirty, died in London in 1963, leaving behind her a sheaf of terrifying poems. Since then, and especially in the past year, poem after poem has been written to her memory by people who never knew her work while she was alive. The fable of "her abrupt, defiant death," as Robert Lowell puts it, sees her as immolated on the altar of a cruel society, her poems the outraged by-product of her last agony. But to

*Reprinted with permission from the *Atlantic Monthly*, 218, No. 2 (August, 1966), 76–77.

oversimplify her life, making her into the James Dean of modern poetry, would also be to oversimplify and vulgarize the development of her work.

Sylvia Plath was a greatly but unevenly gifted woman who took the trouble, and had the intellectual resources, to train herself for a decade as a poet. The *Atlantic* and other periodicals published a fair amount of her early work, written in her twenties, and it showed an unusual sense of rhythm, a vocabularly that had a long, accurate reach, and a protean talent kept under severe control.

The early poems, many of them published in a collection called *The Colossus* (published first in London; then in a shortened version by Knopf, 1962, $4.00), seemed to have no absolute necessity for being: they read like advanced exercises. She wrote a lot of prose as well, including a novel, but none that I have read seemed to me much out of the ordinary. Sylvia Plath's talent, though intensely cultivated, did not bloom into genius until the last months of her life, when, if we may take the internal evidence of the poems in *Ariel* (also published first in London; Harper & Row, $4.95) as our guide, she stood at the edge of the abyss of existence and looked, steadily, courageously, with holy curiosity, to the very bottom. It is not a matter for personal praise or personal blame that she did so; but the resultant poetry has a bone-chilling authority that could not have been achieved except by steady staring. No artifice alone could have conjured up such effects; yet such is the paradox of art, these poems would never have come into being without the long, deliberate, technical training that had preceded them. We can only perform with true spontaneity what we have first learned to do by habit.

Every artist, and almost everyone else, at one time or another fetches up against the stark facts of life and death. No one can avert his gaze at such a time without some degree of self-betrayal, even though he may be turned to stone if he continues looking. The greatest writers have been able to record these terrible moments against the larger canvas of ordinary life, adjusting the threatened catastrophes of death and destruction among related and contrasting themes of life and hope and renewel. It has become fashionable—or if not fashionable, at least common—for poets to set down their autobiographical crises, first person and second person and all, as a qualifying confession to admit them to the fraternity—a kind of professional good-conduct pass. All the difference in the world, however, lies between such antics, performed always with an audience in mind, whether explicitly in the poem or implicitly in its tone, and, on the other hand, such terrifying lines as these, from several of the poems in *Ariel*. No matter to whom these may be addressed, they are written for nobody's ears except the writer's. They have a ritual ring, the inevitable preface to doom.

From "Lady Lazarus"

> Dying
> Is an art, like everything else.
> I do it exceptionally well.

I do it so it feels like hell.
I do it so it feels real.
I guess you could say I've a call . . .

Herr God, Herr Lucifer,
Beware
Beware.

Out of the ash
I rise with my red hair
And I eat men like air.

From "Lesbos" (one mother speaks to another)

You say you can't stand her,
The bastard's a girl.
You who have blown your tubes like a bad radio
Clear of voices and history, the staticky
Noise of the new.
You say I should down the kittens. Their smell!
You say I should drown my girl.
She'll cut her throat at ten if she's mad at two.
The baby smiles, fat snail,
From the polished lozenges of orange linoleum.
You could eat him. He's a boy.
You say your husband is just no good to you.

From "Death & Co."

I do not stir.
The frost makes a flower
The dew makes a star,
The dead bell,
The dead bell.

Somebody's done for.

From "Elm"

I know the bottom, she says. I know it with
        my great tap root:
It is what you fear.
I do not fear it: I have been there . . .

I am inhabited by a cry.
Nightly it flaps out
Looking, with its hooks, for something to love.

From "The Applicant"

First, are you our sort of person?
Do you wear

A glass eye, false teeth or a crutch,
A brace or a hook,
Rubber breasts or a rubber crotch,

Stitches to show something's missing? No, no? Then
How can we give you a thing? . . .

A living doll, everywhere you look.
It can sew, it can cook,
It can talk, talk, talk.

It works, there is nothing wrong with it.
You have a hole, it's a poultice.
You have an eye, it's an image.
My boy, it's your last resort.
Will you marry it, marry it, marry it.

To be given over to poems like these is to stand at the poet's side frozen, but powerless to reach a hand out as she falls. Though the poems have humor in them ("I guess you could say I've a call"), it is gallows humor. They carry little of the playfulness that is contained in most poetry. Their hectic, breathless rhythms give plenty of evidence that they were written in dead earnest, as stays against confusion that were at best only momentary. What else is there to do when you are "inhabited by a cry"? Nothing but to set down what you see, what strikes you, without compunction or consideration. That is what these poems have done. It is all poetry *can* do in the situation.

The poems in *Ariel* are poems of defeat except in one sense: that they exist at all. It would be preposterous to suggest that the experience embodied here is unique; but it would be a lie to suggest that experience alone could have written these poems, that they could have been written by anyone but a true poet. They are a triumph for poetry, in fact, at the moment that they are a defeat for their author.

To have prepared, with all the devices and techniques of an art, for the awful catastrophe which you alone were fitted to face is to have sacrificed for art more victims than life can dispense with. One even infers, from the grim joy of some of these poems, that at the moment of writing, Sylvia Plath's life was eagerly consuming all its careful preparations. The candle is burnt out, and we have nothing left but the flame.

"Perfection Is Terrible; It Cannot Have Children . . . ."

Barbara Drake*

It is her vision of life's imperfections which gives forceful birth to Sylvia Plath's poetry. The poems in *Ariel* tell us that life is a kind of sickness, that in living we are wounded to death. But for all their sardonic humor, their catalogues of injury and failings, their pleas for anaesthesia, these are not poems of nihilism.

There is none of the righteous negation, for example, which often mars works denouncing an existing order. If the speaker of these poems sometimes extracts herself from the fabric of the work, it is, more often than not, to take a cool, ironic look at her own failings. The "Birthday Present" asks:

> Is this the one I am to appear for,
> Is this the elect one, the one with black eye-pits
>   and a scar?
> Measuring the flour, calling off the surplus,
> Adhering to rules, to rules, to rules.
> Is this the one for the annunciation?
> My god, what a laugh!

There are no demands for reform, either within or without the self. If there is one thing about these poems with which we wish to tamper, it may be their cutting objectivity, this lack of expressed morality. You show us the world, we might say to the poet; what are we to *do* about it? But the integrity of the vision is such that these works bend neither to prescribe nor escape. In "Years" she says:

> O God, I am not like you
> In your vacuous black,
> Stars stuck all over, bright stupid confetti.
> Eternity bores me,
> I never wanted it.
>
> What I love is
> The piston in motion —

Perhaps these poems could be accused of trying, weakly, to straddle a philosophical fence. In "Tulips," the hospital patient says:

> I didn't want any flowers, I only wanted
> To lie with my hands turned up and be utterly empty.
>
> The tulips are too red in the first place, they hurt me.

While in "Berck-Plage," the stiff, white face of a man who has died in a bed elicits the exclamation: "This is what it is to be complete. It is horrible."

*Reprinted with permission from the *Northwest Review*, 9 (Summer, 1967), 101–103.

Neither the horrible perfection of death nor the painful imperfection of life is satisfactory. What, then, do these poems utter?"

Generally considered "confessional" poetry, the poems of Sylvia Plath make us intensely aware of an individual voice, a decisively personal character, but display none of the more uncomfortable associations of the word. "Daddy," perhaps the most personal and vituperative of the poems, escapes being what it might have become in a more truly "confessional" treatment, a nasty harangue or the hacking of a helpless scapegoat. There is hatred here, and frustration. But the speaker is as much object as the instrument of the poem. She says, "If I've killed one man, I've killed two—"

In this, as in a number of the poems, such as "Lady Lazarus" and "The Applicant," a kind of nursery rhythm and repetition appears, which gives the poem the intensity of ritual. "Daddy" becomes a communal expurgation of evil, embodied in a figure as broad as a continent and inescapable as the sky.

> There's a stake in your fat black heart
> And the villagers never liked you.
> They are dancing and stamping on you.

True, our retrospective knowledge of the poet's impending death imbues the poems with a sacramental quality, as if each utterance signifies a ceremonial purification, or gives voice to painful ecstasy to which death is the inevitable conclusion. But such an approach, besides being unnecessary to the experience of these poems, renders them less rather than more accessible, for it so much as assumes, here are the gimmicks of poetry, while beyond those velvet ropes is the soul of this woman; overstep them and despair.

In many ways, the poems which make up *Ariel* are no more confessional, for example, than *Gulliver's Travels* or *Through the Looking Glass*. Like those works, her poems conjure madness in things which seem, in their customary perspective, most real. Life itself, viewed close-up, is a phantasma of honeycombs and old scars, clattering mouths and marbled eyeballs. A character exists in a poem as a black boot or a letter through the mail, "White and blank, expansive as carbon monoxide." Our "loving associations," the smile of a husband and child, are also little hooks that tear flesh. Love, death, knowledge, emotion, human entanglements, all "are the isolate, slow faults/That kill, that kill, that kill."

[Review of *Ariel*]   Robert L. Stilwell*

Ariel, by the late Sylvia Plath, has surely become the most talked-about volume by an American poet since John Berryman's 77 *Dream Songs* and Roethke's posthumously published *The Far Field*. That its poems grew out of terrible and shattering and finally unbearable experiences, no one who reads them could gainsay for a moment; and certainly it is difficult not to be moved to (and by) speculation about those experiences, so far as they are hinted — and rendered — within the cryptic *in extremis* privacy of the poetry itself. But to suspend one's critical attention as somehow impertinent, to indulge the brittle fervors of biographical gossip and instant-mythos, means to default the poems that survived the experiences and that bestow upon them their defining form. The most useful enterprise, as always, is to cut through the swirling fog of talk and to determine, so far as possible, what these final poems come to as poems: an enterprise abetted not at all by Robert Lowell's rhapsodic three-page "Foreword."

Perhaps the first point that requires making is that, contrary to most of the reviews and review-articles that I have come across, the poetry within *Ariel* does not penetrate darknesses into which no poet had previously ventured. Emily Dickinson with a handful of her most harrowing zero-at-the-bone poems on madness and dying, Roethke in page after page of his middle-period work — these are only two of the poets who had been there before and who returned to create triumphant poetry. (Anne Sexton in *To Bedlam and Part Way Back*, Lowell, and Hayden Carruth in "The Asylum" are other poets who have employed some of the same subject-matter, although far less triumphantly.) However, it was by no means necessary that Sylvia Plath's poems *should* explore darkness never before charted. A darkness searched remains a darkness, still capable of generating whatever poetry, major or minor, a later poet can achieve. If I were compelled to formulate a single comprehensive statement about these poems (a dubious undertaking at best), I should prefer not to suggest that they are poems "about" psychosis, although to a degree this is unquestionably true. I would maintain, rather, that they are poems which find their fullest analogies in the visions and emotional states and awful insights of psychosis — a distinction that seems to me useful and not mere quibbling. Throughout *Ariel*, language hardens, or seeks to harden, on the truth of a shriek. In a world of outrages and "vulturous boredom", a world lit by "cobra light", things come to live with the devouring horror of hallucination:

> I am mad, calls the spider, waving its many arms.

> And in truth it is terrible,
> Multiplied in the eyes of the flies.

*Reprinted with permission from *Sewanee Review* (as "The Multiplying of Entities: D. H. Lawrence and Five Other Poets"), 76 (July-Sept., 1968), 520–35.

> They buzz like blue children. . . .

Madness and suicide—especially suicide—are guessed at, touched obsessively like sores, fondled like razor blades. The "birthday present" in the poem by that title is really death:

> What is this, behind this veil, is it ugly, is it beautiful?
> Is it shimmering, has it breasts, has it edges?
>
> Let us sit down to it, one on either side, admiring the gleam,
>
> The glaze, the mirrory variety of it.
> Let us eat our last supper at it, like a hospital plate.

In "Lady Lazarus" a suicide-attempt is figured with what are probably the most chilling lines in the book:

> I rocked shut
>
> As a seashell.
> They had to call and call
> And pick the worms off me like sticky pearls.

For the life of me, I cannot escape the conviction that to experience any five or six of the poems from *Ariel*—say "Death & Co.", "Elm", "Lady Lazarus", "Getting There", "Lesbos", and "The Bee Meeting"— is to have experienced all forty-three of them. Too many frightful imaginings, too similar in setting and burden, soon begin to extinguish one another. I am convinced, also, that some of these poems disclose failures of language, moments in which, to levy on Sylvia Plath's own image, the words become "riderless". (Anyone who doubts this might glance at the conjunction "mirrory variety" in one of the lines quoted above, at the metaphoric shambles of the poem entitled "Words", or at the circular string of uncontrolled conceits in "Cut".) At the same time, putting up with repetitions and weaknesses enables one to come upon a poem like "Contusion," in which

> The size of a fly,
> The doom mark
> Crawls down the wall.

One cannot, of course, offer a sure prediction; but I should guess that *Ariel* will linger as a very specialized and rather subterranean book of poems, that A.M. theses will be written on it (doubtless several are already under way), and that it will not, finally, add a major dimension to the poetry of the 1960's. Time—or whatever it is that decides—will confirm the truth or error of these surmises.

Collecting Her Strength [*Crossing the Water*]

Peter Porter*

This is the second posthumous collection of poems from Sylvia Plath's official publisher. The first, *Ariel*, containing poems written just before her death, was one of the most powerful books since the war. *Crossing the Water* consists of poems written in 1960 and 1961, after *The Colossus* was published but before her final intense period of creation. It's important to stress that they are not *Ariel* left-overs, but poems of the brief interregnum between her strange precocity and full maturity. A further volume, *Winter Trees*, will follow shortly, taking us up to *Ariel* itself. It might have been a good idea to issue one carefully-edited collected edition rather than bring out everything piecemeal, but the logistics of the Plath inheritance are nothing beside the advantages of possessing the poems. *Crossing the Waters* is full of perfectly realised works. Its most striking impression is of a front-rank artist in the process of discovering her true power. Such is Plath's control that the book possesses a singularity and certainty which should make it as celebrated as *The Colossus* or *Ariel*. Once more death has all the best parts, but his disguises and metamorphoses are doubly audacious. In "Mirror," for example, the little, four-cornered god denies it has any preconceptions, but when a woman bends over it she sees not only her own agitation but the fate which awaits her:

> In me she has drowned a young girl,
> and in me an old woman
> Rises towards her day after day, like a
> terrible fish.

In this period of Plath's poetry, objects come towards the reader like frightening Greek messengers. The gifts are not even ambiguous; they are seen wearing their proud colours of destruction. The language is that carefully judged half-formal, half-vernacular one she perfected in *Ariel*. It's capable of bearing the full weight of the grand style while staying true to the sharpest observation of reality. As John Frederick Nims pointed out, submerged iambics glisten like reefs under her expressionist surfaces. The "I" of these poems is usually changing, as often as not reaching full authority only in terror. In "Love Letter," she is as fanciful as any metaphysical, but the transformation scene is a matter of life and death:

> I started to bud like a March twig:
> An arm and a leg, an arm, a leg.
> From stone to cloud, so I ascended.
> Now I resemble a sort of god
> Floating through the air in my soul-shift
> Pure as a pane of ice. It's a gift.

*Reprinted with permission from *New Statesman*, 81 (June 4, 1971), 774–75.

So speaks the apprentice "Lady Lazarus." The vignette, frequently in three-line stanzas, is a form she is especially successful in. The title poem is one case: the scene is a lake with a boat on it, as normal as if she were writing a barcarolle. But with a few changes of harmony and a straightforward summoning of death, she makes it the lake of Hell:

> Cold worlds shake from the oar.
> The spirit of blackness is in us, it is in the fishes.
> A snag is lifting a valedictory, pale hand;
> Stars open among the lilies.
> Are you not blinded by such expressionless sirens?
> This is the silence of astounded souls.

Only a truly remarkable poet could afford to rely upon so much downright statement and mix it so surely with metaphor. When she sets an elaborate metaphorical machine in motion, as with "In Plaster," she pursues it as circumstantially as if she were Poe, but there are no ghostly props and no fustian either. In this poem, the plaster-of-paris cast is not just a convenient device to embody schizophrenic otherness, it becomes one of two persons in a closet drama. It could be *Huis Clos* or Isherwood's Mr. Norris bound to his dreadful satellite, Schmidt. The end becomes tragic wish-fulfillment:

> I'm collecting my strength; one day I shall
>   manage without her
> And she'll perish with emptiness then, and
>   begin to miss me.

In the security of theorising, it makes bad art to find death's chrysalis in every stage of life. But Sylvia Plath runs counter to our schools of "life-enhancing" critics — she deals in what most people cannot accept. And we, her legatees, profit by her courage. The last poem in the book is from hospital, mankind's alma mater. It's called "Among the Narcissi," and is a picture of an old man (an old world perhaps?) recuperating on a garden walk. While there is poetry, there is life:

> There is a dignity to this; there is a formality —
> The flowers vivid as bandages, and the man mending.
> They bow and stand: they suffer such attacks!
> And the octogenarian loves the little flocks.
> He is quite blue; the terrible wind tries
>   his breathing.
> The narcissi look up like children, quickly
>   and whitely.

Crossing the Water   Paul West*

Had Sylvia Plath been ugly, and not died in so deliberate a manner, I wonder if she would have the standing she has. Maybe so; she seems an unusually good poet, at her best pithy and stark, with a passion for minute accuracy in recording the physical, and not afraid to be caustic or discordant. Something muscular shows up in her work, as unusual in woman poets as visceral self-pity seems common. And (this perhaps gathered from living among the English) she has a way of putting catastrophe casually, without frills, and you wince at the zombie decorum with which she does it. It's precarious, though, only a bit more decorum than it is a shambles; its tautness might snap and scatter. Reading her is like standing on the San Andreas fault or crawling on a glass roof; she sets up a nervewracking excitement after which, as the poems end, you feel drained and down. She cannot be read aloofly.

On the other hand, there is the cult which finds her a seraphic cosmic victim, a self-elected St. Joan of the post-natal clinic, whose every word is loaded with unimpeachable witness. Male reviewers and critics, in England especially, permitted themselves a breaking of the waters; after years of magistrally rebuking poets whose diction wasn't crisp enough, they gushed out on the occasion of *Ariel* (1966), so much so that a new form of verbal solecism — the Plathitude — came into being. One had never realized that these taskmasters of the London poetry playground had any gush in them, anything but calipers and spirit level. When a Yukio Mishima disembowels himself and has himself beheaded, your English literato finds it a piece of tasteless oriental exhibitionism, not in the well-bred or even the fish-and-chips tradition. When a Sylvia Plath does away with herself, she sets off a chain reaction that has more to do with atavistic, sacrificial rituals — Venus romanticized — than with the excellence or unevenness of her writing (which was evident in *The Colossus*, 1960). The novelist, so-called, will always seem a mercantile figure, whereas the poet, so-called, will always seem a visionary, with one foot in myth and one eye on Orpheus. The poetry is in the pituitary. After which it is almost beside the point to note that Sylvia Plath's recently reissued autobiographical novel, *The Bell Jar*, is hardly as well written as her weakest poems; yet the cult touts it, extols it.

Now comes a book of "transitional" poems, most of which Sylvia Plath wrote between 1960 and 1963, one of which, the title poem, a dim and flimsy thing, "reveals just how deeply the poet felt the hardness of life *and* death." Or so the blurb has it, with that knowing italicization of "and" to tell us tritely this was a *complete* poet. In fact the book is rich with fastidious irony, with a juicy *Schaden-freude* that doesn't go too deep, something neither histrionic nor simplistic; we read about the insubstantiality of being

*Reprinted with permission from *Book World* (*Chicago Tribune*), January 9, 1972, p. 8.

someone—some *one*—in a world of instant certitudes. Here is Plath on
sheep:

> The black slots of their pupils take me in.
> It is like being mailed into space,
> A thin, silly message.
> They stand about in grandmotherly disguise,
> All wig curls and yellow teeth
> And hard, marble baas.

Observant indeed. Here she is on anaesthesia:

> When I was nine, a lime-green anesthetist
> Fed me banana gas through a frog-mask.

On skin:

> Skin doesn't have roots, it peels away easy as paper.

On blackberries:

> I come to one bush of berries so ripe It Is a bush of flies,
> Hanging their blue-green bellies and their wing panes
>   in a Chinese screen.

Chrysanthemums:

> Now I'm stared at
> By chrysanthemums the size
> Of Holofernes' head, dipped in the same
> Magenta as this fubsy sofa.

A drained fish-pond:

> The baby carp
> Litter the mud like orangepeel.

   Observation as innovative as this functions as all-round allusiveness, as
if to suggest everything has been tested by the senses—counterpart to one
poem that ends, "Everything has happened." It is homework done on the
world of things which, although inseparable from us in the ecological tissue, were not created to return our sentient stare. There is always in Plath a
sense that this, right here, is as far as the mind may be able to go; so, instead
of hermeneutics, settle for a precise look, a concise delineation, something
solid to grip while investigating human emotions (which may be just as enigmatic as sheep, anaesthesia, or skin). Her dense specificity makes her
people more present than their emotions do. For example, the crystalliza-
tion in the fourth line of the following not only points the statement as a
whole but almost supplants it:

> And my grandfather moped in the Tyrol,
> Imagining himself a headwaiter in America,
> Floating in a high-church hush
> Among ice buckets, frosty napkins.

In that line grandfather becomes a third entity along with the buckets and the napkins; imagining them into being he exists for us in terms of them only — like the surgeon who calls tissue-slices his "pathological salami," an image in which the mind (Plath's transposed into his) has gone as far as it descriptively can and the yield of its effort becomes an emblem too of all the mind wants said but can't find. This is Plath's forte: definitions with an incomplete agnosticism, the stock-in-trade of one she calls "Fido Littlesoul, the bowel's familiar." The rationale comes in the poem "Last Words":

> I do not trust the spirit. It escapes like steam
> In dreams, through mouth-hole or eye-hole. I can't
>   stop it.
> One day it won't come back. Things aren't like that.
> They stay . . .

And the Zoo Keeper's wife proves it on our pulses:

> Your two-horned rhinoceros opened a mouth
> Dirty as a bootsole and big as a hospital sink
> For my cube of sugar: its bog breath
> Gloved my arm to the elbow.
> The snails blew kisses like black apples.
> Nightly now I flog apes owls bears sheep
> Over their iron stile. And still don't sleep.

In the long haul things aren't enough, are too much: Holding on to them, you become beholden to them, nearly lapse into being one; and the last few poems in this collection, all short, blunt, short-winded lines, emphasize the thingness of lines themselves:

> The month of flowering's finished. The fruit's in.
> Eaten or rotten. I am all mouth.
> October's the month for storage.
> This shed's fusty as a mummy's stomach:
> Old tools, handles and rusty tusks.
> I am at home here among the dead heads.

This is the laconic stasis of Plath's mature manner, with her eye as retentive as ever but her mind like a child's head banging repeatedly against a wall. The idiom evokes Shakespeare's Poor Tom and some Old English riddles; the lines add up to something they don't wholly propel. They enact the difference between a poem that unfurls or unfolds and a poem that is all halts. Her span of confidence is usually only a line's length and she seems glad, after each completed sortie, to return to the left-hand margin which is fixed and static. She stabs a period at the line's end to stop it coming after her into the next. The lines cage her in and she shrinks within her confines.

Crossing the Water (lame title to be foisted on such a skillful phrase-smith) is a substantial eyeful from an unflagging sharp sensibility; a small pageant in insistent vernacular; a book of vivid austerities in which Plath advances from the release of saying almost anything, so long as it's with an engraver's precision, to the containment of saying literally next-to-nothing — a nextness of which her sense was to become woundedly acute. Her later poems tell us how close you can go before you fall in.

Damaged Instruments
[*Crossing the Water*]
Douglas Dunn*

The poems in Sylvia Plath's *The Colossus* are largely flawed by a rhythmical and lexical vulgarity. However, many of them are very good poems, there is a powerful sense of them having come from a single, eccentric imagination, and they are full of strange and startling expressions. They are also identifiably by the author of *Ariel*. For example, there are forecasts of *Ariel*'s subject-matter, that evolution of psychological background, domestic oppression and public and private pain, into a private and ultimate specialisation. In order to achieve that unique and powerful poetry it was necessary to abandon the earlier clotted style. She herself said of the *Ariel* poems: ". . . I have found myself having to read them aloud to myself. Now this is something I didn't do. For example, my first book *The Colossus* — I can't read any of the poems aloud now, I didn't write them to be read aloud. In fact, they quite quietly bore me. Now these very recent ones — I've got to say them. I speak them to myself. Whatever lucidity they may have comes from the fact that I say them aloud." I doubt if many people find most of *Ariel* exactly lucid, but there is a quite obvious liberation of tone and freedom of movement in her later verse which is unlike anything in *The Colossus*. It will be reasonable to suggest that the compulsion to dramatise what she had come to see as her identity was so strong, and so artistically felt, that it was necessary to devise a way of writing that would be a literary version of the identity she was obsessed with fulfilling — in other words she had to find her "own voice", that unriddable cliché.

The poems in *Ariel* were written in 1962 and 1963. Between then and the poems in *The Colossus* (written between 1956 and 1959) Plath was perhaps feeling towards her final style, although it seems more likely, bearing in mind that legendary remark about writing three poems a day seven days a week at four in the morning, that the final style was realised very quickly. In this new collection, *Crossing the Water*, Ted Hughes has collected a number of poems written in this so-called "transitional" period. Many have already been printed in magazines and in two private press selections by the Turret Press and the Rainbow Press, and another volume, *Winter Trees*, is promised.

Crossing the Water is much freer in style than the first book. There is still something formulaic and precious about her phrase-making: ". . . a

*Reprinted with permission from *Encounter* (August, 1971), pp. 68–70.

valedictory, pale hand"; or "Black, admonitory cliffs." However, there is more of that zany, accurate and unexpected imagery that is so central to the style of *Ariel*, and also the first book. Alert, nervous, and often domestic, it is one of her peculiar strengths:

> Now, in valleys narrow
> And black as purses, the house lights
> Gleam like small change
>
> The city melts like sugar
> Now the pills are worn out and silly as classical gods
>
> All morning, with smoking breath, the handy-man
> Has been draining the goldfish ponds.
> They collapse like lungs . . . .

This demotic kind of simile-making is very feminine. She mocks the masculine world with flurries of domestic detail. The irritation and peevishness of this is profound miles beyond the fashionable nonsense of Women's Lib, and it is an essential strand of what Alvarez has called "the terrible unforgiveness of her verse . . . violent resentment that this should have been done to *her.*"

But by quoting disjointed excerpts I don't want to give the impression that the book is a mere happy hunting ground of stray felicities, important only in relation to *Ariel*. Sustained poems of great quality are gathered in this book. "In Plaster", for example, is a monologue spoken by an invalid about the plaster mould that encases her, and which has become an image of her death. Despite the morbid whimsy on which the poem is founded, it is a remarkable poem objectifying a state of mind, and it leads her to frightening statements:

> She wanted to leave me, she thought she was superior,
> And I'd been keeping her in the dark, and she was resentful,
> Wasting her days waiting on a half-corpse!
> And secretly she began to hope I'd die.

"Blackberrying" is a poem of menacing description. Like many others in the book it is made from direct statements — "The only thing to come now is the sea" — leading into surprising language and imagery — "and a din like silversmiths / Beating and beating at an intractable metal." Above all, however, the new ingredient in her poetry of this period is an improved sense of drama, a much stronger narrative interest, as well as an accompanying thinning out of the clots that made that kind of writing impossible in *The Colossus*, although she came close to it in "The Disquieting Muses."

What struck me most after reading *Crossing the Water* was not just that it was so good, or that none of the poems there had been thought good enough for *Ariel*, but that *Ariel* itself represents such a unified stretch of work, such a strong and tragically magnificent working out of a single complicated theme. Only one poem in the new book might be at home in *Ariel*. "The Tour", a parable of a confrontation between the safe life and the terrors of endangered existence, set entirely in a female context, has all that harrowing vernacular directness of her best-known poems, "Daddy" and "Lady Lazarus". However, it is the imaginative power of a poem like "In Plaster" or "Insomniac" that forecasts what I consider to be her best poem — "The Bee Meeting." There is something shrill about "Daddy" and "Lady Lazarus" which, although understandable as overstatements, seem to attain a theatrically, an interior melodrama, that I find hard to take.

> Nightlong in the granite yard, invisible cats
> Have been howling like women, or damaged instruments.

Crossing the Water is an indispensable book, and Sylvia Plath one of that handful of modern poets whom intelligent readers will feel, more and more, that they have no option but to try and understand.

Winter Trees   Damian Grant*

Faber have indicated that we may expect the complete edition of Sylvia Plath's poems early next year. Meanwhile we have here the second of two volumes of poems left unpublished at her death in 1963, and now published by Ted Hughes (who introduced them in the Summer, 1971 edition of *Critical Quarterly*). *Winter Trees* is the slimmest as well as the last of Sylvia Plath's collection; there are nineteen poems here on forty printed pages. But there is ample further evidence of her endless imaginative resource in the restatement of her familiar themes: all proceeding, ultimately, from the "divided self," the self which is alienated, oppressed, disembodied, dissolved. We meet again the familiar images, particularly the (characteristically schizoid) image of the mirror, which appears in all but two of these poems and seems to haunt them with its inevitability and its destructiveness:

> Mirrors can kill and talk, they are terrible rooms
> In which a torture goes on one can only watch.

We are dazed again by the complicated use of colours, almost as a symbolism, to signify states of mind, attitudes; the alienating absolutes of black and white, the terrifying violence red almost always means, the uncertainty of blue, which can signify the cold night-blue of the moon ("What blue, moony ray ices their dreams?"), blue angels — "the cold angels, the abstrac-

*Reprinted with permission from *Critical Quarterly*, 14 (Spring, 1972), 92–94.

tions," or the sky-blue of a child's eyes; and the occasional consolation of the organic colours, brown and green.

In these poems a woman is on trial before herself, and spared nothing. A woman who longs for the unconscious life of trees: "Knowing neither abortions nor bitchery, Truer than women, / They seed so effortlessly!"; a woman who has sacrificed herself to the will of another person: "I am his. Even in his Absence, I / Revolve in my Sheath of Impossibles"; a childless woman who sees her menstrual cycle as a reproach to her futility: "The womb Rattles its pod, the moon / Discharges itself from the tree with no-where to go"; a woman who is tormented by the simple exacerbation of being, to whom the air is "a mill of hooks." A woman recalling the abortion that saved her from having a deformed child: "The dark fruits revolve and fall. / The glass cracks across, The image Flees and aborts like dropped mercury"; a woman imagining to herself the future of her fatherless child:

> You will be aware of an absence, presently,
> Growing beside you, like a tree,
> A death tree, colour gone, an Australian gum tree —
> Balding, gelded by lightning — an illusion.
> And a sky like a pig's backside, an utter lack of attention.

A woman addressing her separated self (in the difficult poem "Lesbos"), a self full of hatred, on the subject of her schizoid child ("Her face is red and white, a panic"), her impotent husband who is kept as "An old pole for the lightning" of her moods, and the impossibility of her own reintegration: "We should meet in another life, we should meet in air, / Me and you," but "Even in your Zen heaven we won't meet." She must simply suffer the discord of her "two venomous opposites" floating in "The smog of cooking, the smog of hell."

But the most important poem in this collection is certainly the poem for three voices, "Three Women," which was broadcast by the BBC in 1962 and published four years ago in a limited edition. In this vividly successful dramatic experiment (which must surely be due for another hearing) three women offer a commentary on their contrasting experiences in a maternity ward "and round about": one woman who gives birth to a child and is fulfilled, a second who has a miscarriage, and a third who suffers the death of her new-born baby. The violence implicit in female physiology, the violence of the phallic intervention into this, the violence of childbirth (recalling Berryman's *Mistress Bradstreet*) are all detained here in the marvellous focus of Sylvia's Plath's imagination:

> He flew into the room, a shriek at his heel.
> The blue colour pales. He is human after all.
> A red lotus opens in its bowl of blood. . . .

and resolved, finally, in post-natal amnesia and its confirming images of peace and growth:

Dawn flowers in the great elm outside the house. . . .
                    . . . The little grasses
Crack through stone, and they are green with life.

Only a detailed analysis — or, better, an attentive reading of the poem —
could possibly provide a sufficient idea of its total poetic effect, unravel the
complex triple fugue of its counterpointed themes and images.

Awesome Fragments [*Winter Trees*]   Alan Brownstone*

Winter Trees contains the radio-piece, 'Three Women', written between *The Colossus* and *Ariel* — the stage of the poems in the recently-pub-
lished *Crossing the Water* — and the rest are 18 poems from the period of
Ariel itself. A note states that the poems in *Ariel* were 'more or less arbitrar-
ily chosen', with the implication that the poems in the new book could be
given equal status with them. Yes, with a few exceptions they can: some,
like "Purdah," "Lesbos" and "The Swarm," are so familiar from anthology
publication that one hunts the indexes of the previous Plath volumes convinced that they have appeared before. All of which argues the overriding
need for a Plath "Collected" which sorts out all the extant work into chronological order, as far as that can be established, and enables the reader to
grasp something more of the extraordinary creative process which led to the
last poems. At the moment, it's a case of trying to fit batches of awesome,
alarming fragments into a picture the final dimensions of which are not
made at all clear.

Nearly all the poems here have the familiar Plath daring, the same feel
of bits of frightened, vibrant, indignant consciousness translated instantly
into words and images that blend close, experienced horror and icy, sardonic control. Like the woman in "Stopped Dead," she is constantly "hung
out over a dead drop"; yet the moment enables her to look around, elaborate on the terror of the situation, and resolve it all into a coherent statement. There is a kind of Plath poem which *seems* as if it exists for its own
sake, with contrived or arbitrary bizarreness, apparently unrelated to felt
experiences. The signs are a certain easiness or glibness, instead of a feeling
of *necessity* about the images. Here, "Brasilia" is like this, with its odd failure fully to realise its theme and the strange reliance on an inverted conven-
tionality at the end ("O You who eat / People like light rays, leave / This one
/ Mirror safe, unredeemed / By the dove's annihilation, / The glory / The
power, the glory"). "Gigolo" has the facile ghastliness of "My mouth sags, /
The mouth of Christ / When my engine reaches the end of it." And what
would have been redrafted, clarified, extended ("By Candlelight," "Lesbos?") we may never know. But in "The Courage of Shutting-Up," "The

*Reprinted with permission from *New Statesman*, 82 (October 1, 1971), 446–48.

Rabbit-Catcher" and "The Swarm" we have the chilling immediacy, the terrible fineness of some of the best poems in *Ariel*:

> Jealousy can open the blood,
> It can make black roses.
> Who are they shooting at?

> It is you the knives are out for
> At Waterloo, Waterloo, Napoleon,
> The hump of Elba on your short back,
> And the snow, marshalling its brilliant cutlery
> Mass after mass, saying Shh!

The Girl Who Wanted to Be God
[*Letters Home*]   Jo Brans*

"The girl who wanted to be God," Sylvia Plath called herself in her diary at seventeen, and somehow the poignant past tense of the phrase lays the burden of her death at thirty on us once again. Of all our American literary suicides, hers is the heaviest to bear. Young, smart, pretty, talented, enterprising, and disciplined, the best product of America, she had, as we say, everything going for her. Our Puritan roots tingle indignantly at the waste of it all. What went wrong? we ask, and, It had better be good, we mutter angrily. Here are two books which seek to answer that question, but which probably only add to the confusion.

Letters Home consists of a portion of the 696 letters Sylvia Plath wrote to her family, especially to her mother, from the fall of 1950 when she began her freshman year at Smith to the week of her death in February 1963. Selected and edited with commentary by her mother, the letters included might mostly have been composed by Dame Kindness, who is the object of her ironic observer's bitter scorn in a poem written just before Plath died: "Sugar can cure everything, so Kindness says." From the schoolgirl beginnings on, the most consistent tone of the letters is bright insincerity, indicated by all kinds of giveaways to anyone conscious of style, especially of the clarity and certainty of Sylvia Plath's style in poetry. Here they flock in numbers, those triple exclamation marks, those parenthetical asides ("What a life!"), those bromides ("Dearest-Mother-whom-I-love-better-than-anybody"), those cute closings ("xxx Sivvy"), all the devices mercilessly banished from the poetry, if indeed they ever had the temerity to venture into that stark territory.

One has no wish to hurt Mrs. Plath, who has suffered enough, ~~and who~~

*Reprinted with permission from *Southwest Review*, 61 (Summer, 1976), 325–28, 330.

doubtless believed these letters, as mothers will. My point is simply that we can learn very little of the Sylvia of the poetry, the only Sylvia in whom we can take a legitimate interest, from these letters. The attitudes taken by the poetry and by the letters toward any specific incident of Plath's life are so disparate as to lend complete credibility to the theory of the divided self of the artist. For example, the letters in March, 1961, describing an emergency appendectomy focus on the usual aspects of a hospital stay, the food, the other patients, the good-natured nurses. Yet "Tulips," the poem which came from the same experience, shows a patient "learning peacefulness," falling in easily with nothingness and death:

> I didn't want flowers, I only wanted
> To lie with my hands turned up and be utterly empty.
> How free it is, you have no idea how free—
> The peacefulness is so big it dazes you,
> And it asks nothing, a name tag, a few trinkets.
> It is what the dead close on, finally; I imagine them
> Shutting their mouths on it, like a Communion tablet.

The tulips of the title are a strident burst of pure color, of involuntary life, "like dangerous animals" driving the persona away from the "white," "quiet," "snowed-in" world she craves.

One other instance. In 1956 Sylvia Plath married the British poet Ted Hughes. In the late summer of 1962, in the last year of her life, she broke with him, ending what she had insisted throughout the letters to be an idyll of poetic and personal fulfillment for them both. In June of that same summer, just before the fatal break, Mrs. Plath visited the young couple in their home in Devon. Of that visit she writes:

> The welcome I received when I arrived . . . was heartwarming. The threshold to the guest room . . . had an enameled pink heart and a garland of flowers painted on it . . . Sylvia said proudly, "I have everything in life I've ever wanted: a wonderful husband, two adorable children, a lovely home, and my writing." Yet the marriage was seriously troubled, and there was a great deal of anxiety in the air. . . . When I left on August 4 . . . it was the last time I saw Sylvia.

The daughter's efforts at saving face evidently failed, and from that time forth she resisted all her mother's attempts to get her and the children to come to America, or Mrs. Plath's offers to return to her. To her brother Warren Sylvia writes: "I hope you can tactfully convey to mother . . . that we should not meet for at least a year. . . . After this summer, I just could not bear to see her; it would be too painful and recall too much." She obviously regretted the break in composure, the genuine exposure of feeling, to her mother. Though the weekly letters and the forms of feeling persist ("I was so glad to have your letter saying you got *my* letter"), the poems tell a different tale, even find the mother responsible for the end of the marriage, as in "Medusa":

> I didn't call you.
> I didn't call you at all.
> Nevertheless, nevertheless
> You steamed to me over the sea,
> Fat and red, a placenta
> Paralyzing the kicking lovers . . .
>
> Who do you think you are? . . .
>
> Off, off, eely tentacle!
>
> There is nothing between us.

In addition to questions raised by this discrepancy between poetry and letters, we rightfully question the reliability of the letters because of their editing. Hardly a letter of those already "selected" is without its ellipsis, and most letters have many. The answer to our original query, What went wrong?, gradually falls in these cautiously written, selected, and edited letters into the following pattern: Sylvia Plath was martyred, ironically enough, by the American success saga that she lived, from all-A student to Fulbright fellow to financially independent poet at twenty-five or so. Such success is created by and carries with it a continuing and obsessive drive for perfection. Any failure, however small, can lead to a response "magnifying a situation all out of proportion," as Mrs. Plath says. Thus Plath's first suicide attempt in 1953 between her junior and senior years at Smith was in her mother's mind clearly triggered by a series of "failures" — to get into Frank O'Connor's writing class, to make progress on her honors thesis, even, absurdly, to learn shorthand. Her second, successful attempt Mrs. Plath also explains rationally and reductively: "Her physical energies had been depleted by illness, anxiety and overwork, and although she had for so long managed to be gallant and equal to the life-experience, some darker day than usual made it seem impossible to pursue." A mere indisposition, a mother's pefect rationale. The beauty of it is, it blames no one, not even Plath herself. . . .

To "know" Sylvia Plath, finally, we must return to the poems, where she created her most singular self. To comprehend her art we must submit to her myth, a myth of a life governed by "fixed stars," but of a genius often triumphant. She called the bitterest of her poems "comic," and they are, blackly so, in the frequency and energy with which the persona escapes her sex and kills off her own destroyers. The poems in *Ariel*, written at the height of her poetic powers, show the creator while working to be androgynous. In "Ariel," the persona is metaphorically somehow both sperm and womb, the creation autogenetic. In "Stings," the persona definitively separates herself from "unmiraculous women, / Honey-drudgers. / I am no drudge / Though for years I have eaten dust / And dried plates with my dense hair" and reveals herself to be the most creative member of the hive, the queen bee emergent:

They thought death was worth it, but I
Have a self to recover, a queen,
Is she dead, is she sleeping?
Where has she been,
With her lion-red body, her wings of glass?

Now she is flying
More terrible than she ever was, red
Scar in the sky, red comet
Over the engine that killed her —
The mausoleum, the wax house.

"Letters Home: Correspondence 1950–1963"

Carol Bere*

Since her premature death in 1963, the Sylvia Plath cult has proliferated, and she seems to have become the martyred high priestess of contemporary poetry. To a great extent the myth has been fed by feminist fuel and
reams have been written about Plath, the super-achiever who fell victim to
both the repressions of the woman's role and society's willingness to constrain female artists. Her brief career has generated a surge of psychological
studies that explore the relationship of female creativity to madness and suicide. Over-analyzed poems such as "Daddy," "Lady Lazarus," and "Lesbos," have been cited as testimony while the very real development of Sylvia
Plath, the poet, has been largely ignored.

Letters Home, the recently published letters of Plath to her mother,
while compulsively interesting reading, will do little to dispel the myth.
True, the collection does reveal Plath's indefatigable discipline and ambition, yet the portrait that emerges is finally unreal. Plath strove relentlessly
to create a singular image; ironically, the Plath who emerges in this collec
tion seems to be a persona fused by relatives and editors.

Over 600 letters were written during the period of 1950-1963, yet less
than 400 have been included in this volume. The majority of these letters
appear to have been selected to stress "Sivvy's" love of life, "gay philosophy," and continued resourcefulness. Rarely does she rail at circumstances,
and the stilted, romanticized superlatives that proclaim her ability to cope
are often embarrassing. The letters of the crucial last six months of Plath's
life are marred by obvious gaps in information and disconcerting ellipses.
Separated from her husband, alone with two infants, ill, yet at the height of
poetic creativity — the period of Ariel and Winter Trees — Plath is finally
permitted (or permits herself) to drop the stoic mask: "I guess I just need
someone to cheer me up by saying I've done all right so far."

*Reprinted with permission from Ariel, 8, No. 4 (October, 1977), 99–103.

Perhaps the person who emerges with most clarity in *Letters Home* is Mrs. Plath herself. Largely in an effort to correct the damaging portrait of the mother in the autobiographical novel, *The Bell Jar,* Mrs. Plath has attempted to show how Sylvia "manipulated experience" and "fused parts of my life with hers." Yet from beneath the outlines of Mrs. Plath's personal history, which is narrated with aggravating restraint, a life of self-sacrifice — and one lived mostly vicariously — surfaces.

Unfortunately, Mrs. Plath has exposed a minefield for psychological exegetes as she relates a story of childhood loneliness, denied academic opportunities and resentment of her husband. Otto Plath, the poet's father and a noted biologist and professor at Boston University, was a demanding, authoritarian figure. In order to circumvent potential marital problems, Mrs. Plath, in her words, became more "submissive," gave up a teaching position that she enjoyed and devoted herself entirely to her family. Her irritation is barely veiled as she recounts a life revolving around her husband's work, THE BOOK, and of evenings spent editing and typing, THE CHAPTER. The resentment was compounded when Otto Plath, who would not listen to the advice of physicians, died leaving Mrs. Plath a young widow, with two children and no life-insurance policies.

Thereafter, Mrs. Plath moved to Wellesley, Massachusetts, with her parents, worked tirelessly teaching medical-secretarial techniques at Boston University and gave herself totally to her children. The pressures that Sylvia Plath must have felt to excel, to both repay and justify her mother's efforts, must have been excessive. In a letter written to her mother while she was on scholarship at Smith College, Plath conveys a permeating theme of the collection, that of filial gratitude: "You are the most wonderful mummy that a girl ever had, and I only hope that I can continue to lay more laurels at your feet. Warren and I both love you and admire you more than anybody in the world for all you have done for us all our lives. For it is you who has given us the heredity and the incentive to be mentally ambitious."

Curiously, Plath seems to have felt a recurrent need to explain herself to her mother, which she does in inordinately formal syntax: "My main concern in the next year or two is to grow as much as possible, to find out, essentially, what my real capabilities are, especially in writing and studying, and then to play my future life in consistency with my abilities and capabilities." Or, more tellingly, there is the letter in which she recapitulates the year's haul of prizes and awards. Finally, with the collapse of her marriage to the British poet Ted Hughes, and with what must have been a tragic sense of having failed her mother, Plath writes: ". . . as you can see, I haven't the strength to see you for some time. The horror of what you saw and what I saw you see last summer is between us and I cannot face you again until I have a new life: it would be too great a strain."

Outwardly, the Smith College letters replay the typical studies-dates-clothes syndrome of many college campuses of the 1950's and the jargon frequently is a distillation of English novels and ladies' magazines. But there are disturbing elements in the correspondence. Underlying the buoyant, artificial accounts of weekends at Yale or studies with renowned authors is a compulsive determination to perfect the self — to avoid mediocrity, to build a "strong inner life," to prepare oneself for the "big moments." To compromise at less than the full life — the honors, the publications, the great love, the family — is to fail. Thus, the letters convey a sense of deferred expectations and a romanticized craving for experience.

Later, at Cambridge, she writes of her love for Ted Hughes: "I feel that all my life, all my pain and work has been for this one thing. All the blood spilt, the words written, the people loved, have been a work to fit me for loving . . . I see the power and voice in him that will shake the world alive. Even as he sees into my poems and will work with me to make me a woman poet like the world will gape at; even as he sees into my character and will tolerate no fallings away from my best right self." The psychological weight of this commitment to the marriage must have been enormous.

The importance of *Letters Home* as a key to understanding Plath, the poet, must ultimately be confronted. On a surface level, the collection will be an invaluable source for many of the early poems. The influence of Emily Dickinson, Theodore Roethke and the primitive painters can be tagged easily from comments and inserted poems. The admitted influence of the powerful Hughes, both on the subject matter and technique of *The Colossus*, is evident, yet Plath did retain her individuality. Hughes attacks all of creation in words that appear to erupt spontaneously from some natural, untapped source. Plath, conversely, is a more willed poet who explores her themes in direct, economical language. But her early poems, as Plath herself acknowledged, were "exercises," and it is on the late poems of *Ariel* and *Winter Trees* that she will be judged.

To resolve the obvious discrepancies between the Sivvy of the letters "singing" her "native joy of life" and the violent, destructive poet of *Ariel*, some critics have asserted that Plath suffered from a divided self. This assessment is too facile. Many of Plath's letters to her mother, while undeniably egocentric, were still assurances that she was succeeding at what must have been a mutually accepted blueprint for her "life experience." It would be unlikely that she would deliver less to a woman who asserts that ". . . my motherhood was the most important thing in my life. It was what my whole life went to."

It was in the last period, however, when the poetic sensibility and the life merged incontrovertibly that Plath assumed her own voice. Although she realized that "I am writing the best poems of my life; they will make my name," little is advanced about the incredible depth and marked technical assurance of these poems. Sadly, we are left with Mrs. Plath's words which can only perpetuate what is already an overworked Plath literary machine: "She began at 4 A.M. each morning to pour forth magnificently structured poems renouncing the subservient female role, yet holding to the triumphant note of maternal creativity in her scorn of 'barrenness'." Surely, Plath's poetry deserves more.

Living and Dying [*Johnny Panic*]   Douglas Hill*

Those who would deal in the legend of Sylvia Plath, who would buy and sell the myths and mystifications surrounding the image of a woman propelled by psychosis into a fury of poetic creation and a compulsion to destroy herself, do her actual career— her dedication to craft and her precocious artistic commitment — something of a disservice. After all, over a ten-year span she published 170 poems, a novel, a verse play, and a considerable number of shorter prose pieces. Such an achievement suggests that she hardly needs to be rescued from anybody, even if the cultists, quite understandably and often persuasively, have overemphasized the apocalyptic nature of the end of her life and art. This volume should help correct distortions; it also will remind us how much more there is to be learned, and indicates how frustrating that search is going to be.

The best of the stories collected here (there are non-fiction pieces and journal excerpts as well) are as indelibly distinctive as *The Bell Jar* and the finest poems. In flowing perceptions of terror— in the title story, for instance— Plath exposes the world as a refraction of consciousness, consciousness as a version of the world. Into this split — other / self, real / surreal, phenomenal / intuitive— her imagination dives, her dream descends. The dream *is* often destructive— of the narrator "Johnny Panic" and "The Wishing Box," of the hero in "The 59th Bear"; it's the dream of a moment, one commentator has said, both girlish and deadly. Plath's special talent is not merely the creation of that moment but the naming of its shattered pieces. Even the weaker stories share this power; they have flashes of intense vision, but lack the consistent pressure.

Plath's truest voice is the most painful, the one closest to the nerve. "I must write about the things of the world with no glazing." Her best prose has an aggressive innocence, a jumping eagerness to see and spell experience in her own alphabet. Like Hemingway in his early stories, she often appears to want to strip down rhetoric to a point where object and self everywhere meet but never touch. The form and rhythm of the stories, too, can be brilliantly open—chopped, jerky, elliptical, but always clear and focussed however erratic.

Among the bits of non-fiction prose, the autobiographical "Ocean 1212-W" is essential ("I sometimes think my vision of the sea is the clearest thing I own"). So is "Context," a five-paragraph assessment of her poetry for

*Reprinted with permission from *Canadian Forum*, 58 (June, 1978), 323–24.

London Magazine ("The poets I delight in are possessed by their poems as by the rhythms of their own breathing"). The real stunner, though, is the first of the four journal passages, printed here, from the time of her Fulbright studies at Cambridge. Parts of it are naive and self-conscious, if not trite, but even when Plath strikes a conventional pose for herself, it's a totally engrossing and often revealing one. There's not enough of it, however; the selection gives only the barest sampling of the range and quantity of her unpublished material.

Literary judgments aside, the question of when, how, and by whom Plath's works are to be edited and presented is now — as it has been for fifteen years — absolutely crucial. Even granted an inhuman amount of tact, taste, and impartiality, Sylvia Plath's mother and husband — Aurelia Plath and Ted Hughes — ought not to have the exclusive responsibility of deciding what the world is to know of her. No wonder we have a legend on our hands.

Hughes's editorial decisions in this volume may raise some eyebrows, but I'm basically in sympathy with most of them. To divide the public prose into "more successful" and "other" is of course arbitrary, but considering what he had to work with, I see no other course he could have followed that would have given as useful a picture, tantalizingly partial though it is, of Plath's development and continuity. (He's had limitations: a postscript to his Introduction, added when the book was in proof, reports the emergence, in the States, of "a large number" of manuscripts formerly belonging to Mrs. Plath.)

Where Hughes is less convincing, as was Mrs. Plath in her selection of the letters, is in his argument — essentially with himself — for restricting publication of the most personal and potentially defamatory journals. It's best to quote him:

> I am more and more inclined to think that any bit of evidence which corrects and clarifies our idea of what she really was is important, insofar as her writings persuade us of her importance. But living people figure everywhere even in her most private discussions with herself, and — an editor has to face it — some things are more important than revelations about writers.

It's a tough choice: since I can hardly expect to play a large part in Plath's diaries, I'd opt for complete publication and hope for understanding or thick skins on the parts of those who do. At least that way I might be spared such speculations and ambiguities as arise from the knowledge that the single Cambridge entry Hughes prints in this book — the single "personal" as opposed to "literary" entry — was written less than a week before Plath met him for the first time, a meeting sufficiently impressive that she described him in a letter to her mother a few days later as "the only man I've met who'd be strong enough to be equal with."

There's another sort of inference to be drawn — tentatively, to be sure — from Hughes's editorial control, this from the Introduction itself. On his own evidence, I'd support his implicit claim that he both understood and helped Sylvia Plath, fully and honourably, at the extremes of their relation — in the spiritual business of connecting poetically with an artist and in the practical business of getting through the days and dirty dishes with one. He was good with her images and with her sinus trouble; he understood her terribly and trivially. What he seems to have missed was the necessary middle, the kind of support, the quality of love or understanding, that might have made it possible for her to live. So she, too, may have been unable to find this middleground: Plath killed herself that morning, we know, in the grip of an iron winter's desperation, but not before setting out bread and butter and two mugs of milk for her children.

To be fair, I'd say Hughes is sensitive to his lack. He calls the work of Plath's last year "liberation." If the term applies, surely it includes her attempt at liberation from him. Hughes's introductory remarks quietly imply a recognition of this.

The acolytes of Confessional or Extremist poetry have emphasized, over and over, the tremendous risks involved in Plath's "murderous art." This basically admiring view finds the source of her creative energy in self-destructiveness (A. Alvarez), and the imagination of dying as the climactic experience of living (Charles Newman). The cultivation of derangement, dying as *the* mode of life — enticing and fashionable as these attitudes are, they ignore, or try to overwhelm by rhetorical force, the moral aspects of the relation between aesthetic value and suicidal madness. Such an approach may ultimately be unfair to Plath.

I don't know if this question can be settled. Certainly we need to look at more evidence; even if we get it all, the secrets may stay hidden and the answers remain suppositions. The publication of *Johnny Panic* is important in part because it can make these issues live once more, can put the hard crystals of Plath's reputation into solution again for another generation to analyze. The book also adds a good fifty ineradicable pages to the anthology of contemporary consciousness.

Sylvia Plath [*The Collected Poems*]   Laurence Lerner*

The most important book of poetry published this year is Sylvia Plath's *Collected Poems*. "About time too" might be one's first, understandable reaction. It is 19 years since she died, and ten years since the last of the posthumous volumes: now at last everything has been gathered together, and edited with care and tact by Ted Hughes. All good things are worth waiting

*Reprinted with permission from *Encounter*, 58 (January, 1982), 53–54.

for, and reading through the volume makes it clear that she was one of the most remarkable poets of her time.

Let us take not one of the really well-known *Ariel* poems, but, to start with, a lesser-known piece that is short enough to be quoted in full. "Mirror" was written in 1961, and published in *Crossing the Water:*

> I am silver and exact. I have no preconceptions.
> Whatever I see I swallow immediately
> Just as it is, unmisted by love or dislike.
> I am not cruel, only truthful —
> The eye of a little god, four-cornered.
> Most of the time I meditate on the opposite wall.
> It is pink, with speckles. I have looked at it so long
> I think it is a part of my heart. But it flickers.
> Faces and darkness separate us over and over.
>
> Now I am a lake. A woman bends over me,
> Searching my reaches for what she really is.
> Then she turns to those liars, the candles or the moon.
> I see her back, and reflect it faithfully.
> She rewards me with tears and an agitation of hands.
> I am important to her. She comes and goes.
> Each morning it is her face that replaces the darkness.
> In me she has drowned a young girl, and in me
>   an old woman
> Rises toward her day after day, like a terrible fish.

This is a witty poem in the best sense, not only in the precision of the details, and the verbal sprightliness, but in the amusing self-importance given to the mirror. It is not as wild as, say, "Lady Lazarus" or "Fever 103°": its inventiveness shows no sign of spilling over into free association or surrealism. Yet it implies those other, more disturbing poems, and satisfying as it is in itself, it takes on a deeper resonance in the context of Sylvia Plath's work. Is the woman who bends over the mirror, for instance, to be seen as the author? We cannot say, but if she is, there is an extra irony in knowing that she is not yet 30 when she sees an old woman rising towards her; and the obsessive concern with itself given to the mirror takes on an extra resonance if it echoes the similar obsession in the author of the poem. This poem steps back from the terrible intensity of the experiences of *Ariel* while inviting us to remain aware of them. I find it an almost perfect poem, stronger for its limitations.

It undercuts at least one popular view of Sylvia Plath, that her early work is controlled, formal, even superficial, and the later poems make true contact with her anxieties, and so are imbued with a new power. There is some truth in this, but it should not be taken too rigidly. Here we have a late poem that gains force from its ability to stand back. True, it does not stand back in quite the same way as the poems of *The Colossus* do. Take "Spinster," written five years earlier:

> Now this particular girl
> During a ceremonious April walk
> With her latest suitor
> Found herself, of a sudden, intolerably struck
> By the birds' irregular babel
> And the leaves' litter. . . .

What is the difference? Is it just the greater formality of this poem in half-rhymes and regular stanzas? Is it the echo of Auden in the way the half-rhymes are used for sinister effect? There seems to be the same disturbing experience behind it as behind "Mirror": both, in their different ways, keep a superb distance from hysteria.

Yet it is not difficult to find poems in *The Colossus* that would seem at home in *Ariel* — the marvellous "Lorelei", for instance. The fatal lure of a siren's song provides the perfect subject for Sylvia Plath, obsessed as she was with the horrible beauty of dying, and this poem blends its death-wish with a cool awareness of its folly:

> Sisters, your song
> Bears a burden too weighty
> For the whorled ear's listening
>
> Here, in a well-steered country,
> Under a balanced ruler. . . .

The impudent assurance of the pun ("well-steered") reminds us of detachment while mocking it slightly: like all her best poetry, it neither surrenders to hysteria nor escapes from it. And the haunting last line ("Stone, stone, ferry me down there") is enriched by the stone-like qualities of the underwater shapes of which we have glimpsed a vision.

Of course in a poetic career that lasted only seven years we would expect continuity. In stressing this, and in praising the control of the early poems, am I suggesting that the great frenetic outbursts which have become so famous are artistically inferior? Some enthusiasts for "confessional poetry" would say at this point, So much the worse for art; but that is a very superficial conception of the relation of art to experience. Artistic success that destroys the living nerve for the sake of an elegant pattern produces only literary exercises, but there is a deeper and more necessary art that seizes the experience and brings it to life in language, involving the reader's emotions, where artlessness might leave him cold and even resentful. It is the miracle of a poem like "Lady Lazarus" that though it seems a wild and incoherent outpouring of terror and self-hatred, it also has the true control of art. Not, this time, through the imposition of any formal metrical pattern, but through the use of repetitions that capture the frenzy of the speaking voice and find a pattern in it, and above all through the deliberate self-dramatisation that presents suicide as a form of role-playing, almost of comedy:

> Dying
> Is an art like everything else.
> I do it exceptionally well.
>
> I do it so it feels like hell.
> I do it so it feels real.
> I guess you could say I've a call.

The last line can be said with a giggle, as a boast, or as wry self-deprecation, and each implies the possibilities of the other. The poem has deservedly become one of the best-known of our time.

A Note of Triumph [*The Collected Poems*]

Katha Pollitt*

Literary evaluations of Sylvia Plath have a way of turning into sermons, in which critics forsake close reading in favor of moral pronouncements on whatever issues strike them as pertinent to her case. Is life worth living? Most critics think it is. Is madness admirable? Most agree it is not. Are men the enemy? A chorus of cheers from feminists. Can one justifiably connect one's small, private, middle-class life with fascism, war and the Holocaust? Yes, claims A. Alvarez, for whom Plath is the ultimate literary risk-taker. No, argues Irving Howe, who is not only outraged by Plath's appropriation of the death camps to her personal situation but does not understand what, exactly, she was so upset about, anyway. The very fact that Plath was a woman has dazed many a strong mind. For Stephen Spender she is "a priestess cultivating her hysteria"; for Robert Lowell she is "hardly a person at all, or a woman," but Dido, Phaedra, Medea. George Steiner sees her poems as propelled by "the need of a superbly intelligent, highly literate young woman to cry out about her especial being, about the tyrannies of blood and gland, of nervous spasm and sweating skin, the rankness of sex and childbirth in which a woman is still compelled to be wholly of her organic condition." And you thought men sweated too.

What lies behind these responses is Plath's suicide — she killed herself, as all the world knows, in the winter of 1963 after her husband, the British poet Ted Hughes, left her for another woman. She was not, as many feminists like to think, unknown at the time of her death. Hughes's reputation was more established, true, but Plath had won her share of grants and prizes, had been widely published in magazines and had received favor-

*Reprinted with permission from the *Nation*, 234 (January 16, 1982), 52–55.

able, although not very insightful, reviews for her first book of poems, *The Colossus*, which came out in 1960. It was the posthumous publication of *Ariel* in 1965, though, that made her fame — the wrong kind of fame, for it was based on the notion that her poems could be read as if they were a suicide note that "explained" her death. The possibility that her poems made a literary shape of their own has only recently been considered.

Probably nothing could have prevented the sensationalizing of Plath's work. Her voice, once she found it, was too strong, too strange, not to have struck a note of challenge, her life too brief and intense not to have been packaged as that of yet another doomed female genius. It must be said, though, that the way in which her work was presented to the public did little to bring about a better understanding of it. There was the chronologically jumbled release of her poems in the two post-*Ariel* volumes, *Winter Trees* and *Crossing the Water* (both 1971). There was the publication of still more poems in tiny limited editions and the failure to publish others at all. Most important, though, was the fact that *Ariel* itself, as printed, was not the manuscript of that name completed by Plath three months before her death but a selection put together by her executors in an order of their choosing.

The published book contained poems written after Plath's manuscript had been completed, an addition for which we must be grateful. But it omitted poems Plath herself had chosen for the book: "Mystic," "Purdah," "Brasilia," "The Jailer" and others. This editorial decision meant that late poems of great distinction were out of circulation while Plath's literary place was being debated; those that did belatedly appear, in *Winter Trees*, were mingled with poems Plath had put aside, and were discounted along with them.

Worse, the published *Ariel* destroyed the artistic pattern of Plath's manuscript. The *Ariel* we know ends on a note of absolute despair, and virtually invites the reader to luxuriate in the *frisson* of knowing that a week after writing "Edge" ("The woman is perfected. / Her dead / Body wears the smile of accomplishment"), Plath would herself be dead. The actual manuscript ended quite differently, on the note of triumph sounded by the magnificent cycle of Bee Poems, whose subject is the reclaiming of an autonomous womanly self. Its final word, as Plath noted, was "spring." Would it have made a difference to her reputation, I wonder, if Plath's pattern had been preserved, with the last poems added as a separate section? Or even if a complete edition of her poems had appeared, say, ten years ago, when interest in Plath was still high?

Well, better late than never. Plath's image may be too firmly established by now for any information short of news that she is alive and living in Brazil to alter it, but those who care can at long last have her work entire, in a handsome edition chronologically arranged, introduced and annotated by Ted Hughes. It is a beautiful book, prepared with seriousness and love.

Every poet should be so well served — although I do think most would prefer to forgo the hefty appendix of high school and college verse included here.

Complete collections often have an unintended effect: instead of displaying a poet's accomplishment, they subtly diminish it. Swamped by their pale, sluggish brothers and sisters, the special poems seem less and less unusual. We put the book away with the thought that the poet was, after all, quite right to have left half his work in the drawer.

That is not what happens here. One reason is that Palth was a superb craftsman who never, Hughes tells us, abandoned a poem until it had "exhausted her ingenuity." She wrote recalcitrant poems and failed poems, but none that were idle or blathering or tentative. With very few exceptions, every poem has a shape of its own. Another reason is that she was dazzlingly inventive. Even poems that fail to come off frequently contain lines of extraordinary loveliness. "Ouija" may bog down in Stevensish rhetoric, but it opens with eerie splendor: "It is a chilly god, a god of shades, / Rises to the glass from his black fathoms." The dreadful "Leaving Early," a savage account of a visit to an elderly woman who has somehow incurred the poet's hatred, offers the startling image of the poet "bored as a leopard" in her hostess's fuggy living room.

But the most important source of the pleasure to be found in these pages is the fact that Plath's was one of those rare poetic careers — Keats's was another — that moved consistently and with gathering rapidity and assurance to an ever greater daring and individuality. She was always becoming more distinctly herself, and by the time she came to write her last seventy or eighty poems, there was no other voice like hers on earth. Her end may have been tragic, her character not what we would choose in our friends, but her work records a triumph. Chronologically arranged, her 224 adult poems make a kind of diary of artistic self-discovery that is exhilarating to contemplate.

It was not an easy process. *The Collected Poems* shows just how hard Plath worked to transform herself from a subdued, well-mannered student of Auden, Eliot, Ransom and Lowell into the effortlessly associative poet of the late work. Discards vastly outnumber "book poems" in the entries for 1956–59, the years Plath was working on *The Colossus*, and it's hard to disagree with her verdicts. For all their skill, the rejects strike me as devitalized, strangled by the very technical proficiency that was later to be so liberating:

> Loam-humps, he says, moles shunt
> up from delved worm-haunt;
> blue fur, moles have; hefting chalk-hulled flint
> he with rock splits open
> knobbed quartz; flayed colors ripen
> rich, brown, sudden in sunglint.
>   ("Ode for Ted")

The Colossus is a book of considerable interest quite apart from the fact that it was written by the author of *Ariel*. "Black Rook in Rainy Weather," "The Disquieting Muses," "Full Fathom Five," "All the Dead Dears" and many others have a controlled, melancholy beauty and a redeeming wit. Yet all but a handful — the musical, dreamlike "Lorelei," the playful "Mushrooms" and "The Thin People" — have about them a quality of having been willed into existence, of having fought for breath against an anxiety or depression that threatened to engulf them:

> Leaning over, I encounter one
> Blue and improbable person
>
> Framed in a basketwork of cat-tails.
> O she is gracious and austere,
> Seated beneath the toneless water!
> It is not I, it is not I.
>
> No animal spoils on her green doorstep.
> And we shall never enter there
> Where the durable ones keep house.
> The stream that hustles us
>
> Neither nourishes nor heals.
>   ("The Burnt-out Spa")

"A fury of frustration," she wrote after completing the elegant pastoral "Watercolor of Grantchester Meadows." "Some inhibition keeping me from writing what I really feel."

It is certainly cause for wonder that this same poet should a mere three years later be turning out poems like "Daddy," "Lady Lazarus" and "Elm" with the speed, in Hughes's phrase, of urgent letters. Nonetheless, critics who deny a continuity between the early and late Plaths — usually to dismiss one in favor of the other — will want to rethink their positions in light of the wealth of evidence provided here for a broadly continuous development. As the chronological arrangement makes clear, Plath found and lost her voice many times. "The Stones," the first poem that hints at the new manner, was followed by a raft of poems in the old. The old bobs up long after the new has established itself: the Lowellian exercise "The Babysitters" postdates "The Rival" and "Tulips."

On the deeper level of themes and images, there was not so much a rift as a reformulation. Throughout her career, Plath worked with a tightly connected cluster of concerns — metamorphosis, rebirth, the self as threatened by death, the otherness of the natural world, fertility and sterility — and applied them all to what she saw as the central situation of her life, the death of her worshipped father when she was 9 years old and the complex emotions of loss, guilt and resentment it aroused in her even as an adult. But where the early Plath is autobiographical, Freudian ("Electra on Azalea

Path," "The Colossus"), the later Plath is working in another mode entirely — of fixed symbols, drama and myth.

Jon Rosenblatt has argued that the late poems are governed by a vision of "negative vitalism," a conviction that all life is at the mercy of a cosmic, merciless principle of death, of which the dead father — along with God, male-dominated marriage, fascism, war and mass society — is only an aspect. Judith Kroll, who has traced the profound influence on Plath of Robert Graves's *The White Goddess*, makes a similar point, and shows how Plath cast her life in the form of a ritual drama of death and rebirth which the poems enact. "Tulips," "Ariel," "Daddy" and "A Birthday Present" are thus not confessional poems in which the poet displays her wounds but dramatic monologues in which the speaker moves from a state of psychological bondage to freedom, from spiritual death to life, with suicide, paradoxically, standing as a metaphor for this transformation. In the late poems, Plath enters the world of death — the hospital room in "Tulips," the death train in "Getting There," the fever-induced fantasy of Hades in "Fever 103°" — suffers a ritual death and emerges reborn. This explains why Plath described Lady Lazarus, who is a kind of professional suicide ("One year in every ten I manage it"), as having "the great and terrible gift of being reborn. . . . She is the Phoenix, the libertarian spirit, what you will":

> Herr God, Herr Lucifer
> Beware
> Beware
>
> Out of the ash
> I rise with my red hair
> and I eat men like air.
> ("Lady Lazarus")

The impact of "Ariel" has been so great that other late poems, as well as the "transitional" ones of the early 1960s, have been overshadowed. One of the accomplishments of *The Collected Poems* will be, I hope, to remind us of the strength of much of this work. Any poet less rapidly evolving than Plath would have been tempted to rest on such laurels as "I am Vertical," "Wuthering Heights" and "Parliament Hill Fields." It is a great thing, too, to see late poems like "Stopped Dead," "Purdah" and "The Jailer" placed, finally, at the culmination of Plath's career where they belong.

All these poems, but especially the late ones, fill out and qualify our sense of Plath's vision. To give but one instance: The critics who see her work as a rejection of life, and the feminists, too, will have to come to terms with the tenderness and purity of Plath's maternal feelings, as displayed in "Brasilia," "Child," "For a Fatherless Son" and her radio verse play *Three Women*.

If Sylvia Plath were alive now, she would be 49 years old — younger than Adrienne Rich, John Ashbery, Philip Levine and W. S. Merwin, younger, incredibly, than Allen Ginsberg. It is often said that when she died, she had gone as far as poetry could take her, and indeed, the very last poems do seem to leave no way out. I cannot believe, though, that a poet as fertile and energetic and fearless as Plath here shows herself to be could ever have been reduced to silence by her own imagination. Had she lived, like Lady Lazarus, she would surely have transformed herself yet again, as she had done before. "The loss to poetry has been inestimable," wrote A. Alvarez after her death. Surveying the current state of poetry, one can see how sadly right he was.

An Interesting Minor Poet?
[*The Collected Poems*]   William H. Pritchard*

During Sylvia Plath's short life of just over 30 years, she saw only one book of her poems published: *The Colossus* (1960). She had prepared a second one, even worked out the order of its poems, and that appeared as *Ariel* in 1965 after her death, with a number of poems added which were written in her final months. Two further volumes were published posthumously: *Crossing the Water* (1971), containing mainly earlier poems, and *Winter Trees*, in the same year, containing 18 late ones plus "Three Women," a lugubrious "poem for three voices" written for the BBC. The result of such piecemeal, though perhaps advisable, publication was to create confusion in our minds about those remarkable seven years (1956–1963) in which 224 poems were written and finished. Now, 18 years after her death by suicide in February 1963, we are at last given a thoroughly responsible presentation of the poems in chronological order, more than a third of them not previously published in book form. The old volume titles have been dropped, and poems are simply grouped under their appropriate year, dated by month and day whenever possible. The result is to make her appear an altogether larger and more satisfying poet than this reader had taken her to be.

Reading these poems through in chronological order calls into question the received idea of the clever craftswoman producing beautifully shaped objects, almost too beautifully shaped, who suddenly achieved a "breakthrough" into — in the phrase of one of that book's reviewers — the "raw genius" of the later, *Ariel* poems. You could even read it as a lesson in liberation, with the early volume coming at the end of those evil 1950s (and she went to Smith too!) and the later one heralding, along with Robert

*Reprinted with permission from the *New Republic*, 185 (December 30, 1981), 32–35.

Lowell and Anne Sexton and lesser talents, a confessional freedom from the repressive, whether prosodic or personal:

> What a thrill —
> My thumb instead of an onion.
> > — "Cut"
>
> Dying
> Is an art, like everything else.
> I do it exceptionally well.
> I do it so it feels like hell.
> > — "Lady Lazarus"

Never mind that in both poems, as in so many of her other late ones, there was not only a bitter but a mockingly self-lacerating and playful wit, a pure revel in felicities of language ("My thumb instead of an onion" — some fun there after you get through wincing) which the desperateness of her running-out life somehow gave birth to. Too many readers, younger ones especially, approached these later poems with religious awe as if "Sylvia" (or as they would now say, "Plath") were to be treated in a manner befitting Jesus Christ; it was she who had died for our sins — so the distressed young student might feel, especially if female. Of course the backlash wasn't long in coming. One college newspaper in the early 1970s printed 24 Sylvia Plath jokes, grisly riddles the mildest of which by far went "Why did SP cross the road?" "To be struck by an oncoming vehicle."

Ted Hughes has done an exemplary job in editing these poems, writing notes to them year by year (one only wishes for more notes, since they are so interesting), and giving us a generous selection of the juvenile pre-1956 poems. And he strikes the right note in his introduction when he remarks that "her attitude to her verse was artisan-like: if she couldn't get a table out of the material, she was quite happy to get a chair, or even a toy. The end product for her was not so much a successful poem, as something that had temporarily exhausted her ingenuity." The right note, for surely she was one of the most ingenious poets in this latter half of our century; and to speak of her in terms of artisan and chair-maker, rather than transmitter of pure inspiration from heaven upstairs or downstairs hell, does justice to her resourcefulness and skill as a maker.

She did not always do justice to herself in this respect; or rather, she sometimes spoke as if formal ingenuity and true feeling might not be compatible. For example, this remark made about "Point Shirley," a poem she completed in January of 1959: "Oddly powerful and moving to me in spite of rigid formal structure." "Point Shirley" was written at the time she had begun to attend (along with Anne Sexton and George Starbuck) Robert Lowell's writing seminar at Boston University, and the poem's debt to Lowell's work is evident. But consider its opening two stanzas, in which her grandmother's house is evoked:

> From Water-Tower Hill to the brick
>   prison
> The shingle booms, bickering under
> The sea's collapse.
> Snowcakes break and welter. This year
> The gritted wave leaps
> The seawall and drops onto a bier
> Of quahog chips,
> Leaving a salty mash of ice to whiten
>
> In my grandmother's sand yard. She
>   is dead,
> Whose laundry snapped and froze
>   here, who
> Kept house against
> What the sluttish, rutted sea could do.
> Squall waves once danced
> Ship timbers in through the cellar
>   window;
> A thresh-tailed, lanced
> Shark glittered in the geranium bed —
>
> Such collusion of mulish elements
> She wore her broom straws to the nub.

This may have been, as her biographer Edward Butscher says it was, a deliberate attempt to capture Lowell's seaside grays; but the strict stanza, the rhymes and half-rhymes, above all the careful syntax and enjambed lines — even running over from one stanza to the next — show an attention to (in Frost's words) "the sound of sense" that is compelling and demanding of any reader's agility. The continuations and suspensions which the speaking voice must make to navigate these lines are surely central to the poem's power. If we may correct Sylvia Plath, it moves us not in spite of but partly because of its "rigid formal structure." And it is quite different from anything Lowell had done in *Lord Weary's Castle* — where the blank verse proceeds in a breathless, hurtling way — or was doing in *Life Studies*, which appeared in 1959.

During the preceding two years, Plath had grown extremely skilled at rendering sentence sounds in poems which this volume allows us to read for the first time. Here is the opening of "The Great Carbuncle" (1957):

> We came over the moor-top
> Through air streaming and green-lit,
> Stone farms foundering in it,
> Valleys of grass altering
> In a light neither of dawn
> Nor nightfall, our hands, faces
> Lucent as porcelain, the earth's
> Claim and weight gone out of them.

And it continues just as expertly. Imagine deciding, as evidently she did, that such a poem was not quite good enough to be included in her first book! When she spoke (in another remark quoted by Hughes) with respect to the admirable "Mushrooms" (which did make *The Colossus*) of "my absolute lack of judgment when I've written something: whether it's trash or genius," she spoke with her characteristic either / or absoluteness. But "The Great Carbuncle," or "Above the Oxbow" (here my Connecticut River sentimentality may be intruding), or "In Midas' Country," or "Child's Park Stones" (a first rate poem), or "Green Rock, Winthrop Bay" are not trash — perhaps not genius either, but something else, less sensational: assured performances, with a technical control wholly adequate to sustain the observant, grave, responsive presence that makes itself felt audibly over the carefully tracked course of stanza and whole poem. John Frederick Nims said it succintly when he suggested that young writers should be advised to "forget *Ariel* for a while; study *The Colossus*." With the new volume, this study can more intelligently take place.

If she could only "let things slip a bit," said a reviewer in admiration of her earlier poems, she will do something really special. What happened in fact was that she let them slip with a vengeance into the "stream of repulsions" (the phrase is Hugh Kenner's) that inform the poems from the last months of her life. Ted Hughes left her in October of 1962. During that month she wrote or finished 25 poems, including the ones for which she is best known. Beginning with one new to me, "The Detective," we read on through, among others, the bee poems, "The Applicant," "Daddy," "Medusa," "Lesbos," "Fever 103°," "Cut," and "Lady Lazarus." Much adjectival overkill has been employed by reviewers attempting in desperation of vocabulary to outdo the poems themselves, and George Steiner, never at a loss on such occasions, has referred to "Daddy" as the "Guernica of modern poetry." But really it is nothing of the sort, reading now like a very clever, very nasty, very hopeless horror song which holds us partly by its resourceful way of exploiting our reticence and embarrassment at what we are hearing:

> I have always been scared of you,
> With your Luftwaffe, your gobbledygoo.
> And your neat mustache
> And your Aryan eye, bright blue.
> Panzer-man, panzer-man, O You —

Poor Otto Plath, a diabetic professor of biology at Boston University who had the misfortune to combine the diabetes with gangrene and bronchopneumonia, so double-crossed his daughter by dying too soon, scarcely deserved such a tribute (I know, it's really a myth). And the stanza, indeed the whole poem, contains much that is repellent about Plath's poetry: the clever "gobbledygoo," a word like the one English teachers used to write on freshman themes; the relentless caricaturing of another, in tough baby-talk, all done in the interests of "art." And the panzer-man repetition. Earlier in

"Daddy" we hear that "The tongue stuck in my jaw": "It stuck in a barb wire snare. / Ich, ich, ich, ich," and the poet's tongue sticks also in "Elm" ("These are the isolate slow faults / That kill, that kill, that kill"), in "The Bee Meeting" ("They will not smell my fear, my fear, my fear"), in "The Applicant," and elsewhere. There are many more questions now, fired off by an "Ich" whose tongue really isn't stuck at all, but extraordinarily adept and daring in its leaps and spins; like the one done around the first line of "Lady Lazarus," "Dying is an art":

> I do it so it feels like hell.
> I do it so it feels real.
> I guess you could say I've a call.
>
> It's easy enough to do it in a cell.
> It's easy enough to do it and stay put.
> Its the theatrical
>
> Comeback in broad day
> To the same place, the same face, the
>   same brute
> Amused shout:
>
> 'A miracle!'
> That knocks me out.

A brilliant show, but there may be a problem about how many times one wants to watch it again. That is why encountering it here, as poem #198 in a chronological sequence, is a very good thing for its continued life. She had done, could do so much with words; now she had to do this, *would* do this new turn.

But as "Lady Lazarus" goes on to say, "There is a charge . . . a very large charge / For a word or a touch / Or a bit of blood." The sad joke is that the reader — surrounded by all those other poets in the imaginary museum who can be summoned up in a twinkling for a performance — really doesn't have to pay very much to watch the show. It was Sylvia Plath who paid the charge in full, and one feels in reading the final 12 poems in this collection, those written in the month and the days of 1963 which preceded her death, form a sort of coda, or perhaps a rehearsal for a new part to be played somewhere else.

The mood is set by the bleakly wonderful "Sheep in Fog" ("My bones hold a stillness, the far / Fields melt my heart") and holds largely through until the last poem, "Edge," in which "The woman is perfected. / Her dead / Body wears the smile of accomplishment." But just before the finality of "Edge" comes "The Balloons," a touching surprise after the histrionic agonies of more sensational Plath-poems. For four stanzas, composed with that fluidity of motion she had grown so expert at achieving years before, these "Guileless and clear / Oval soul-animals" are celebrated for being themselves, for living with the mother and her children since Christmas, for keeping them company. Two last stanzas address the daughter:

> Your small
>
> Brother is making
> His balloon squeak like a cat.
> Seeming to see
> A funny pink world he might eat on
>   the other side of it,
> He bites,
>
> Then sits
> Back, fat jug
> Contemplating a world clear as
>   water.
> A red
> Shred in his little fist.

This was finished a week before she died, and unlike the balloons it remains with us, in its own words

> Delighting
> The heart like wishes or free
> Peacocks blessing
> Old ground with a feather
> Beaten in starry metals.

For years I have endorsed Irving Howe's limiting judgment of Sylvia Plath as an "interesting minor poet." But I don't think anyone who submits to this collection is likely to be comfortable with that judgment. She was rather, was indeed — as the expression goes — something else.

The Journals of Sylvia Plath   Nancy Milford*

Her published journals begin in the summer of 1950, just before she enters Smith College, when she is 17. (Although we are told by her editor, Frances McCullough, that she began keeping a diary when she was a child, no portions of it are printed here.) They are marked by an immense will to succeed, and she is as relentless in her dedication to her craft as she is in her search for a self from which to shape it.

Why has it taken nearly 20 years for these "curtailed" journals to be published, let alone "The Collected Poems?" Is it because these journals are dominated from the first by the twin thrusts of sex and vocation, which are,

*Reprinted with permission from the *New York Times Book Review* (May 2, 1982), 1, 30–32.

unfortunately for her, linked to idealized domesticity and female dependence? Listen to her voice as she records meeting Edward James Hughes in Cambridge, England, where she's a Fulbright Scholar. It is February 26, 1956. She's 23.

"Then the worst thing happened, that big, dark, hunky boy, the only one there huge enough for me, who had been hunching around over women, and whose name I had asked the minute I had come into the room, but no one told me, came over and was looking hard in my eyes and it was Ted Hughes. I started yelling again about his poems and quoting: "most dear unscratchable diamond" and he yelled back, colossal, in a voice that should have come from a Pole, 'You like?' and asking me if I wanted brandy, and me yelling yes and backing into the next room . . . and bang the door was shut and he was sloshing brandy into a glass and I was sloshing it at the place where my mouth was when I last knew about it.

"We shouted as if in a high wind . . . and I was stamping and he was stamping on the floor, and then he kissed me bang smash on the mouth [omission]. . . . And when he kissed my neck I bit him long and hard on the cheek, and when he came out of the room, blood was running down his face. [Omission.] And I screamed in myself, thinking: oh, to give myself crashing, fighting, to you."

There are extraordinary things to notice here: the fierce passion of their meeting, as if they were in combat, and that it is he who kisses and she who draws blood; the stunning urgency with which she records wanting him, without equivocation. And, finally, of course, the omissions. For who can tell from this docked text what provoked her bite? Surely it serves to confirm:

> Out of the ash
> I rise with my red hair
> And I eat men like air.
> ("Lady Lazarus,"
> 23–29 October 1962)

But does it? Here is what was cut between the galleys and the published book:

". . . and I was stamping and he was stamping on the floor, and then he kissed me bang smash on the mouth and ripped my hairband, off my lovely red hairband scarf which has weathered the sun and much love, and whose like I shall never find again, and my favorite silver earrings: hah, I shall keep, he barked. And when he kissed my neck I bit him long and hard on the cheek, and when we came out of the room, blood was running down his face. His poem 'I did it, I.' Such violence, and I see how women lie down for artists. The one man in the room who was as big as his poems, huge, with hulk and dynamic chunks of words; his poems are strong and blasting like a high wind in steel girders. And I screamed in myself, thinking: oh, to give myself crashing, fighting, to you."

What has been deleted is his action: he kisses and he rips, he takes and he keeps. Those are not small details. What we are left with instead is a text pared to her reaction. This seems to me a disservice to both of them.

She had been waiting for him for years. The following entries are written when she is 17:

"I have too much conscience injected in me to break customs without disastrous effects; I can only lean enviously against the boundary and hate, hate, hate the boys who can dispel sexual hunger freely, without misgiving, and be whole, while I drag out from date to date in soggy desire, always unfulfilled."

"After a while I suppose I'll get used to the idea of marriage and children. If only it doesn't swallow up my desire to express myself in a smug, sensuous haze. Sure, marriage is self-expression, but if only my art, my writing, isn't just a mere sublimation of my sexual desires which will run dry once I get married. If only I can find him . . . the man who will be intelligent, yet physically magnetic and personable. If I can offer that combination, why shouldn't I expect it in a man?"

Once at Smith she continues to turn the question in her mind, but it is always the same question: Can I marry and have children and continue to write?

"I dislike being a girl, because as such I must come to realize that I cannot be a man. In other words, I must pour my energies through the direction and force of my mate. My only free act is choosing or refusing that mate."

"I wonder if art divorced from normal and conventional living is as vital as art combined with living: in a word, would marriage sap my creative energy and annihilate my desire for written and pictorial expression . . . or would I [if I married] achieve a fuller expression in art as well as in the creation of children?"

Early in 1953, she's 20 now and writes, "I need a strong mate: I do not want to accidentally crush and subdue him like a steamroller . . . I must find a strong potential powerful mate who can counter my vibrant dynamic self: sexual and intellectual . . ." And in April of the same year after Russell Lynes of Harper's has bought three of her poems, "Let's face it, I am in danger of wanting my personal absolute to be a demigod of a man. . . . I want a romantic nonexistent hero."

After she has met Hughes, but less than two weeks have passed, he is again in Cambridge.

"Please let him come; let me have him for this British spring. Please, please. . . . Oh, he is here; my black marauder; oh hungry hungry. I am so hungry for a big smashing creative burgeoning burdened love: I am here; I wait; and he plays on the banks of the river Cam like a casual faun."

By June she will have married him in a ceremony secret from everyone but her mother, who is there to bear witness.

There is an awful convention at work here, but can it truly be called commonplace? Who knew in the heart of the 50's the cost not only of domesticity, but of the violence to the self involved in loving that "black marauder"—that fierce and equally talented romantic hero who would father us into our fullest selves and art. It was a devastating bargain and not a woman I can think of has not paid her dues, in her own voice, which if she is a writer is her only coin. One becomes increasingly cautious these days about throwing stones, for the breakage comes dear, and close to home.

After she has married, her mood is for a while celebratory, "And here I am: Mrs. Hughes. And wife of a published poet. Oh, I knew it would happen. . . . Ted's book of poems—The Hawk in the Rain—has won the first *Harper's* publication contest. . . . I knew there would be something like this to welcome us to New York! We will publish a bookshelf of books between us before we perish! And a batch of brilliant healthy children. . . . I am so glad Ted is first . . . it is as if he is the perfect male counterpart to my own self. . . ."

She finishes out her year at Cambridge and accepts a teaching position at Smith for the following fall. Her mother treats them to a summer on Cape Cod. Plath frets about her work, her "bright glittery" adolescent success is behind her and she fights "to make the experience of my early maturity available to my typewriter." She casts a green eye at the competition, Donald Hall and Adrienne Rich, "and only 16 poems published in the last year." And she's tough on herself.

"Worst: it gets me feeling so sorry for myself that I get concerned about Ted: Ted's success, which I must cope with this fall with my job, loving it, and him to have it, but feeling so wishfully that I could make both of us feel better by having it with him. I'd rather have it this way, if either of us was successful: that's why I could marry him, knowing he was a better poet than I and that I would never have to restrain my little gift, but could push it and work it to the utmost, and still feel him ahead."

Her little gift, indeed, when what she wished and worked for was to be, "The Poetess of America (as Ted will be The Poet of England and her dominions). Who rivals? Well, in history Sappho, Elizabeth Barrett Browning, Christina Rossetti, Amy Lowell, Emily Dickinson, Edna St. Vincent Millay—all dead." Marianne Moore and Edith Sitwell are her "aging giantesses," and among the living she lists only the female poets: May Swenson, Isabella Gardner, "and most close, Adrienne Cecile Rich," toward whom she felt both rivalrous and admiring. Adrienne Rich was a scant three years older and when they met at Radcliffe that spring Plath eyed her closely: "little, round and stumpy, all vibrant short black hair, great sparkling black eyes and a tulip-red umbrella: honest, frank, forthright and even opinionated."

She was careful to scrutinize the work and the lives of other women who wrote, and she paid particular attention to those whose sexual choices were at odds with hers.

"Am reading Elizabeth Bishop with great admiration. Her fine originality, always surprising, never rigid, flowing, juicier than Marianne Moore, who is her godmother."

"Independent, self-possessed M.S. Ageless. Bird-watching before breakfast. What does she find for herself? Chess games. My old admiration for the strong, if lesbian, woman. The relief of limitation as a price for balance and surety. . . ."

It is worth noting that these reflections about other women's lives are made when Plath is pregnant for the first time. Before that she fears being barren, and is rhapsodic about what she's missing.

"I would bear children until my change of life if that were possible. I want a house of our children, little animals, flowers, vegetables, fruits. I want to be an Earth-Mother in the deepest richest sense. . . . And what do I meet in myself? Ash. Ash and more ash. . . . Ted should be a patriarch. I a mother."

When she knows she is going to have a child she is considerably cooler, even funny. "Children might humanize me. But I must rely on them for nothing. Fable of children changing existence and character as absurd as fable of marriage doing it. Here I am, the same old sour-dough."

Isn't this precisely why we read a writer's journals? Not as a key to the poetry, but to know about the life from which the poems sprang. Poetry is never simply autobiography; even if its heat and urgency is stoked by the dilemmas of ordinary life, it is an act of transformation. For even among the so-called "Confessional" poets, whether Lowell, Berryman or Plath, their revelations are not to be confused with fact. Hidden, shaped, toyed with and mercilessly reworked, fabricated even, the facts of their lives become the instruments of their art. Even journals tell only a kind of truth — taken on the run, or when the mood is foul, when one is feeling too dim, or pressed to make the real work, which is the poetry. Still, a journal must be a record clear of the filtering hands and mind of a biographer, and clear, too, of anyone as deeply implicated in her life, and her work, as Mr. Hughes is. Finally, it seems to me disingenuous to suggest that these Journals can be used as a gloss to Sylvia Plath's poetry when they do not cover the period, 1959–1963, when her major work got written.

Mr. Hughes has something quite extraordinary to say about all this in an essay titled "Sylvia Plath and Her Journals," submitted too late for the American edition, but which is printed in the current issue of the quarterly, Grand Street.

"The motive in publishing these journals will be questioned. The argument against is still strong. A decisive factor has been certain evident confusions, provoked in the minds of many of her readers by her later poetry. "Ariel" is dramatic speech of a kind. But to what persona and to what drama is it to be fitted? The poems don't seem to supply enough evidence of the definitive sort. This might have been no bad thing. . . . But the circumstances of her death, it seems, multiplied every one of her statements by a wild, unknown quantity. The results, among her interpreters, have hardly been steadied by the account she gave of herself in her letters to her mother, or by the errant versions supplied by her biographers." Fair enough. I have not read her biographers, but I have read her "Collected Poems," annotated by Mr. Hughes, and her "Letters Home," with notes provided by her mother, Aurelia Plath. The Journals should be crucial. They are. They are also a peculiarly broken record; Mr. Hughes calls them "curtailed." But by whom, if not by him, and why? Notice the pronouns, for they are chilling.

"Two other notebooks survived for a while after her death. They continued from where the surviving record breaks off in late 1959 and covered the last three years of her life. The second of these two books her husband destroyed, because he did not want her children to have to read it (in those days he regarded forgetfulness as an essential part of survival). The earlier one disappeared more recently (and may, presumably, still turn up)."

In the Foreward published here, his wording is different enough to be striking.

"Two more notebooks survived for a while, maroon-backed ledgers like the '57–'59 volume, and continued the record from late '59 to within three days of her death. The last of these contained entries for several months, and I destroyed it because I did not want her children to have to read it (in those days I regarded forgetfulness as an essential part of survival). The other disappeared."

To within three days of her death? I'm a betting woman: the earlier notebook will surface. Mr. Hughes is hardly unaware of what he's done; again he writes in Grand Street, "we cannot help wondering whether the lost entries for her last three years were not the more important section of it. Those years, after all, produced the work that made her name."

Between the close of 1959 (when Plath was 27 and these Journals essentially cease) and her suicide in February, 1963, this is a rough chronology of what happens. Plath and Hughes return to England to live; in April 1960, their first child, a girl, is born. In October "The Colossus," Plath's first book of poetry, is published in England. In January and February of 1961 Plath suffers a miscarriage, has an appendectomy, and The New Yorker offers her a contract to permit them the first reading of her poems for the year. During the spring and summer of 1961 she writes "The Bell Jar," becomes pregnant with their second child, and moves to Devon. In January 1962 a son is born. Sometime in the summer of 1962 Hughes begins an affair which leads to their separation in October. Plath has just turned 30, the babies are $2^{1}/_{2}$ and 9 months old; they are with her. She writes 25 poems in the month of October, by December she moves with the children to London. In January 1963 "The Bell Jar" is published in England under the pseudonym Victoria Lucas.

It was the coldest winter in England since the War, pipes froze and broke, water leaked or didn't come at all, babies caught cold. At the end of the month she began to write again, completing 12 poems before her death on February 11, 1963.

The question about these Journals is always the same: who is doing the cutting? And why? There is almost no rage expressed in these Journals, no sex described, but everywhere suggested. Why, for instance, in an entry that describes two teenagers dancing, is the boy's erection omitted while Plath's breasts are allowed "aching firm against his chest." Gracious sakes. And can we believe that this woman would have recorded no response to childbirth in her Journals? No woman living would have made such cuts without the pressure of a male hand. It is not enough for Mr. Hughes to tell us that "This is her autobiography, far from complete, but complex and accurate." Not in the face of such crucial missing material: the two years after her first suicide attempt in 1953: the entire period of her courtship with Hughes between April 1956 when she returns to him in England and their marriage in June: the entire last three years of her life, with the exception of certain character sketches which Mrs. McCullough tells us "were separate from her regular journals, and are all that survive in prose from this period, though she was also at work on a second novel." This too, 130 manuscript pages of a novel called "Double Exposure," is lost.

In a cautionary letter to Norma Millay, Edna St. Vincent Millay's surviving sister and her estate, Edmund Wilson wrote, "I don't think you ought to try — as people's families so often do — to supress the tragic aspects [of her life] because they might be painful or shocking. . . . Her poetry is not the work of a being for whom life could ever have been easy or gone along at a comfortable level. It will always give the lie to any too respectful biography . . . but it will also always be there to make the casualties of her life seem unimportant."

Against the immense seriousness of Sylvia Plath's quest for herself, and the perhaps monstrous and unrelenting self-observation that could not in the end sustain her, we will usefully place her poetry, her letters, and these Journals. She would be 50 this October. Instead she is forever caught in her 30th year, the fever heroine.

> The blood jet is poetry,
> There is no stopping it.
> You hand me two children,
>   two roses.
> ("Kindness," 1 February 1963.)

ESSAYS

The Transfiguring Self:
Sylvia Plath, a Reconsideration
Leonard Sanazaro*

In the four months before her death, Sylvia Plath, at the age of 30, composed some of the most controversial and widely read poetry of the twentieth century. She achieved her artistic virtuosity despite repetitive bouts of flu that affected her and her two small children. But pressed by her desire to overcome the recent break-up of her marriage and exhausted by ill health and her compelling desire to write herself to great success, she succumbed in a period of extended depression and tragically ended her own life on a bleak February morning in London in 1963. Nine months later, ten of the late poems appeared in *Encounter Magazine* and began what can only be termed a phenomenon of serious contemporary literature. With the continual publication of the Plath legacy, interest in the life and work of this disturbing artist has grown and intensified in the nearly two decades since her death. And this year, with the awarding of the Pulitzer Prize to *The Collected Poems*, we are directed toward a more serious re-evaluation of her artistic achievement.

The excesses of Plath criticism, that growing body of work by her numerous advocates and detractors, most accurately reflect the very dilemma the poetry ultimately presents its readers. Either the poems are thoroughly immersed in the poet's biography and rendered incapable of independent existence as works of art; or they are defensively divorced from the poet's life and interests, thus denuding them of the important personal and world milieu in which they came to being.[1] Dubious an achievement as it certainly seems, few poets have elicited so clear a division of the readership approaching their work. But in either case, both excesses distort and fail finally to treat the emotional and intellectual complexities of the poems themselves. When available, primary biographical data surrounding specific poems can be used effectively to illuminate their creator's particular emotional concerns at the time of their composition. This information, in conjunction with a detailed textual analysis, can yield a greater understanding of the larger, universal themes that run throughout Plath's *oeuvre*.

*Reprinted with permission from the *Centennial Review*, 27, No. 1 (Winter, 1983), 62–74.

I

By October 30, 1962, Plath had completed most of the major works now contained in *Ariel* and *Winter Trees*.[2] At that time in an interview with Peter Orr for the BBC, Plath had identified her poems as rising immediately from "the sensuous and emotional experiences I have."[3] These late poems were inevitably influenced by the intense pressures and disturbing experiences of the previous two months: a troubled and uncertain marriage and a growing sense of financial and personal vulnerability in her roles of wife and mother. In several letters written to her mother toward the end of September, 1962, Plath had repeatedly expressed a desire to "get my independence again," and "get control of my life."[4] And in the succeeding letters of October, after the disintegration of her marriage, Plath's sense of urgency grew more immediate in response to her mother's repeated requests for her to return to the United States. On October 9, she writes: "I should say right away America is out for me. I want to make my life in England. If I start running now, I will never stop. . . . *I must make a life all my own as fast as I can* . . . the flesh has dropped from my bones. But I am a fighter" (Plath's italics).[5] And again on October 16, she writes:

> . . . it would be psychologically the worst thing to see you now or to go home. I have free doctor's care here, cheap help *possible* though not now available, and a home I love and will want to return to in summer to get ready to leap to London. *To make a new life.* . . . I feel only a lust to study, write, get my brain back and practise my craft. . . . I have no desire but to build a new life. Must *start here.* . . . I must not go back to the womb or retreat. I must make steps out . . . I am fighting against hard odds and alone.[6]

Two days later she wrote to her brother urging him to help their mother see "how starting my own life in the most difficult place — here — not running, is the only sane thing to do."[7] One critic, Judith Kroll, believes Plath's desire for a "a new life" manifests itself in a number of late poems — particularly "Ariel" and "Fever 103°" — as a need to detach herself from the "old patterns that had dominated her life and her very conception of self."[8] But rather than concerning themselves with the detachment from one state in order to reach another, a number of late poems are direct experiences of religious transfiguration in which the various female personae suffer themselves into a creation of a new self. Composed within a span of ten days and sharing structural similarities, these poems share a common thematic concern as well which is defined specifically in religious contexts. "Purdah," "Lady Lazarus," "Fever 103°," and "Ariel" all dramatically illustrate the individual's urgent drive toward liberation and self-definition.[9]

In "Purdah" the speaker, a member of a harem, is imprisoned and dehumanized by the veils of a curtain devised for the subjugation of women in Oriental societies. Not only does the veil separate her from the world at large; it also confines the dynamic, active self and effects a division of her personalilty. Ultimately the "purdah" is the system of male domination, and the poem is the process of the speaker's emergence from that system.

At the beginning of the poem she characterizes herself in terms of images that are transmutable. She is "Jade—Stone . . ." and "enigmatical" only "shifting" as the intensity of light alters in the course of the day. But as the poem proceeds we discover her to be "Cousin" to the moon, an image of transformation. Like the moon, she "gleams like a mirror" and revolves in a "Sheath of impossibles," able to change from one condition into another. This power to self-transform is given impetus as the possessive bridegroom approaches the "purdah" behind which the speaker is concealed. His title of "Lord of the mirrors" implies her obligation as a member of the harem to reflect his lordliness. In this sense, she is his "valuable" and "his / Even in his / Absence." Against this domination, she will ultimately revolt and "unloose" to freedom through his assassination.

The two allusions at the beginning and end of the poem fix the speaker's condition in a religious context. The opening allusion refers to the Biblical story of Eve's creation from Adam's rib:

> Jade—
> Stone of the side,
> the agonized
>
> Side of a green Adam, I
> Smile, cross-legged,
> Enigmatical,

The use of the corresponding "green" of the jade figurine, Eve, with the condition of newly created man, a "green Adam," serves to establish a new mythos in the story of "Purdah." The characters of the poem are newly created like the characters of the Genesis story, and in that context the drama they enact achieves a ritualistic level. The ritual murder of the bridegroom in the poem and the emergence of the woman as independent at its conclusion signal the end of male domination and, indeed, the end of the concept of woman as mere extension of the man. No longer a Jade figurine, she emerges, finally, from the "small jeweled / Doll he guards like a heart."

The closing allusion, "The lioness, / The shriek in the bath, / The cloak of holes" also functions similarly by raising the action of the poem to the level of ritual drama. The lioness that is unloosed refers to the first play of the Orestia in which Clytemnestra avenges the sacrifice of her daughter, Iphigenia, at the outset of the Trojan War by throwing a netlike robe over her husband, Agamemnon, and stabbing him as he steps from the ritual bath.[10] This assassination of a male for his sacrifical abuse of the female establishes the final motif of Plath's poem. The woman is possessed in the basest fashion possible; she is no longer a consciousness; she is pure object, a jade figurine "priceless and quiet." For this dehumanization, like Clytem-nestra, she exacts her revenge.

Another poem in which the female transfigures is "Lady Lazarus." The character performs a bizarre circus act for the "peanut-crunching crowd." She dies and revives.[11] But the central issue of the poem is not only the spectacular deaths of Lady Lazarus. Her death and rebirth here are achieved against the polarities revealed to us in the poem's conclusion, that of God and Lucifer. The speaker warns these deities to "beware." From her self-immolation she will arise like the phoenix and devour men. This willfulness to arise and devour humankind in the form of a self-fulfilled deity points up the impotence of the traditional concepts of good and evil. Neither God nor Lucifer is able to exact punishment for the atrocities man heaps upon man: "my skin / Bright as a Nazi lampshade, / My right foot / A paperweight." Thus the speaker characterizes them earlier as "Herr Doktor" and "Herr Enemy" and turns with the bitterest irony to say: "Do not think I underestimate your great concern."

In this light, the death and revitalization of Lady Lazarus contrast sharply with the poem's biblical context. The speaker is perfected in the Nietzschean sense of the word.[12] Unlike the Jewish Lazarus of the *New Testament* who must await Christ to summon him back to life from his deathly paradise, Lady Lazarus does not simply die but reduces herself to ashes and revives herself in flames by the strength of her own will. In this way, the efficacy of an exterior redemptive and punitive power is denied; the center of power becomes the individual's ability to create the self.

A number of critics view Plath's use of holocaust imagery as a means by which she enlarges her own emotions and sensationalizes her own biography.[13] However, the central issue of such a poem as "Lady Lazarus" is not merely the dramatization of personal emotion and biography. Judith Kroll believes that the late poems in which Plath employs Nazi imagery are a means to the construction of a cogent mythicized biography of the ritual victim.[14] Jerome Mazzaro in "Sylvia Plath and the Cycles of History" believes poems like "Lady Lazarus" to be historical enlargements that illustrate the individual's reversal of passivity and a mastery of the "dialectic of wills."[15] And Jon Rosenblatt points out that Plath's combined use of personal material and holocaust imagery allows her to invent a dramatic structure that moves in areas of feeling previously untapped in modern poetry.[16] In any event, to view these works as exhibitionist and self-pitying is to obscure and even ignore both their artistic complexity and their rich theological significance. Plath said specifically that her poems had come:

> . . . out of the sensuous and emotional experiences I have, but I must say that I cannot sympathize with these cries from the heart that are informed by nothing except a needle or a knife, or whatever it is. I believe that one should be able to control and manipulate experiences, even the most terrifying, like madness, being tortured, this sort of experience, and one should be able to manipulate these experiences with an informed and intelligent

mind. I think personal experience is very important, but certainly it shouldn't be a shut-box and mirror-looking, narcissistic experience. I believe it should be relevant, and relevant to the larger things, the bigger things such as Hiroshima and Dachau and so on.[17]

II

It is evident then that the core of Plath's poetic experience was personal experience, but for her the creation of art necessitated control and manipulation by the "informed and intelligent mind." This was, of course, the contrast to what she characterized as "cries from the heart" and as a "shut box and mirror-looking, narcissistic experience." The characterization of individual suffering, if it was to have any meaning to the modern mind, was then dependent upon a broader field of reference to achieve universality of meaning. These were "the larger things, the bigger things," where man has perpetrated the grossest inhumanity upon his fellow man. Contrasted to these, the theological touchstones become specific landmarks which signal the sufferer's distance from any form of action or definition not resulting from the individual's self-realization. Therefore, in order for poems to have deep psychic impact on the modern reader, they had to be at once enactments of personal suffering divorced from the human and individualized.[18] The woman of "Purdah" and Lady Lazarus both exemplify this personal-depersonalization.

Another example is the woman of "Fever 103°" who tries to duplicate Christ's ascension into heaven.[19] But against this religious context, Plath poses images of hell and the Inquisition. In an earlier version of the poem she recorded for the BBC, this antithesis is even more clear.[20]

The poem initially questions the meaning of *pure*. The woman tells us that the "tongues of hell / Are dull," that they are, in fact, as dull as the "triple / Tongues of dull, fat Cerberus" who now "wheezes" as he guards the gates of Hades. These metaphorical "tongues of hell" no longer speak a message of fear to mankind and are no longer capable of serving as sufficient expiation for sinfulness. Cerberus, the terrifying three-headed monster of Greek mythology, is both "dull" and "fat." In his antiquity, he "wheezes" rather than roars and is "incapable" of cleansing man of his feverish sinfulness. The fires of hell are now the products of men; they have their "autos-da-fe" and are "purple," "gold-crusted," and filled with ill-tempered capriciousness. It is they who assume responsibility for punishment; they "sit with their hooks and crooks and stoke the light." With "crooks," reference to the traditional shepherd's staff of Christ, they perpetrate divine authority. In their pomposity and arrogance, they "stoke" the fires of hell as if they were the inferno of an earthly furnace. The lives of men are the "tinder" for their fires. The "indelible smell" of the "snuffed candle" refers to the climax in the act of excommunication before the final punishment, death by burning at the stake, is exacted. In the image of the candle, Plath makes an amazing transition by introducing a personal voice. This speaker identifies with it. By envisioning the smoke from its extinguished taper as scarves, she comes to fear an accidental death like that of the dancer, Isadora Duncan, in 1927. This smoke is "yellow" and "sullen"; and because it is the product of man's inhumanity, it not only threatens the speaker but pervades and poisons the entire atmosphere. Ultimately characterized as "radiation," it embodies the diametrical opposite of the blessing delivered by Christ in the Sermon on the Mount. The sin is no longer ideological fraud and human brutality; it becomes the penultimate looming spectre of atomic destruction embodied by Hiroshima.[21]

At this juncture, the exact midpoint of the eighteen stanza poem, the poem makes a natural break. Besides insinuating a personal voice into the experience of the poem, the first half is concerned with establishing an inclusive historical milieu against which the persona will transfigure. This milieu is the reality of man's sinfulness which permeates his history. The second half begins with a direct reference to the speaker's condition, one of illness. In three days and three nights, the speaker has been purified. She tells us, "I am too pure for you or anyone." These three days reflect the three days Christ spent in the underworld before his final transfiguration and ascension into paradise. Like Him, the speaker is transfigured. Her skin is "gold-beaten" and "infinitely delicate and infinitely expensive." She possesses both "heat" and "light" resembling a huge glowing flower that bursts into bloom. As she ascends, she finally fades to invisibility. Describing herself as "pure acetylene," she has transfigured from her physical body into pure spirit, her "selves dissolving" to paradise.

When one remembers the initial question posed in the opening line of the poem — "Pure? What does it mean?" — the unity of the fragments of the speaker's experience is impressive. She surmounts evil by moving from the expansive historical level to that of the interpersonal. She abandons her lover. "Your body / Hurts me as the world hurts God," so that her "selves" can peel away, "old whore petticoats," revealing finally a being which throbs with heat and light. To transform the self through the evil constraints of its history, both personal and historical, is to achieve a vibrant lucidity and clarity. Plath had said of the poem: "This poem is about two kinds of fire — the fires of hell, which merely agonize, and the fires of heaven, which purify. During the poem, the first sort of fire suffers itself into the second."[22]

Thus purification can occur only in the broadest sense if each individual confronts himself or herself at the most personal level of his or her own consciousness. This individual must achieve a transcendence from the agonized history of mankind's sinfulness.[23] Once again, power lies in the individual's ability to realize the self.

III

In "Purdah," "Lady Lazarus," and "Fever 103°," the self is realized in a variety of experiences. In the first the self achieves freedom from male oppression; in the second, it is no longer bound by the traditional constraints of good and evil; and in the third, the purified self arises from the imprisonments of history. But in "Ariel," the shortest poem of the group, the self appears to suffer obliteration.

Annette Lavers, one of Plath's earliest critics, saw in "Ariel" a final "orgastic ecstasy" in which the horse's gallop stands as a double symbol for the "pulsating rhythm of life, and for the dispersion of the individual" into blank eternity.[24] Later Judith Kroll interpreted the experience of the poem to be one of "ecstatic union" in which the individual undergoes "a final letting go of self which yields an ultimate reconciliation."[25] Most recently, Jon Rosenblatt has viewed the poem as one which "entices us into a kind of death — the experience of abandoning our bodies and selves."[26] However, all of the other poems of this period concern themselves with the preservation and re-creation of the self. To interpret the central experience of "Ariel" as a complete loss of self for whatever reason, be it a desire for orgastic finality or ecstatic union, is to ignore the implications of both Plath's immediate emotional situation at the time of its composition and the previous poems to which it bears similarity.

Two days before the composition of the poem,[27] on October 25, 1962, Plath wrote her mother:

> . . . I believe in going through and facing the worst, not hiding from it. That is why I am going to London this week, partly, to face [people] and tell them happily and squarely I am divorcing . . . so they won't picture me as a poor country wife. I am not going to steer clear of these professional acquaintances just because they know. . . .
>
> Now don't feel helpless anymore. I am helped very much by letters. . . .[28]

The realistic tone of the letter with its balanced focus on practical details does not reflect the desire for self-obliteration critics so often perceive in the poem. Rather here is a woman voicing firm resolve in the face of altered personal circumstances and expressing a determination to survive as a professional and as an artist. Also the imagery of earlier poems stressing rebirth and transformation is similar to that of "Ariel."

In the transitional poem "Blackberrying" [*Collected Poems*, pp. 168–69], Plath had used the images of "berries" and "blood" to express ideas of sisterhood and communion. At the end of the poem the speaker is strengthened by the landscape to face the vast hostility of the sea. In "Love Letter" [*CP*, p. 147], another transitional poem, the speaker ascends like the dew to "resemble a sort of god." In the ascent she is "pure as a pane of ice."

Similar processes are at work in "Ariel," but Plath had come to express them in more immediate and ritualistic terms.

Judith Kroll correctly identifies the allusion the title of the poem makes to "Ariel" as the altar of sacrifice or the "altar of God." She goes on to point out that the horse in the poem is actually called "God's lioness" and that Plath had written "lioness of God" at the top of the manuscript. But the meaning of sacrifice and its relationship to the speaker's experience in the poem needs to be clarified and sufficiently developed.

Among the ancient Israelites, the rite of sacrifice was an act of purification and reconciliation. When an animal was sacrificed, it represented a

> . . . transference of the iniquities of the people to the [animal] to be driven forth [and] was affected by the priest laying his hands upon its head and confessing all their sins over it to bear them away to a solitary land. The carcasses of the [animal] slain as a sin-offering were to be taken without [the city] and destroyed by fire.[29]

These rites of sacrifice are central to the experience and meaning of "Ariel." The poem begins at dawn:

> Stasis in darkness.
> Then the substanceless blue
> Pour of tor and distances.

The opening lines both make a philosophical statement and establish the speaker's initial condition. It is static and blank; there is no change. But as black yields to blue, stasis yields to motion, the "Pour of tor and distances." This process, besides reflecting a gradual lightening, as may take place in the sky at dawn, also intimates the movement of the speaker's mind. The allusion to "tor" (an ancient sacrificial altar at the top of a hill) and "distances" not only establishes a motif for physical movement but also for the quasi-movement of consciousness in dreaming. "God's lioness" specifies a place, ancient Jerusalem, the altar of God, but also identifies the animal upon which the speaker of the poem rides, "how one we grow."[30] From this point of identification, the images of movement and riding are intensified by the detailing of specific leg parts, "heels and knees." The verbs also express action more directly: "pivot," "splits," "passes," and "catch." But suddenly the process is interrupted. The speaker is lifted out of the action. What remains is residue. As if observing from a vantage point above, she views the transfiguration of the old self. The allusion to Lady Godiva, the devoutly religious wife of the Earl of Leofric, works much in the same way as the religious allusions of the earlier poems.[31] Here the old self is a "White / Godiva," a corpse that represents the tight constrictions of religious stagnation expressed as "dead hands, dead stringencies." What matters is the transfiguration, the birth of the new self. As "the child's cry melts in the wall," the old self is carried off by the sacrificial animal which transforms to other types of offerings — vegetation, "wheat" and water, "a glitter of seas." The old self dies like the dew, "suicidal," that "flies into the red / Eye, the cauldron of morning."

At the conclusion of the poem, the day has begun — the process from night to daylight completed. For the speaker, the process is the metamorphosis of consciousness.

In centering a number of her late poems in the experience of transfiguration, Sylvia Plath employed all the dynamism of her skill to illustrate the individual's drive to self-creation. "Purdah," "Lady Lazarus," "Fever 103°," and "Ariel," in many ways the best of her poetry, are essentially but one expression of the individual's battle for self-definition and liberation. Unfortunately her suicide on February 11, 1963, has come to overshadow the meaning of much of the late poetry and its vital significance. Yet as we approach the second decade since her death, it is hoped we come closer to a better understanding of her vibrant contribution.

Notes

1. The opposite poles in Plath criticism may be represented by such essays as Robert Phillips' "The Dark Funnel: A Reading of Sylvia Plath," *Modern Poetry Studies*, 3 (1972), 49–74, and Hugh Kenner's "Sincerity Kills" in *Sylvia Plath: New Views on the Poetry*, Gary Lane, ed. (Baltimore: The Johns Hopkins University Press, 1979), pp. 33–44.

2. The poems were "Lady Lazarus," "Stopped Dead," "Nick and the Candlestick," "Medusa," "Purdah," "Amnesiac," "Fever 103°," "The Rabbit Catcher," "Ariel," and "Daddy." Gary Lane and Maria Stevens, *Sylvia Plath, A Bibliography*. (Metuchen, New Jersey: The Scarecrow Press, Inc., 1978). pp. 60–61.

3. Peter Orr, *The Poet Speaks*. (London: Routledge & Kegan Paul, 1966), p. 169.

4. The full quotations read: ". . . I must at all costs make over the cottage and get a live-in nanny next spring so I can start trying to write and get my independence again. . . ." (September 23, 1962, p. 461) and: "I am sorry to be so worrying at this time when your own concerns are so pressing, but I must get control of my life, the little I have left." (September 26, 1962, p. 463) Sylvia Plath, *Letters Home: Correspondence 1950–1963*, edited and with commentary by Aurelia Schober Plath (New York: Harper & Row, Publishers, 1975).

5. Plath, *Letters Home*, p. 465.

6. Plath, *Letters Home*, pp. 468–69.

7. Plath, *Letters Home*, p. 472.

8. Judith Kroll, *Chapters in a Mythology*. (New York: Harper & Row, 1976), p. 173.

9. Sylvia Plath, *The Collected Poems*, (New York: Harper & Row, Publishers, 1981), "Fever 103°," pp. 231–32, was composed on October 20, 1962; "Ariel," pp. 239–40, on October 27, 1962; "Purdah," pp. 242–44, on October 29, 1962; and "Lady Lazarus," pp. 244–47, was composed and re-worked from October 23, thru October 29, 1962, inclusively.

10. Judith Kroll points out the allusion to Agamemnon's assassination for a different end. *Chapters*, p. 157.

11. Plath had long been interested in the story of Lazarus. As early as February 19, 1956, she recorded in her journal: "I feel like Lazarus: that story has such a fascination. Being dead, I rose up again, and even resort to the mere sensation value of being suicidal, of getting so close, of coming out of the grave with the scars and the marring mark on my cheek which (is it my imagination) grows more prominent. . . ."
Sylvia Plath, "Cambridge Notes," in *Johnny Panic and the Bible of Dreams: Selected Short Stories, Prose, and Diary Excerpts*. (New York: Harper & Row, Publishers, 1979), p. 249.

Also Plath had included in the "Cambridge Manuscript" of her early poems an early piece entitled "The Aerialist." In this poem the girl dreams of her circus performance and then awakens. I quote stanza two and six.

> Nightly she balances
> Cat-clever on perilous wire
> In a gigantic hall,
> Footing her delicate dances
> To whipcrack and roar
> Which speak her maestro's will.

and:

> Tall trucks roll in
> With a thunder like lions; all aims
> And lumbering moves
> To trap this outrageous nimble queen
> And shatter to atoms
> Her nine so slippery lives.

Plath, *Collected Poems*, pp. 331–31.

12. Plath was familiar with Nietzsche as early as 1954. In an undergraduate essay, "The Age of Anxiety," she quotes from *Thus Spake Zarathustra* extensively. She also composed several early poems in the Nietzschean mode. One, "Notes on Zarathustra's Prologue," contains the lines: "Go flay the frail sheep in the flock / And strip the shroud from coward's back." My thanks to Ms. Saundra Taylor of the Lilly Library, Indiana University, Bloomington, for supplying these early writings by Sylvia Plath. All unpublished Plath material is under the copyright of Mr. Ted Hughes.

13. See George Steiner's "Dying is an Art," in *The Art of Sylvia Plath*. (Bloomington: University of Indiana Press, 1970). p. 218, and Irving Howe's "A Plath Celebration: A Partial Descent," in *Sylvia Plath: The Woman and the Work*. (New York: E.P. Dutton, 1979), pp. 230–232.

14. Kroll, "The Mythic Biography in the Late Poetry," *Chapters*, pp. 108–121.

15. Jerome Mazzaro, "Sylvia Plath and the Cycles of History," in *Sylvia Plath: New Views on the Poetry*. (Baltimore: The Johns Hopkins University Press, 1979), p. 234.

16. Jon Rosenblatt, *Sylvia Plath: The Poetry of Initiation*. (Chapel Hill: The University of North Carolina Press, 1979), p. 146.

17. Orr, *The Poet Speaks*, pp. 145–46.

18. Jon Rosenblatt points out how Plath's poems permit "the reader to understand what is occurring with only the slimmest reference, or no reference at all, to the poet's biography." *Sylvia Plath*, p. 146.

19. Judith Kroll mistakenly notes a similarity to the Assumption of the Virgin Mary and distinguishes the poem as "farce." The action of the poem parallels more accurately the final ascension of Christ due to the speaker's later reference to three days and nights of purification. See *Chapters*, p. 178.

20. Eileen Aird, "Variants in a Tape Recording of Fifteen Poems by Sylvia Plath," *Notes and Queries*, 19 (February 1972), 54–61. The lines are v.3, 1.1 after the *Ariel* version:

> O auto dá fe, the purple men
> Gold-crusted, thick with spleen,
> Sit with their hooks and crooks and stoke the light.

21. "Fever 103°" contains clear references to the visual images of Alain Resnais's film, *Hiroshima, Mon Amour*. Note this description of the film's opening scene: "One strange thing about the opening scene is that the bodies are covered with a glistening substance that could be ashes or dew. It may be perspiration produced by their lovemaking, but, since the scene is set in Hiroshima, it could be radioactive dust." The nature of Resnais's art also bears relation to

Plath's poem since he too represents experiences as fragmented sensory perceptions [where] "time dimensions are combined; the characters try desperately to hold on to the past; love and death are juxtaposed as the two most intense experiences in life," (p. 202). See Marsha Kinder and Beverle Houston, *Close-up: A Critical Perspective on Film* (New York: Harcourt, Brace, Jovanovich, Inc., 1972).

22. Plath, *Collected Poems*, p. 293.

23. Plath had told Peter Orr in an interview at the time of the reading that: "I am not a historian, but I find myself being more fascinated by history and now find myself reading more and more about history . . . and I think that as I age I am becoming more and more historical." *The Poet Speaks*, p. 169.

24. Annette Lavers, "The World as Icon," in *The Art of Sylvia Plath*, p. 120.

25. Kroll, *Chapters*, p. 180.

26. Rosenblatt, *Sylvia Plath*, p. 147.

27. Judith Kroll, who had access to the Plath manuscripts of the late poems, was able to make this observation. Its composition date is that of Plath's birthday. *Chapters*, p. 180.

28. She also wrote her mother telling her: "On my birthday, if it's nice, I'll be at my horseback riding lesson . . ." *Letters Home*, p. 477.

29. E.O. James, *The Ancient Gods*. (New York: G.P. Putnam's Sons, 1960), p. 155.

30. Kroll, *Chapters*, p. 181.

31. Chambers Encyclopedia, 1973 ed., s.v. "Lady Godiva." The derivative of Godiva's name may also have relevance here. It comes from the old English *godgifu*, meaning "gift of god." Plath used word derivatives in several poems to add another level of meaning. See "A Life," [*CP*, pp. 149–50] and "Medusa," [*CP*, pp. 224–225].

The Americanization of Sylvia   Alicia Ostriker*

Sylvia Plath's first published book of poems, *The Colossus* (1960), received the mild critical commendation usually accruing to competent, promising, and rather mediocre first books. Her second, appearing posthumously after her suicide in 1963, provoked a violent and brief literary cultism, some highly excited critical acclaim and nervous critical attack,[1] and a rain of elegies and tributes by fellow poets. Since many of the poems in *Ariel* deal, directly and passionately, with illness, death, suicide and rage, it is not surprising that commentary on Plath typically identifies her poetry with her biography, declaring, for example, that "the long, escalating drive toward suicide and the period of extraordinary creativity . . . actually coincided . . . or were at least two functions of the same process."[2]

In this respect sophisticated critics resemble naive readers. I have refereed more than one angry classroom debate between Plath defenders and Plath antagonists in which it was perfectly clear that the issue was the morality of suicide. Had the poet the "right" to kill herself? Was she "self-indulgent?" The questions can of course be pushed further. Was her death society's fault, for romanticizing "extremism" and burn-out in artists? Was

*Reprinted with permission from *Language and Style*, 1, No. 3 (Summer, 1968), 201–12 and Ostriker's *Writing Like a Woman* (Ann Arbor: University of Michigan Press, 1982).

it Otto Plath's fault, for being an authoritarian papa and inscribing feminine passivity upon his little daughter forever? Should we blame the self-
sacrificing Aurelia Plath for being a model of wifely submissiveness and
because she forced Sylvia to become the appallingly and unrelievedly en-
thusiastic-and-grateful-and-happy American Girl of *Letters Home*? Was it
that the "absolutely white person" (see "In Plaster") of Sylvia's social facade
was so unyielding and disruption-proof as to press all anti-social impulses
back into the private self, where they rankled and festered? Or did Sylvia
create the Good Girl mask because she herself feared volcanic forces
within? Did Ted Hughes really kill Sylvia? ("But she *picked* him," half the
class leaps to remark.) What if we shift our camera backward from this particular life, until we see Plath sharing a frame with other inconsolable children, such as Hemingway and Berryman, who were perhaps doomed from
the moment of their fathers' suicides, though they fought fate as long as they
were able? Think of that old notion of the curse on a family, so central to
Greek tragedy. Or the Old Testament remonstrance: "The fathers have
eaten sour grapes, and the children's teeth are set on edge." We would love to
refute that, if we could. Or, shifting still further back, must we ask if some
people are congenital emotional hemophiliacs — if you cut them they cannot
make scar tissue, they simply keep bleeding — and if so, what is the connection between such a condition and the genesis of poetry?

I do not think such questions are improper, provided we see how the
multiplicity of answers must lead us finally to a sense of mystery. We do not
know why some people destroy themselves, just as we do not know why
some people destroy others. "Why look'st thou so?" asks the wedding guest.
"With my crossbow I shot the Albatross," says the Ancient Mariner. Consequences follow, but why did he shoot it? Coleridge cannot say. Our frustrated wish to clear up the mystery and label the package "Someone Else:
Not Me" might lead us to understand that what we are really asking about is
our own agitation. This too is proper. No failure to distinguish art from life
is quite so stupid as pretending that poetry is some kind of sterile swabbed
tissue of language uninfected by the poet's life and incapable of infecting
the reader's life.

My own response, on first reading *Ariel*, was a thought compounded of
something like *Good God, it's real* and *Damn, she did it* — as if having "done
it" were a triumph — and a physical sensation like that of being slapped
hard: rush of adrenalin, stunned amazement. I was stealing time to read. In
those days I stole whatever time I could from the demands of family and the
demands of freshman classes. Either set of duties was inherently infinite,
infinitely guilt-producing. Often it seemed I never slept. It was very late,
my husband and two babies were asleep, it was icy and windy outside the
apartment as I sat under the lamp and moaned my way through poems
written in the hours before the sound of the milkman and the cries of children, during the last six months of Plath's life.

If I ask myself in retrospect precisely what I mean by *Damn, she did it*, the answer is complex ("like everything else," as the poet herself might observe). Most obviously: she had dared to kill herself, as in all probability I never would. This made her somehow an aristocrat and me a peasant gasping at her nobility. Of course I too wanted annihilation. Second: she had permitted herself emotions which for me were forbidden, and which I spent a considerable amount of effort attempting to repress. Self-loathing, that drug. Loathing of others, especially my near and dear. Desire to kill as well as die. Fury of the trapped animal. Plenty of TNT in that kitchen cabinet. The authenticity of this poet's hatreds was for me nailed down of course by their rootedness in a feminine body and their location among domestic arrangements. It was justified by her terror and anger at war and her sense of helplessness in the face of brutality, which I shared and share. I also shared her understanding of maternal love and ecstasy in poems like "Morning Song" or "Balloons," her fierce grasp of life in poems like "Tulips," the celebration of womanhood and rebirth that closes the bee poems (which, by the way, Hughes tells us were originally intended to conclude *Ariel* itself; for unspecified reasons he moved these poems away from the manuscript's close, thus altering its emotional plotline.)[3] The fact that this woman knew the nature of specific female pleasures, however tenuously, however they failed to save her, made the downward spin of her whirlpool even more seductive to my mind.

And then: as a poet, oh, as a poet, she had done it. She had contrived not merely to feel freely but to state clearly. As a poet, greedy, I wanted her bag of tricks.

Fifteen years later I resemble Sylvia less than I first imagined. In middle age I am a peasant, thick-skinned and concerned with survival, in a way that the sensitive young woman I was could not have anticipated. I want to live to be a hundred. I see myself wrinkled and sage, dropping off the branch in the ultramarine cold, very late in the season, a twilight scene with snow flurries. But to my first encounter with Plath I date the initial stirrings of a realization (practical not theoretical, and not her realization but mine) that to accomplish this intention will require, for me, reconciliation with a self that wants to kill or die. Not denial, not "indulgence:" reconciliation. It is an understanding I share with many other women, taught by Plath to recognize the underside of our womanly propriety. At the same moment as we are pulling ourselves from martyrdom's shadows to some sort of daylight, we honor her for being among the first to run a flashlight over the cave walls.

But it is the bag of tricks, the art, that I still admire unreservedly, having found it inimitable. Or rather I should say I found it impossible to steal from and get away with, since a Plath device in someone else's poem can be spotted miles off, like a giraffe meandering over tundra. And what strikes me now, reading through Plath's *Collected Poems*, is how she achieved a voice that is not only distinctly her own but distinctly American, through an almost complete reversal of stylistic direction. For the weakness of Plath's earliest work is that it is derivative and safe in style if not substance; and the strength of the poetry from 1960 on is achieved by means of a technique that has nothing to do with safety, everything to do with risk.

The American grain Plath belongs to is that part of our writing which, since the nineteenth century, has been deliberately antibelletristic, deliberately naive, programmatically occupied with climbing over the enclosures of established forms, and perpetually re-insisting that the true function of the writer is the documentation of physical and emotional facts, in a fashion as close to journalism as possible. Has any other nation produced so many major writers who started out as journalists? At any rate, from Whitman's installation of the muse amid the kitchenware to Williams' filthy Passaic, from Melville's encyclopedic turgidity to Hemingway's "true" sentence, from *Walden* to *Let Us Now Praise Famous Men* — and consider writers like Twain, Sherwood Anderson, Ring Lardner, John Dos Passos, E.A. Robinson, Edgar Lee Masters, Carl Sandburg, Robert Frost, to name at random a few majors and minors and indicate the boundaries — the native American tradition continually produces writers who write as if art were literally supposed to represent life without falsification, and as if it were preferable to have real toads at the expense of imaginary gardens. An example: "I went to the wood because I wished to live deliberately, to front only the essential facts of life," says Thoreau in *Walden*, "to shave close, to drive life into a corner and reduce it to its lowest terms, and, if it proved to be mean, why then to get the whole and genuine meanness of it and publish its meanness to the world; or if it were sublime, to know it by experience, and be able to give a true account of it in my next excursion."

Most nineteenth-century Americans, including Thoreau, favored the sublime. Emerson did not choose to suppose that the transparent eyeball would ever behold anything displeasing. Whitman acknowledged that to face Fact meant to face Death, but tried to be cheerful about it. Intimations of the whole and genuine meanness surface only occasionally, in Melville, late Twain, and Dickinson. Think of Dickinson's "I heard a fly buzz," or "The sky is low, the clouds are mean," or the bird on her garden walk who "bit an Angleworm in halves / And ate the fellow, raw." Meanness is a dominant twentieth- rather than nineteenth-century convention. Yet even Thoreau remarks characteristically, a few lines after the passage I have just quoted, "If you stand right fronting and face to face to a fact, you will see the sun glimmer on both its surfaces, as if it were a cimeter, and feel its sweet edge dividing you through the heart and marrow, and so you will happily conclude your mortal career. Be it life or death, we crave only reality. If we are really dying, let us hear the rattle in our throats and feel cold in the extremities; if we are alive, let us go about our business." Notice, now, the striking resemblance between Thoreau's image of the lethal swordlike "fact" and the conclusion of *Ariel*'s "A Birthday Present," in which the unopened gift is also a desired, unconfronted fact:

Only let down the veil, the veil, the veil.
If it were death

I would admire the deep gravity of it, its timeless eyes.
I would know you were serious.

There would be a nobility then, there would be a birthday.
And the knife not carve but enter

Pure and clean as the cry of a baby
And the universe slide from my side.

Or compare Thoreau's not quite serious recommendation, "If we are really dying, let us hear the rattle in our throats and feel cold in the extremities," with Plath's "Dying / Is an art, like everything else. / I do it exceptionally well. / I do it so it feels like hell. / I do it so it feels real." And compare both with Dickinson's "I like a look of Agony, / Because I know it's true."

The difference between *The Colossus* and *Ariel* lies in the poet's advancing will and ability to do it, technically, so it feels real, without veils. If Plath commits herself in her first book to "tending, without stop, the blunt / Indefatigible fact," ("Night Shift") she often fails. It is not a question of themes, which are implicitly as brutal in *The Colossus* as in *Ariel*. Several of the poems in *Ariel* are precisely re-visions of poems in *The Colossus*. The astonishing change occurs in the typical occasions employed, the diction, and the form of the poems. One could summarize the change by saying that having learned to see the skull beneath the skin, she threw away the skin.

The first book is safer in many ways. It depends on past tradition, and this is not simply a matter of allusions to classical and European literature and art, although the allusions are there. It obeys, as most academic poetry in the 1950s did, that line of T.S. Eliot's criticism which cautions severely against the shallowness of merely personal ideas, and reasonably asserts that writing which assimilates the past can have a philosophical assurance, a firmness and density of texture, otherwise unavailable. Poems like "The Manor Garden," "Two Views of a Cadaver Room" (one view is in a medical school, the other a Breughel painting), "Hardcastle Crags," "Point Shirley," "Watercolor of Grantchester Meadows," and others, as their titles indicate, hang themselves onto places, or works of art or architecture. They are descriptive-meditative poems, out of Wordsworth by Auden or Lowell. They have a distance, usually, a sense of meditation completed. They seem assured, stable, controlled. Some of the more personally analytical — or psychotic — pieces such as "The Thin People" or "The Disquieting Muses" in *The Colossus* fail to follow this line. And the poet throws it off in *Ariel*, retaining nothing bookish or archaic-sounding beyond a few titles and a few minor references. For Plath, who had been so earnestly the good student, the sincere imitator "adhering to rules, to rules, to rules," it is a radical break.

Is the loss of density and firmness worth it? Compare the first book's poems about her father, "The Colossus" and "Full Fathom Five," with the later "Daddy." The titles tell all. The earlier poems have some strength and passion, but also a saving, self-protective primness. Father is a shattered statue, or a submerged kingly titan. The "archaic trenched lines / Of your grained face shed time in runnels." He is formally addressed: "O father, all by yourself / You are pithy and historical as the Roman Forum," or "Old Man, you surface seldom." There is a lyricized death wish, "Your shelled bed I remember. / Father, this thick air is murderous. / I would breathe water," and a classicizing scorn, "Perhaps you consider yourself an oracle, / Mouthpiece of the dead, or of some god or other." Well and good, but not the same thing as "You do not do, you do not do / Any more, black shoe / In which I have lived like a foot." Or "At twenty I tried to die / To get back, back, back to you. / I thought even the bones would do." Or a more contemporary historical (not literary) accusation, "Not God but a swastika . . . Every woman adores a Fascist / The boot in the face."

In the earlier poems some hard language loses its bite because of the distance imposed by an objective tone, allusion used only as illustration, and the fact that the ironies are lavished on easy game, not yet turned against the poet herself. In the later poems (as these quotations only begin to indicate) hysteria veiled becomes hysteria unveiled, what it feels like, without logical development or analysis, self-indulgent, regressive, shrilly repetitive, exaggerated — and of course ultimately pathetic, ultimately ridiculous, like a child having a tantrum. Think of the bravado of the last line: "Daddy, Daddy, you bastard, I'm through," where "through" should mean she has successfully punctured him ("a stake in your fat black heart"), is finished with her attachment to him, and has emerged from something like a tunnel. We believe her not at all. The more she screams the more we know she will never be through. It is the same with the famous ending of "Lady Lazarus," where the poet warns she will rise from the dead and "eat men like air." That men do dread the avenging maenad Plath evokes here is unquestionable. At the same time, her incantation is hollow. She is impersonating a female Phoenix-fiend like a woman wearing a Halloween costume, or a child saying "I'll kill you" to the grownups, or Lear bellowing "I will do such things — / What they are yet I know / not, but they shall be / The terrors of the earth." She is powerless, she knows it, she hates it. The reader may fear, but must also pity.

"Daddy" and "Lady Lazarus" are typical, for the "I" at the center of an *Ariel* poem is commonly childish and incomplete, moving the poem along by sheer will, and forcing the reader into disequilibrium. At times the reader may be forced to identify with Plath's antagonists, the loving tormentors against whom certain poems are acts of fury. "You" are the leering crowd craving a look at her scars, you are Herr Doktor, Herr Enemy, you are the husband whose cool normality is killing her, you are the inane lady friends, the obscenely clinging mother in "Medusa," you are Daddy. This combination of a refusal of a traditional literary locus, dramatic and arrogant assertion of a self which is totally unstable but is the only self she has, and enraged attack on an outside world seen as stupidly and brutally stable, produces a poetry which continually threatens to slide into absurdity.

She undertakes a similar gamble with her language. In *The Colossus*, the language is neutrally literary (with complex sentences, parallelisms, inversions, compound epithets) most of the time, privately symbolic (rather like early Roethke) some of the time, colloquial occasionally and in the best pieces. In *Ariel*, the American language rises gap-toothed from the waves. It is brusque, businesslike, and bitchy. It deflates everything it touches. It grins behind and through the literary language, exploiting it. It makes a wife-to-be:

> A living doll, everywhere you look.
> It can sew, it can cook,
> It can talk, talk, talk . . .
> You have a hole, it's a poultice.
> You have an eye, it's an image
> My boy, it's your last resort.
> ("The Applicant")

It explains abortive suicide:

> I have done it again.
> One year in every ten
> I manage it —
> A sort of walking miracle, my skin
> Bright as a Nazi lampshade . . .
> My face a featureless, fine
> Jew linen.
> ("Lady Lazarus")

It disposes of a lady friend's advice:

> You say I should drown the kittens. Their smell!
> You say I should drown my girl . . .
> I should sit on a rock off Cornwall and comb my hair.
> I should wear tiger pants, I should have an affair.
> We should meet in another life, we should meet in air,
> Me and you.
> ("Lesbos")

It responds to a cut:

> What a thrill —
> My thumb instead of an onion.
> ("Cut")

As a version of Donne's "Therefore ask not . . . It tolls for thee," it summarizes:

> The dead bell.
> The dead bell.
> Somebody's done for.
> ("Death & Co.")

"Doomed" would have been the obvious "literary" word here; "done for" does not so much evoke *timor mortis* as express contempt for literature alongside dread of death.

Here the gain is clear, since everybody likes the shock of recognition from a good mimesis of the spoken tongue. Novelists with an ear for idiom will sell. Playwrights who have it will prosper. But there is an equivalent risk. Colloquial meat decays — nobody cares how people talked twenty years ago — and the only thing that can preserve it fresh is salt. Readers apparently *remain* delighted with language such as men did use, if and only if it is funny, or its author ironic. Where Plath's colloquialism is "straight" it will probably dissolve shortly into its English background, having served its purpose of helping her write the tongue she spoke, and leaving poems perhaps a little thinner than they needed to be. It will be a permanent asset, I would guess, in the poems where it turns most spitefully against itself — "The Applicant," "Lady Lazarus," "Cut," "Death & Co.," "Lesbos," "A Birthday Present," "Daddy" — as if to prove that a world which talks like this, therefore thinks like this, therefore is like this, shallow and nasty, cannot deserve one's survival.

This ironic streak, in *Ariel*, even engages itself to something as technical as prosody. Plath's musical ear, like her ear for vernacular, is dead keen. Yet in her early work it seems to function almost decoratively rather than organically. Meter in *The Colossus* is usually fairly loose, rhymes fashionably false, and so on. But the prosodically conscious reader is led to play can-you-find-this, as in a picture puzzle book: terza rima in "Sow," "Lorelei," "Full Fathom Five," "Man in Black," "Snake-charmer," "Medallion," rime royale in "The Eye-Mote," three-line *a*-rhyme stanza in "Bull of Bendylaw," couplets in "The Thin People," all cleverly disguised, lines broken with apparent irregularity turning out time after time to serve complicated and static stanza patterns. *Ariel* is less patient. Poems drop into and out of formal verse as if time were too dear to spend rewriting. If something happens to fall into meter, fine. If it doesn't, the devil with it. This is a free verse always approaching the older, stricter disciple, and gaining power from the tension. But the rationale of free verse in *Ariel* is not just a matter of variety, speaking voice, or even asserted emotionalism, but an attraction-repulsion toward formality as if to write the perfectly polished, formal poem would be to die. The verse correlates with her scorn, or fear, of everything orderly and finished, and with her paradoxically simultaneous feeling that the moment of death, which is her epitome of total organization, is desirable. In "Berck-Plage," she explains about an old man's sheeted corpse, "This is what it is to be complete. It is horrible." A few lines later she declares, "It is a blessing, it is a blessing." Similarly, her repeated device of carrying rhymes and assonances over irregularly from stanza to stanza, instead of enclosing them within stanza units, reinforces a cultivation of speed-effects which is also paradoxical. She explains that "What I love is / The piston in motion;" yet the various journeys she undertakes in this book by spiritual horse or nightmare rail, while they seem, in violent motion, the antithesis of death's static perfection, inevitably turn out to be hurtling as fast as they can toward the point of extinction.

This connection between the idea of dying and the idea of formal beauty explains why Plath's most conspicuously musical moments tend to be the most annihilating. A curious thing happens in several of the poems, where she will seem to be talking around and about, and then suddenly hit her stride and go by like a blue streak. The mechanics of this effect of intensification involve alliterations, assonances, and rhymes coming fast and repeatedly, and the echoes of sound reinforcing semantic links — sometimes accretively, as in "The flesh the *grave cave ate*" or "How you *jump* . . . "Th*umb* st*ump*," or more subtly in the close of *Ariel*'s title poem, which may be about a runway horse (as we have been told) or may be about masturbation:

> . . . I
> Foam to wheat, a glitter of seas
> The child's cry
> Melts in the wall,
> And I
> Am the arrow,
> The dew that flies,
> Suicidal, at one with the drive
> Into the red
> Eye, the cauldron of morning.

Or sometimes the echoes work ironically, as in the lines from "Lady Lazarus" which I have already quoted, where the terms *well, hell, real, feels, call,* all have their meanings viciously transformed by each other's presence:

> Dying
> Is an art, like everything else.
> I do it exceptionally well.
> I do it so it feels like hell.
> I do it so it feels real.
> I guess you could say I've a call.

If meter and rhyme in these poems forfeit their usual function of providing part of a consistent sense of decorous normality in poetry, or retain suggestions of order and beauty only to reveal the poet's terror of order and beauty, Plath's late imagery similarly avoids decorativeness, and sometimes forfeits coherence, for the sake of truth to the immediately experienced private fact. Plath's imagery is commonly considered her greatest asset, and is often labelled "striking," which misses the point that the virtue of an image, in poetry or elsewhere, consists minimally in its novelty, maximally in its accuracy. Some of the effects that had the strongest impact on me on first reading—the restriction of her spectrum to primary colors, the harping on white for purity and death, red for life and violence, the obsession with objects that are bare and bald, the sinister smiles, the embodied bones and hair—seem in retrospect weak and formulaic. Where Plath's imagery is genuinely powerful it is because the poet is fixing her mind not on a handful of shocking words but on complicated sensations which she insists words must be able to convey, and surprising things are constantly falling into place because the poet has a remarkable gift for producing verbal equivalents of physical sensation. Reading "Cut," one feels the weird sinking hilarity which is an immediate response to any accident. Reading "Fever 103°" one can feel the marvelous superiority and euphoria of the burning. Several of the poems withheld from *Ariel* and first published in *Crossing the Water*—"Face Lift," "In Plaster," "Insomniac," "Blackberrying"—are devoted to evocations of extraordinary physical conditions; the last, which carries the poet down a hooked lane of blackberry bushes to a cliff overlooking the sea, is like a long figure for a journey through a birth canal. Her gift for evoking sound, touch, taste, as well as visual sensations, is vigorous. There is also a hard-edge precision in the way Plath can present the *look* of something and its *significance* wrapped neatly together. A few quotations should illustrate these points, and incidentally indicate her range—which is not large, but not so narrow as the commentaries enthralled by her suicide suggest. She can of course be malevolent:

> The butcher's guillotine that whispers 'How's this, how's this.'
> ("Totem")

> Your dissatisfactions, on the other hand,
> Arrive through the mailslot with loving regularity,
> White and blank, expansive as carbon monoxide.
> ("The Rival")

But she can also be comic; in one pleasant piece balloons are "oval soul-animals" and the toddler who bursts one "sits back, fat jug." In the bee series, when she looks inside the bee box,

> It is dark, dark,
> With the swarmy feeling of African hands
> Minute and shrunk for export . . .
> How can I let them out?
> It is the noise that appalls me most of all,
> The unintelligible syllables.
> It is like a Roman mob,
> Small, taken one by one, but my god, together! . . .
> I wonder if they would forget me

> If I just undid the locks and stood back and turned
>   into a tree.
>   ("The Arrival of the Bee Box")

And then she can move from pure sensation, as in "Tulips":

> The tulips are too red in the first place, they hurt me.
> Even through the gift paper I could hear them breathe
> Lightly, through their white swaddlings, like an awful baby . . .
> The tulips should be behind bars . . . They are opening
> Like the mouth of some great African cat . . .

to something that is on a borderline between sensation and hallucination, as at the close of "Berck-Plage" when a dull priest is

> Following the coffin on its flowery cart like a beautiful
>   woman,
> A crest of breasts, eyelids and lips
> Storming the hilltop.

And the last lines of this poem, the funereal fulfillment:

> For a minute, the sky pours into the hole like plasma.
> There is no hope, it is given up.

"Berck-Plage," incidentally, may be the most successful poem in all of Plath's late work. It has a broader scope than any other, more characters, more variety of scenery and activity, and certainly more complexity. It begins by being privately neurotic, concentrating on the author's various obsessions with sex and disease at a seaside spa, where all the other people in the landscape, and all the objects in the landscape itself, appear to threaten, sicken, and demand something of her. But unlike other lyrics which both begin and remain so, "Berck-Plage" works outward to something which is in a sense more real, one particular old man's hospital death and how the world goes on after him. This tale at once confirms, enlarges, and objectifies the poem's initial vision, and the poem gains emotional impact as it grows more "objective," since part of its point is that one is irrevocably separated from other people and can do nothing for them, until at the conclusion it has become public in the way that tragedy is public. The loss is every loss, its details sordid, the survivors helpless, the dead man's deeds "are flying off into nothing: remember us" but nobody shall remember; a ritual performs itself which is like the celebration of a wedding, and at the last moment one almost believes that a miracle of vitality may occur as the sky pours itself into the earth—but no, of course not, "it is given up." Plath's artistic development occurred so rapidly that it is easy to imagine the creation of her work as identical with the consuming of her life. A poem like "Berck-Plage" suggests that far from being at the poetic impasse her intense subjectivity implies, she was even in her last few months prepared to apply the method to matter outside of her own skin.

The method, to summarize, depends on an inability or unwillingness to perform within prior boundaries of socially and historically accepted behavior, plus a feverish craving for what Thoreau meant by "reality," plus the technical skill to represent that reality. The method is a kind of journalism of obsessions — hasty, flashy, but it works. It is a contemporary as well as a perennial American style; we find things like it in our prose, from Kerouac to Mailer, whenever a writer wants to collapse aesthetic distance and be subversive and sensational. We find things like it in painting and graphics — Rauschenberg, Warhol — whenever there is attraction-repulsion toward the slick images, at once trivial and demonic, generated by American commerce.

Some time ago while visiting China I had a conversation pertaining to Plath with an elderly Chinese woman poet who in youth had studied in the United States. She was catching up on events in American poetry subsequent to China's emergence from the Cultural Revolution. The subject was our suicides — Berryman, Plath and Sexton were mentioned — and the way suicide exemplified our culture. Why, she wondered, was western literature in general and American literature in particular so full of mental torment and imbalance, instead of stressing, as the Chinese have done, serenity and balance? Why do we keep encouraging individualism and the cult of experience when we see that it makes people sick?

Why indeed? We in the west apparently adore individual liberty, which includes the liberty to suffer, where China adores collectivity. We have no Confucius teaching the commitment of men's intelligence to order and stability within the concentric circles of self, family, society. China has no Christ. We lack the *I Ching*. They lack the red thread of Romantic Agony. This was not a comfortable conversation for me.

It was also not a private conversation; there were journalists present, though our visit was ostensibly informal. In another city I learned that this same earnest lady had recently been attacked in the Chinese literary press for having published a series of poems too "mystical" for the mass of workers to understand, meaning that the poems had been somewhat introspective and had expressed feelings of loneliness. So there it is: Chinese today are not supposed to have the freedom to contemplate, in a poem of their own language and time, loneliness as a human possibility. We are on the other hand addicted to it though it makes us sick. I remember another poem of Emily Dickinson's, one which begins "The heart asks pleasure first" and concludes with "the liberty to die." In that nutshell rests the connection between American narcissism and American self-destructiveness. We are "free" to slide from one to the other. It is true for us that the blood jet is poetry and that there is no stopping it. Sylvia Plath's poetry is a withering into the truth of a national predicament.

Notes

1. The acclaim, in America, begins with Robert Lowell's encomiastic introduction to the Harper & Row edition, which makes the poet "hardly a person at all, or a woman, certainly not another 'poetess,' but one of those super-real, hypnotic, great classical heroines," another Sappho or Medea; through approvals like "a bitter triumph, proof of the capacity of poetry to give to reality the greater permanence of the imagination," George Steiner, *Newsweek* (June 20, 1966); to the culmination of popularization, "one of the most marvellous volumes of poetry published for a very long time," *Time* (June 10, 1966). The attacks tend to complain of the publicity and cult hoopla, and to express antagonism about the type of personality, e.g., "a kind of female hardness which I find resistable," Marius Bewley, *Hudson Review* (October, 1966), or the type of poetry, e.g., "Subjects are not really examined . . . they become opportunities for the personality to impose itself . . . it is best viewed as a case study," Dan Jaffe, *Saturday Review* (October 15, 1966).

2. M. L. Rosenthal, *The New Poets: American and British Poetry Since World War II* (New York: Oxford University Press, 1967), 83.

3. Eliot, of course, can aim the juggernaut of culture and tradition versus the individual talent as well against errant British writers as against Americans; his essay on William Blake, for example, criticizes idiosyncratic philosophy-poetry by the standard of Dantean classicism in much the same way as the study of Hawthorne criticizes American cultural barrenness by the standard of European culture. Nevertheless, that line of criticism seems particularly applicable to American literature.

Angst and Animism in the Poetry of Sylvia Plath
Marjorie Perloff*

When Sylvia Plath was a little girl spending her summers at Cape Cod, she loved the suppers her grandmother made of cod chowder, "buttery steamed clams," and "lobster pots." "But," she recalled in a BBC broadcast made shortly before her death in 1963, "I never could watch my grandmother drop the dark green lobsters with their waving, wood-jammed claws into the boiling pot from which they would be, in a minute, drawn — red, dead, and edible. I felt the awful scald of the water too keenly on my skin." The little girl who could suffer so profoundly for a lobster was, however, the same child who felt a "polar chill immobilize" her bones when she found out that she would no longer be the only child in the family: her baby brother was born. "I would be a bystander, a museum mammoth," she remembers feeling. "I felt the wall of my skin: I am I. That stone is a stone. My beautiful fusion with the things of the world was over."[1]

The vision of reality that informs the imagery of Sylvia Plath's mature poetry is contained in this casual autobiographical memoir. It has two poles: (1) human beings are, in themselves, simply *things*, objects, machines — "Museum mammoths," but (2) such "thingness" can be tran-

*Reprinted with permission from *Journal of Modern Literature*, I (1970), 57–74.

scended either in the joy or in the suffering that results when man identifies imaginatively with the life of animals, of plants, or of inanimate objects. The central paradox at the heart of Sylvia Plath's poetry is thus that human beings are dead, inanimate, frozen, unreal, while everything that is non-human is intensely alive, vital, potent.

When one examines the recurrent imagery of Sylvia Plath's *Ariel* poems in the light of poetic convention rather than as an expression of the poet's painful and tragic drive toward suicide,[2] it becomes apparent that hers is "oracular poetry" in the tradition of such later eighteenth-century poets as Smart, Cowper, Collins, and Blake, the poets of what Northrop Frye has called "the Age of Sensibility."[3] Both in his essay on this period and in the *Anatomy of Criticism*, Frye makes the distinction between the Aristotelian view of literature as *product* or aesthetic artifact and the Longinian view of literature as the poetic *process* itself. *Catharsis*, he argues, is a concept valid only for the literature of product, in which pity and fear are detached from the beholder by being directed toward objects. But where there is a "sense of literature as process, pity and fear become states of mind without objects, moods which are common to the work of art and to the reader, and which bind them together psychologically instead of separating them aesthetically." Fear without an object is a state of *Angst* or anxiety; Frye cites Cowper's "The Castaway" and Blake's Golden Chapel poem in the Rossetti MS as examples. Pity without an object, on the other hand, "expresses itself as an imaginative animism or treating everything in nature as though it had human feelings or qualities." It ranges from the "apocalyptic exultation of all nature bursting into human life that we have in Smart's *Song of David*," to the "curiously intense awareness of the animal world" found in Burns's *To a Mouse*, in Cowper's exquisite snail poem, in Smart's superb lines on his cat Jeoffrey . . . in the opening of Blake's *Auguries of Innocence*."[4]

In the poetry of process, *catharsis* is replaced by *ecstasis:* the poet as "the medium of the oracle" as in a "trance-like state"; "autonomous voices seem to speak through him, and as he is concerned to utter rather than to address, he is turned away from his listener, so to speak, in a state of rapt self-communion." Metaphor, in such poetry, is accordingly not a way of describing or of evoking an observed world; it is a "direct identification in which the poet himself is involved." Thus, in Cowper's "Castaway," the stricken deer does not have the symbolic status of, say, the albatross of "The Ancient Mariner"; rather, the poet *becomes* the stricken deer.[5]

The poetry of process is not an isolated historical phenomenon; in the late nineteenth century, it is brilliantly revived by Rimbaud, whose "Bateau Ivre," in which the poet's self is projected as the drunken boat of the title, is a paradigm of the oracular mode. Rimbaud himself described the form when he insisted that for the oracular poet, "C'est faux de dire: Je pense. On devrait dire: On me pense."[6] After Rimbaud, the "primitivism" of Cowper and Smart reappears in such poems as Dylan Thomas's "Fern Hill" and Theodore Roethke's "Praise to the End!", but the outstanding modern practioner of the mode is surely D.H. Lawrence, especially the Lawrence of *Birds, Beasts, and Flowers.*

Contemplating his fellow men as they go about their daily tasks, Lawrence is apt to respond as the poet of *angst.* "City Life," for example, is a vision of the paralysis and pointlessness of the modern urban world. In a hallucinatory state, the poet sees "iron hooks" growing out of every face he meets, and he senses that "invisible wires of steel" pull the city dwellers "back and forth to work." Dehumanized, they become "corpse-like fishes hooked and being played by some malignant fisherman on an unseen shore."

The poet's imaginative animism, on the other hand, creates such superb animal poems as "Swan," "Bat," and "Tortoise Gallantry," poems in which the birds and beasts do not represent something else — Lawrence is not a symbolist poet — but which show us what it is like to *be* a bat or a swan. Jessie Chambers wrote in her memoir of the poet that a "living vibration" seemed to pass between Lawrence and "wild things," a vibration that led him to explore what Vivian De Sola Pinto has called "the divine otherness of non-human life."[7] "A Doe at Evening," for example, is a modern version of Cowper's "Castaway." The poet, aimlessly wandering through the marshes, suddenly notices a doe, silhouetted against the sky, and he becomes so obsessed by the animal's "nimble shadow" that he seems to enter her very being:

> Ah yes, being male, is not my head hard-balanced, antlered?
> Are not my haunches light?
> Has she not fled on the same wind with me?
> Does not my fear cover her fear?[8]

The process of self-communion found in the poetry of Rimbaud and of Lawrence is precisely that which occurs in the later poetry of Sylvia Plath. The poet's *angst* or floating fear is expressed in her dehumanization of herself and her fellow men; persons including oneself are objects, things associated with a nameless fear. But the human qualities lacking in persons are found everywhere in the outer world: the poet's "I" can thus become a blue mole, an elm tree, a cut thumb, a race horse. Contrary to the charges levelled against them by Marius Bewley and Stephen Spender,[9] Sylvia Plath's poems do have a "shaping attitude toward experience," a "principle of beginning or ending," but the principle is that of the oracular poem, the poem of process, rather that of the more firmly established symbolist mode of Yeats, Eliot, and Stevens or even that of the elegiac autobiographical mode of Robert Lowell.

II

It is no coincidence that every poem in *Ariel* is written in the first person. The oracular poem, the poem of ecstasis, is by definition one that centers on the self, a poem in which "objectivity" is impossible because the seer, unable to detach himself sufficiently to describe the things outside himself, can give voice only to his own emotional responses. If Sylvia Plath's early poetry strikes the reader as being too "careful" and "seldom exciting,"[10] it is no doubt because prior to 1960, the date that she herself considered the dividing line between Juvenilia and her real poetry,[11] she did not yet understand that third-person description, narrative, or ironic observation were alien to her poetic vision.

The early descriptive mode may be exemplified by "Watercolor of Grantchester Meadows" (1956), perhaps the best known poem in Sylvia Plath's first volume, *The Colossus*.[12] The poem uses a fixed rhyming stanza with an elaborate network of full and approximate terminal rhymes, internal rhyme, alliteration, assonance, and onomatopoeia.[13] The verse line is basically iambic, but the preponderance of monosyllables and compounds produces much secondary stressing and slows up the rhythm decisively as in "Clóudráck and owl-hóllowed willows slánting óver / The blánd Gránta dóuble their white and gréen. . . ." All in all, the sound structure is highly formalized and rather precious.

The same formality characterizes the orderly presentation of the poem's images. Cambridge's Grantchester Meadows, immortalized by Rupert Brooke, is viewed as a tame, pretty place, a subject for a watercolor. In the first stanza, the meadow itself is described: "spring lambs jam the sheepfold," "Each thumb-size bird / Flits nimble-winged in thickets"—"Nothing is big or far." The second stanza in turn centers on the image of the "bland" Granta River, in whose waters "owl-hollowed willows" are reflected: here "The punter sinks his pole" and "Cattails part where the tame cygnets steer." The picture is generalized in Stanza III: "It is a country on a nursery plate," the narrator observes, too "benign" and "Arcadian green" to be quite real. Even the "Black-gowned" students who people the landscape in the final stanza seem implausibly pastoral; they stroll about, "Hands laced, in a moony indolence of love." The reader is unprepared for the sharp reversal of the last three lines: abruptly the narrator informs us that the students are

<blockquote>
unaware
How in such mild air
The owl shall stoop from his turret, the rat cry out.
</blockquote>

The orderly arrangement of precise visual images and the carefully organized sound pattern cannot dispel the reader's uneasy sense that the ambiguous quality of nature, alluded to in the final lines, is never defined or explored. Why is it that the seemingly pastoral landscape is full of menace? Because the individual images in the poem have no larger context, no frame of reference, it is finally impossible to know just what it is that the cry of the mutilated rat portends. Sylvia Plath is, in short, no sort of Imagist; the objective, impersonal poem in which the juxtaposition of images establishes a central meaning is not her mode. It is as if she cannot keep in check the voice that longs to interpret the images, to show what they mean to the perceiving self.

Third-person narrative presents similar problems. "Hardcastle Crags" (1957)[14], for example, is a chronological account of a mysterious walk taken by a nameless young woman through the deep, narrow valley in the Pennines in West Yorks, the southern boundary of the moorland made famous by Emily Bronte in *Wuthering Heights*.[15] As the poem opens, the girl leaves behind the "dark, dwarfed cottages" and "steely street" of the "stone-built" mountain village above the valley and makes for the open moor with its "incessant seethe of grasses / Riding in the full / of the moon, manes to the wind, / Tireless, tied, as a moon-bound sea / Moves on its root." As she walks through this strange, lonely landscape, a "blank mood" invades her mind; the "long wind" assaults her, "paring her person down / To a pinch of flame" and whistling in the "whorl of her ear" until her head, "like a scooped-out pumpkin crown," "cupped the babel." The next stanza contains the poem's central theme:

> All the night gave her, in return
> For the paltry gift of her bulk and the beat
> Of her heart was the humped indifferent iron
> Of its hills, and its pastures bordered by black stone set
> On black stone.

Despite the carefully selected metaphors (black hills that look like iron and are "humped" above the wanderer like black cats), this assertion of nature's indifference to man remains inert. It is difficult to believe that a person in an utterly "blank mood," a trance-like state, could formulate the contrast between man and nature so neatly. Similarly inappropriate precision spoils the end of the poem: the black, ominous silence of the stone landscape was evidently "Enough to snuff the quick / Of her small heat out," but "before the weight / Of stones and hills of stones could break / Her down to mere quartz grit in that stony light / She turned back."

"Hardcastle Crags" suffers from irresolution because its point of view hovers uneasily between that of a detached narrator and that of the character herself. The landscape as seen through the girl's eyes is appealing in its mystery (e.g., "the dairy herds / Knelt in the meadows mute as boulders"), but the third-person narrator intervenes to explain that this landscape "Loomed absolute as the antique world was / Once" and that its stark silence was so oppressive that, in the moment of crisis, the girl "turned back." One senses that Sylvia Plath does not really believe in her chosen theme: the alien and hostile quality of nature.

Moreover, the orderly chronological sequence of images in the poem does not accord with the mental and emotional states that are portrayed. The girl's experience is phantasmagoric, dream-like, and mysterious, but it is conveyed in a straightforward narrative, divided into nine fixed stanzas, whose rather obtrusive sound patterns, as in the case of "Grantchester

Meadows," draw undue attention to themselves. The first stanza, for example, has repeated alliteration of *st*'s and consonance of *k*'s and *t*'s, not to mention such internal rhymes as "rack-Tack-" / "black", such assonance as "m*oo*n-bl*ue*d," and the use of phonetic intensives as in "flint," "struck," "steely," and "tinder."[16]

"Hardcastle Crags" is typical of the third-person symbolic narratives that Sylvia Plath was writing in the mid-fifties. Thus, "The Snowman on the Moor"[17] is the story of a girl's reaction to a bitter argument with her husband and of the hallucinatory incident that leads to their reconciliation. Abandoning her husband by the fireside, the young wife runs out into the snowy night and begs the elements to take her part, but, as it turns out, it is once again nature that rebukes and admonishes the speaker, this time in the shape of a mysterious snowman:

> To the world's white edge
> She came, and called hell to subdue an unruly man
> And join her siege.
>
> It was no fire-blurting fork-tailed demon
> Volcanoed hot
> From marble snow-heap of moor to ride that woman
>
> With spur and knout
> Down from pride's size: instead, a grisly-thewed
> Austere, corpse-white
>
> Giant heaved into the distance . . . .

In the first stanza above, the point of view is that of the girl, whereas in the second, a knowing commentator tells us what happened to "that woman." The effect, as in the case of "Hardcastle Crags," is that the validity of the experience is undercut; the mystery is patiently explained away.

A third poetic mode, found in Sylvia Plath's poetry prior to 1960, is that of ironic understatement, the third-person poem that sets up an Audenesque contrast between two ways of looking at the same phenomenon. The best example of this mode is "Two Views of a Cadaver Room" (1959),[18] a poem that foreshadows Sylvia Plath's later disease and death imagery but is quite unlike the oracular poems of *Ariel*. The poem presents two contrasting views of death: the scientific and the artistic. The girl who visits the dissecting room in Part I sees death simply as decomposition. Four men are "laid out, black as burnt turkey / Already half unstrung." The "white-smocked boys" work on these pitiful cadavers while, elsewhere in the room, "In their jars the snail-nosed babies moon and glow." As if such horror were not enough, "He" (evidently one of the doctors who is her special friend) "hands her the cut-out heart like a cracked heirloom," a morbid token of his affection. The second "view of a cadaver room" is a description of a Brueghel painting that graphically depicts the horrors of war (it can be easily identified as *The Triumph of Death* in the Prado), in whose bottom right-hand corner the painter has placed two lovers who are making music together and are completely unmindful of their surroundings. In Brueghel's vision, the narrator argues, "desolation, stalled in paint / Spares the little country / Foolish, delicate, in the lower right-hand corner." The artist, in other words, shows us the irony of life: although the death cart is not far off, someone is enjoying a brief moment of joy and beauty.

The second part of the poem is highly reminiscent of Auden's famous "Museé des Beaux Arts," in which the speaker observes that "In Brueghel's *Icarus*, for instance: how everything turns away / Quite leisurely from the disaster." But whereas Auden introduces this example as an illustration of his larger theme: "About suffering they were never wrong, / The Old Masters: how well they understood / Its human position; how it takes place / While someone else is eating or opening a window," Sylvia Plath's "two views" of the cadaver room are actually unrelated. The reader's response is not controlled; one wonders how the image of the lovers in the second part is related to the pitiful "snail-nosed babies" of Part I. Which is the more correct view of death?

Auden's detached ironic statement is no more Sylvia Plath's forte than is the symbolic narrative of "Hardcastle Crags" or the imagistic mode of "Watercolor of Grantchester Meadows." Her "real voice," as Ted Hughes calls it, does not appear until the late autumn of 1959, when Sylvia Plath and her husband were writers-in-residence at Yaddo and she was pregnant with her first child. Hughes observes that "at this time she was concentratedly trying to break down the tyranny, the fixed focus, and public persona which descriptive and discursive poems take as a norm" (pp. 85–86). In the "exercises of meditation and invocation" which she and her husband practiced, Sylvia Plath's poems of *angst* and animism were born.

III

The poems in *The Colossus* that were written at Yaddo in 1959 — "Mushrooms," "Blue Moles," "The Burnt-out Spa," "Flute Notes from a Reedy Pond," and "Stones" — are interesting transitional works that forecast Sylvia Plath's later direction. One immediately notices that the new rhythms are much more flexible. "Blue Moles," for example, is written in unrhymed nine-line stanzas whose lines range between three and five stresses. In this poem, the "I" is squarely at the center. Coming across two dead moles "shapeless as flung gloves" on the road, the speaker contemplates the meaninglessness of their fate: the moles resemble bits of "blue suede"; they look "neutral as the stones" as "Their corkscrew noses, their white hands / Uplifted, stiffen in a family pose." Gradually, the speaker becomes obsessed with the death she has witnessed. Entering "the soft pelt of the mole," she imagines what it would be like to be one of these creatures, "moving through their mute room" and "Palming the earth aside." Perpetually, endlessly, the moles are "delving for appendages / Of beetles, sweet-breads, shards—to be eaten / Over and over." And still "the heaven / Of final surfeit is just as far / From the door as ever." The daily night journey of the mole is futile and so, the speaker implies, is the dark journey of her own life.

"Blue Moles," undoubtedly influenced by Sylvia Plath's reading of Theodore Roethke,[19] is perhaps too self-consciously conceived as an oracular poem. The reference to "little victim" in line 6, the rather heavy-handed pun on "duel" in line 8, and the slightly affected announcement, "I enter the soft pelt of the mole," indicate that the poet is still struggling with her new form. But the poem does explore the unusual states of mind to be found in Sylvia Plath's mature work, particularly her acute sensitivity to non-human life.

The title poem of *Ariel* carries the process of identification with the animal kingdom one step further. In the simplest sense, "Ariel" merely relates a morning ride from the moment when the speaker mounts her horse, poised for movement ("Stasis in darkness"), to its culmination in the violent and destructive flight through space. But the poem is not *about* the speaker's favorite horse Ariel nor about the morning ride; rather, girl, horse, and the movement of galloping merge to create something quite different. In the first tercet, for example, it is not certain whether it is horse or rider that is aware of the "substanceless blue / Pour of tor and distances," so that we are immediately prepared for the ecstatic assertion, "God's lionness, / How one we grow, / Pivot of heels and knees!" As the motion accelerates, the speaker cannot distinguish the brown furrow ahead from the brown neck of the horse: both are oddly felt to be beyond her, out of her reach, and she cannot catch up. Vaguely, the new being that is both girl and animal is aware of "Nigger-eye / Berries" on the side of the road, "Black sweet blood mouthfuls" that "cast dark / Hooks" to catch her, but she is immune to their touch. In her new, trance-like state, she sheds the empty shell of her body, her thighs and hair:

> White
> Godiva, I unpeel—
> Dead hands, dead stringencies.

Taken out of herself, she can be part of the foaming wheat, the "glitter of seas" before her. Thus the identity not only of the rider but also of the horse is dissolved: the newly created self is an "arrow" or

> The dew that flies
> Suicidal, at one with the drive
> Into the red
> Eye, the cauldron of morning.
>   (pp. 26–27)

A. Alvarez has observed that "Ariel" is "about what happens . . . when the potential violence of the animal is unleashed. And also the violence of the rider." M.L. Rosenthal writes that the poem ends with the "desolate realization of the plunge into death that is going on."[20] The emphasis of these readings does not seem quite right: surely the ending of the poem recalls Keats's "Now more than ever seems it rich to die," and, in fact, "Ariel" can be read as a modern variant of the "Ode to a Nightingale." At its most intense, life becomes death but it is a death that is desired: the "Suicidal" leap into the "red / Eye" of the morning sun is not only violent but ecstatic. Both horse and rider become disembodied spirit — they are "Ariel."

The poem thus dramatizes what it is like to be taken completely out of one's self, to transcend one's ego in a moment of animistic communion. The structure of the poem, moreover, perfectly renders the experience: the explosive shift from "Stasis in darkness" to the "Suicidal" leap into the "cauldron of morning" is given a formal counterpart in the open tercets, whose abrupt, breathless run-on lines range anywhere from one stress ("Hooks") to four ("Pivot of heels and knees! — The furrow"). There is much less alliteration and assonance than in Sylvia Plath's earlier poetry, the predominant form of sound repetition used being occasional rhyme that creates a kind of echo structure, mirroring the galloping movement: "Pour of tor," "grow" / "furrow", "are" / "dark", "air" / "hair", "I" / "cry" / "eye". The oracular process is completed as the "I" and the "eye" merge; for Sylvia Plath, joy comes in those moments when the human and the non-human, here the self and the sun, are one.

"Ariel" represents one pole of Sylvia Plath's poetic vision; the opposite, the mode of *angst*, has received more critical attention. Such poems as "Daddy" and "Lady Lazarus" have been praised for their "strange kind of terror," their "clear perception of despair," their insight into the "schizophrenic situation."[21] But Sylvia Plath does not, as some critics suggest, exploit the bizarre for its own sake. The grotesque elements in these poems must be seen in their largest context.

"Morning Song," the first poem in *Ariel*, is a good example of the way autobiography can become art. One might note, in the first place, that the poem turns the *aubade* convention inside out: the speaker's dawn is not one of love or joy but one of dimly felt anxiety — motherhood both frightens and fascinates her. The arrival of her baby is utterly puzzling to this young mother: sardonically, she tells the sleeping infant that "Love set you going like a fat gold watch." It is as if the sex act simply set into motion a mechanical process; the clock is wound up and the baby is born. Its initiation into life similarly sounds like an assembly-line process: "The midwife slapped your footsoles, and your bald cry / Took its place among the elements." The infant's cry, in other words, immediately becomes so much dead matter. What should be most living is most dead. Yet it is important to note that the speaker is not simply hostile toward her child. The persistent second-person address, the close bond established between the "I" and the "you," implicate the mother in the child's drama. If her infant is merely a mechanical thing, the poem suggests, it is ultimately because she is one also.

The poet's *angst* transforms the baby into a "New statue" in a "drafty museum," whose parents, their voices emptily echoing the infant's cry, "stand round blankly" like museum walls. The speaker is at a loss to understand her relationship to this new object, whose "moth-breath / Flickers among the flat pink roses" embroidered on his quilt or painted on the nursery wallpaper. She responds mechanically to the baby's cry, stumbling out of bed "cow-heavy and floral / In my Victorian nightgown." Automatically, the infant's "mouth opens clean as a cat's," as the mother begins to nurse. Even the light of dawn is unreal: "The window square / Whitens and swallows its dull stars." In the gray morning hour, the infant, now fully awake, begins to cry:

> And now you try
> Your handful of notes;
> The clear vowels rise like balloons.

Even the human cry becomes an object, a rising balloon. And one feels that both mother and child, the I and the you, are inside the balloon, unable to get you, to have contact with the "normal" world of living creatures.

Whether or not the reader shares Sylvia Plath's response to motherhood is surely irrelevant here. The point is that the images are most carefully chosen to dramatize the speaker's tension, the pull between love and anxiety. It is not that the mother of "Morning Song" does not want to love her baby — clearly she identifies completely with the child and feels totally responsible to it — but that she cannot believe that she herself is human. If one has no identity, the poem implies, having a baby cannot be more than winding a "fat gold watch"; the new world of motherhood is a frozen one where breath is as ephemeral as the life of a moth. "Morning Song" is thus a movingly ironic version of the trite slogans in the so-called "Baby Magazines," which inform the pregnant woman that having a baby is the best thing that will ever happen to her, the greatest miracle on earth. For the self that fears the human condition, however, the "miracle" is not the one that is expected.

"Ariel" and "Morning Song" embody animism and *angst* respectively in relatively pure form. Sylvia Plath's more usual strategy, however, is to combine the two. In "Tulips," for example, the anguish of the "I" is inextricably bound up with the personality with which she endows a bunch of flowers. The speaker is a hospital patient who is recovering from surgery.[22] The world of her white hospital room is a "winter" one; it is perfectly quiet, snowed in, peaceful:

> I am nobody; I have nothing to do with explosions.
> I have given my name and my day-clothes up to the nurses
> And my history to the anaesthetist and my body to surgeons.

The patient's head, propped "between the pillow and the sheet-cuff," is "Like an eye between two white lids that will not shut." Her body is merely a "pebble," and the nurses tend it "as water / Tends to the pebbles it must run over."

Into this white, dead world, in which the speaker's self has become "a

thirty-year old cargo boat," intruders come in the form of red tulips, flowers
sent to the patient to brighten up her room. And now an odd metamorphosis takes place. The seemingly mindless tulips come alive and threaten the
dazed emptiness of the white hospital world. Their redness begins to hurt
the speaker: it "talks to my wound." The tulips now "breathe," they have
"tongues," their red petals become "red lead sinkers round my neck." As the
red flowers become larger and more ominous, the frightened ego withdraws
and shrinks. The flowers watch her and eat her oxygen while she becomes a
"cut-paper shadow"; they have "eyes" but she has "no face." In the final
stanza, the "peace" of the hospital world is exploded:

> The tulips should be behind bars like dangerous animals;
> They are opening like the mouth of some great African cat,
> And I am aware of my heart: it opens and closes
> Its bowl of red blooms out of sheer love of me.
> The water I taste is warm and salt, like the sea,
> And comes from a country far away as health. (p. 12)

The drama is complete: because they become flesh and blood in the speaker's imagination, the tulips force her out of her earlier whiteness, her passive
extinction, and she hates this active intrusion. In her anxiety, she equates
the tulip petals with the "red blooms" of her heart which insists on beating
despite her desire for death. Finally, life returns with the taste of her hot
tears; health is a "far away" country but at least now it is remembered. The
spell of the hospital room is broken.

In this poem, the tulips are not symbols in the conventional sense; the
focus is not on the tulips as natural objects with such and such connotations,
but on the process whereby the "I" finally *becomes* the hated tulip so that
her heart "opens and closes / Its bowl of red blooms." The whole poem is
organized around two central images: white and red — the white of human
extinction and the red of living matter, of non-human vitality, or again, the
white of *angst* and the red of animism. Like a "great African cat" opening its
mouth, the red flower finally absorbs the world of selfhood into its strange
domain: flower petal and human blood become one. The seven-line unrhymed stanzas with their five, six, and seven-stress lines are full of halting
repetitions as the consciousness of the "I" comes to grips with the situation:

> I *didn't want* any flowers, I *only wanted*
> To lie with my hands turned up and be utterly empty.
> *How free* it is, you have no idea *how free*. . . .

Only at the end of "Tulips" when the tension is resolved do the wrenched
accents, the caesuras, and the word repetitions give way to what are almost
regular iambic pentameter lines:

> The wáter I táste is wárm and sált, like the séa,
> And cómes from a cóuntry fár away as heálth.

In the poetry of *angst* and animism, not only flower and animals but even an object may become endowed with human traits. "Cut," one of Sylvia Plath's most remarkable poems, begins with an everyday incident: the speaker cuts her thumb "instead of an onion." But from the opening line — "What a thrill — " — we know that her response to this accidental "Cut" will be quite unusual, that somehow she wants the injury. It is immediately not *her* thumb that is bleeding but a new being outside herself with which she can sympathize. In a series of extraordinary transformations, the bleeding thumb becomes a "little pilgrim" whose scalp "The Indian's axed," and whose "turkey wattle / Carpet rolls / Straight from the heart," and then "a bottle / Of pink fizz." The "pink fizz" in turn becomes a platoon of soldiers, "Redcoats" running "Out of a gap," and the speaker, fascinated by the spectacle, wonders irrelevantly, "Whose side are they on?"

This line, coming precisely at the midpoint of the poem (line 21), is almost unbearably poignant. The girl is so absorbed in the drama of the bloody thumb that she imaginatively enters its self, losing her sense of identity, her rational awareness that this thumb is simply a piece of flesh and blood, a part of *her* body. She knows what it is to be the bleeding wound and her seemingly random question turns out to be the crucial one: whose side are the "Redcoats" on, hers or the side of death? This thought brings her back with a jolt to her own "wounded" condition:

> O my
> Homunculus, I am ill.
> I have taken a pill to kill
> The thin
> Papery feeling.

The series of identifications that follow are most hostile: the thumb now becomes a "Saboteur," a Japanese suicide pilot ("Kamikaze man"), a woman whose "Gauze Ku Klux Klan / Babushka / Darkens and tarnishes." As the poet watches the "balled pulp" of the thumb's "heart" escape, she suddenly understands the truth:

> How you jump —
> Trepanned veteran,
> Dirty girl,
> Thumb stump.
>   (pp. 13–14)

A *trepan* is a "surgical instrument in the form of a crown-saw, for cutting out small pieces of bone, especially from the skull" (OED); the stanza thus presents the image of the thumb as a miniature man with a wounded skull. But "Trepanned" also means "trapped" or "snared" and so the little "veteran" is doubly doomed. The image is particularly effective because the thumb is, of course, literally a trepanned veteran: it survives its battle with the knife but is severely injured, maimed. And now the poem comes full circle: as the blood gushes forth, the images of "Little pilgrim," of the "bottle / Of pink fizz," even of the "Kamikaze man" give way to the more frightening reality: the "Homunculus" who has been addressed so intimately is, in fact, nothing but a "Thumb stump" (the rhyme "jump" / "Thumb" / "stump" emphasizes the ugly truth), and, the poem implies, this "Thumb stump," this "Dirty girl," is none other than the speaker herself.

"Cut" accomplishes a great many things within the space of its ten abrupt four-line stanzas with their run-on lines of two and three stresses and their occasional rhyme. A cut thumb will never be the same after one has read this strange poem in which *angst* and animism are fused, in which an unspecified fear of being alive and an imaginative projection into something alien — a piece of thumb — coalesce. The structure of the poem depends upon the speaker's subtly developing awareness: when the blood begins to flow, the "I," detached from the "you" (her thumb), is fascinated by the spectacle, but, as the wound deepens, the intimately known "you" becomes the "I's" enemy, a "Saboteur," a "Dirty girl" — ultimately a hideous "Thumb stump." "Cut" may be read as a sardonic parody of "The Love Song of J. Alfred Prufrock"; here too the world of "you and I" is a closed one.

The mode of "Cut" and "Tulips" is the basic mode of the *Ariel* poems. In "Fever 103°," for example, the terrified poet becomes an artifact: "I am a lantern — / My head a moon / Of Japanese paper, my gold beaten skin / Infinitely delicate and infinitely expensive." She seems to attach no value to her life, yet her "Words," as the poem by that name testifies, are living creatures; they are "Axes / After whose stroke the wood rings, / And the echoes! / Echoes travelling / Off from the centre like horses." Despite their anguish, the *Ariel* poems also have moments of elation and splendor. The poet as "Paralytic," who is weighed down by the "iron lung / That loves me" and that "pumps my two / Dust bags in and out," is also ecstatic "woman in the ambulance / Whose red heart blooms through her coat so astoundingly" at the unexpected sight of late-blooming, flaming red poppies, etched against an unpromising, gray autumn sky, "Igniting its carbon monoxides":

> O my God, what am I
> That these late mouths should cry open
> In a forest of frost, in a dawn of cornflowers.
> ("Poppies in October," p. 19)

Despite its intensely personal quality, its stress on selfhood, Sylvia Plath's poetry is emphatically not, as is often argued, similar to that of Robert Lowell. In *Life Studies*, the poet is obsessed with his own past, a past he must recover if he is to come to terms with the present and, by implication, with the future. The sense of history, both personal and social, found in a poem like "For the Union Dead" is conspicuously absent from the *Ariel* poems. This is not mere coincidence: for the oracular poet, past and future are meaningless abstractions; emotion, as Northrop Frye has observed, is "maintained at a continuous present."[23] For Sylvia Plath, there is only the given moment, only *now*.

Again, in the poetry of process, persons and places outside the poet's own self have only peripheral interest; one therefore finds little of Lowell's documentary realism in *Ariel*. As in the case of D.H. Lawrence, whom she resembles more than any other poet of our century, Sylvia Plath's "I" would rather be with poppies than with people. It is Lawrence's flower poems — especially his "Andraitx — Pomegranate Flowers" — that stand behind "Poppies in October," and his "November by the Sea" contains in embryo the imagery of Sylvia Plath's "Letter in November," in which the poet is quite literally enchanted by the colors of the autumn leaves:

> O love, O celibate.
> Nobody but me
> Walks the waist-high wet.
> The irreplaceable
> Golds bleed and deepen, the mouths of Thermopylae.
>
> (p. 47)

The less successful poems in *Ariel* are, to my mind, those like "The Swarm" and "Getting There" that try to make a comment on the horrors of war or the viciousness of the Nazi ethos. In an interview of 1962, Sylvia Plath insisted that, although she was naturally concerned about such issues as the "genetic effects of fallout," these contemporary problems were not the mainspring of her poetry: "For me, the real issues of our time are the issues of every time — the hurt and wonder of loving; making in all its forms, children, loaves of bread, paintings, building; and the conservation of life of all people in all places. . . . Surely the great use of poetry is its pleasure — not its influence as religious or political propaganda."[24]

Didacticism is essentially alien to this "ecstatic" poet, whose paradoxical view of life is summed up in an especially touching poem, published in *Critical Quarterly* in 1962 but not reprinted in *Ariel*, which expresses the poet's distaste for the life of a person and her complementary yearning for union with that more intense life that is death.

I AM VERTICAL

> But I would rather be horizontal.
> I am not a tree with my root in the soil
> Sucking up minerals and motherly love
> So that each March I may gleam into leaf,
> Nor am I the beauty of a garden bed
> Attracting my share of Ahs and spectacularly painted,
> Unknowing I must soon unpetal.
> Compared with me, a tree is immortal
> And a flower-head not tall, but more startling,
> And I want the one's longevity and the other's daring.
>
> Tonight, in the infinitesimal light of the stars,
> The trees and flowers have been strewing their cool odors,
> Sometimes I think that when I am sleeping
> I must most perfectly resemble them —

Thoughts gone dim.
It is more natural to me, lying down.
Then the sky and I are in open conversation.
And I shall be useful when I lie down finally:
Then the trees may touch me for once, and the flowers have time
for me.[25]

Notes

1. "Ocean 1212-W," *The Listener*, 70 (August 29, 1963), 312.

2. Most of the reviews of *Ariel* have regarded the poems as thinly veiled autobiography, revealing the mind of a seriously deranged woman. John Malcolm Brinnin, for example, writes, "Many of these poems are magnificent; a whole book of them is top-heavy, teetering on that point where the self-created figure threatens to topple over into self-expression and the diversions of psychopathology," *Partisan Review*, 34 (Winter 1967), 156. See also Dan Jaffee, *Saturday Review*, 49 (October 15, 1966), 29; Francis Hope, *New Statesman*, 69 (April 30, 1965), 687; *Time*, 87 (June 10, 1966). The foregoing reviews are generally unfavorable; the following praise Plath's work enthusiastically but still stress its autobiographical rather than its formal qualities: George Steiner, *The Reporter*, 33 (October 7, 1965), 51–54; C.B. Cox and A.R. Jones, "After the Tranquillized Fifties," *Critical Quarterly*, 6 (1964), 107–22; A.R. Jones, Necessity and Freedom: The Poetry of Robert Lowell, Sylvia Plath, and Anne Sexton, *Critical Quarterly*, 6 (1965), 11–30; Charles Newman, "Candor is the Only Wile: The Art of Sylvia Plath," *Tri-Quarterly*, No. 7, Sylvia Plath Issue (Fall, 1966), 39–64. All further references to articles in *Tri Quarterly* are to this issue.

3. "Towards Defining an Age of Sensibility," *Fables of Identity* (N.Y.: Harcourt, Brace, 1963), 130–37.

4. Ibid., 134–35. See also *Anatomy of Criticism* (Princeton, N.J.: Princeton Univ. Press, 1957), 66–67.

5. *Fables of Identity*, 136–37.

6. *Poesies Completes et Autres Textes* (Paris: Gallimard, 1960), 218.

7. See Chambers, *D.H. Lawrence: A Personal Record* by E.T. (London, 1935), 223; Pinto, "Poet Without a Mask" in *D.H. Lawrence: A Collection of Critical Essays*, ed. Mark Spilka (Englewood Cliffs, N.J.: Prentice-Hall, 1963), 135–36.

8. *The Complete Poems of D.H. Lawrence*, 3 vols. (London: William Heinemann, 1957), 1, 211.

9. See Bewley, *Hudson Review*, 19 (Autumn, 1966), 491; Spender, *New Republic*, 154 (June 18, 1966), 23.

10. M.L. Rosenthal, *The New Poets, American and British Poetry Since World War II* (New York: Oxford Univ. Press, 1967), 83. See also A. Alvarez, "Sylvia Plath," *Tri-Quarterly*, 67.

11. Ted Hughes observes that in 1961 she "dismissed everything prior to *The Stones* written in 1959 as juvenilia, produced in the days before she became herself" ("Notes on the Chronological Order of Sylvia Plath's Poems," *Tri-Quarterly*, 86). My chronology of Plath's poems is based on this article.

12. *The Colossus* was originally published in London in 1961 by Heinemann; in N.Y. in 1962 by Alfred A. Knopf. All references are to the Knopf edition, reissued in 1967; all references to *Ariel* are to the Harper edition of 1966.

13. Each of the poem's four stanzas has the rhyme scheme $a_5 b_5 a_3 b_5 c_3 c_2 a_5$. In the first stanza, all the rhymes except "heard" / "bird" are approximate. The first line contains internal rhyme: "lambs" / "jam"; the second line has alliteration and consonance: "Stilled silvered as

water in a glass"; the fourth has an example of onomatopoeia in "chitters," and the seventh has heavy assonance: "Flits nimble-winged in the thickets, and of good color."

14. *The Colossus*, 20–21.

15. For this background information, see Hughes, *Tri-Quarterly*, 83.

16. The poem has nine five-line stanzas rhyming $a_3b_4a_4b_6a_2$.

17. *Poetry*, 99 (July, 1957), 229–31. This and a score of other uncollected poems await Hughes' permission for book publication. In his article on Plath in *Tri-Quarterly*, Charles Newman lists the most important uncollected poems.

18. *The Colossus*, 5–6.

19. Hughes comments that during this period Plath was reading "closely and sympathetically for the first time — Roethke's poems" (85). Plath said in an interview for the *London Magazine* (New Series, 1, February, 1962, 46) that she particularly admired Roethke's "greenhouse poems." The question of Roethke's actual influence falls outside the area of this essay, but "Blue Moles" is clearly reminiscent of "The Lost Son" and "A Field of Light."

20. Alvarez, *Tri-Quarterly*, 69; Rosenthal, *New Poets*, 85.

21. See Rosenthal, 81; Cox and Jones, *Critical Quarterly*, 111.

22. According to Hughes, the poem was written in March, 1961, and "records some tulips she had in the hospital where she was recovering from an appendectomy," *Tri-Quarterly*, 86.

23. *Fables of Identity*, 133.

24. "Context," *London Magazine*, New Series, 1 (February, 1962), 45–46.

25. *Critical Quarterly*, 3 (1961–62), 140–41.

Doing Away with Daddy: Exorcism and Sympathetic Magic in Plath's Poetry

Guinevara A. Nance and Judith P. Jones[*]

Sylvia Plath's ironic reference to two of her most venomous poems, "Lady Lazarus" and "Daddy," as "some light verse"[1] shows an aesthetic distance that not many of her readers have been able to achieve. Alvarez recalls that when Plath first read these two poems to him, he responded to them more as "assault and battery"[2] than as poetry. Subsequent critical responses to "Daddy" in particular have reacted to the most grizzly stanzas in categorizing the poem as symbolic enactment of patricide and have accentuated its macabre quality by focusing on the parallels between the daddy of the poem and Plath's own father.[3] Readings of the poem as a ritualistic murder have overlooked evidence that the father — whether purely an artistic construct or a derivative of the poet's father — is the fabrication of a persona who attempts to exorcise her childish view of her daddy. Plath has said that "the poem is spoken by a girl with an Electra complex" whose "father died while she thought he was God."[4] Significantly, she refers to the thirty-year old person as a "girl," for the psychological restrictions of an infantile

*Reprinted with permission from *Concerning Poetry*, 11, No. 1 (1978). 75–81.

love and fear of the father have retarded the possibility of autonomy. In the declaration that "You do not do, you do not do / Any more, black shoe,"[5] the speaker recognizes as untenable her puerile perspective of daddy; and the poem depicts her attempts to free herself from an image which she created of the father as deity and demon. Anthony Libby comes closest to recognizing the speaker's participation in the creation of her father when he says that she is as much operator as victim: "She creates the man in black . . . and she finally destroys him" in a destruction that is "internal and theoretical."[6] The process of doing away with daddy in the poem represents the persona's attempts at psychic purgation of the image, "the model," of a father she has constructed. Her methods, however, are more akin to magic than murder, since it is through a combination of exorcism and sympathetic magic that she works to dispossess herself of her own fantasies.

The first twelve stanzas of the poem reveal the extent of the speaker's possession by what, in psychoanalytic terms, is the *imago* of the father — a childhood version of the father which persists into adulthood. This *imago* is an amalgamation of real experience and archetypal memories wherein the speaker's own psychic oppression is represented in the more general symbol of the Nazi oppression of the Jews. For example, the man at the blackboard in the picture of the actual father is transformed symbolically into the "man in black with a Meinkampf look." The connecting link, of course, between each of these associations is the word "black," which also relates to the shoe in which the speaker has lived and the swastika "So black no sky could squeak through." Thus the specific and personal recollections ignite powerful associations with culturally significant symbols. The fact that the girl is herself "a bit of a Jew" and a bit of a German intensifies her emotional paralysis before the *imago* of an Aryan father with whom she is both connected and at enmity. Commenting on the persona in a BBC interview, Plath herself suggests that the two strains of Nazi and Jew unite in the daughter "and paralyze each other"[7]; so the girl is doubly incapacitated to deal with her sense of her father, both by virtue of her mixed ethnicity and her childish perspective. As the persona recalls the father of her early years, she emphasizes and blends the two perspectives of impotence: that of the child before its father and of the Jew before the Nazi. The child's intimidation is clear, for example, in "I never could talk to you. / The tongue stuck in my Jaw"; but the sense of the childhood terror melds into a suggestion of the Jewish persecution and terror with the next line: "It stuck in a barb wire snare."

What Plath accomplishes by the more or less chronological sequencing of these recollections of childhood, and on through the twenty year old's attempted suicide to the point at thirty when the woman tries to extricate hersel from her image of daddy, is a dramatization of the process of psychic purgation in the speaker. The persona's systematic recollection of all the mental projections of her father amounts to an attempt at dispossession through direct confrontation with a demon produced in her imagination.

Both psychoanalysis and the religious rite of exorcism have regarded this process of confrontation with the "trauma" or the "demon" as potentially curative; and from whichever perspective Plath viewed the process, she has her persona confront — in a way almost relive — her childhood terror of a father whose actual existence is as indistinct as the towns with which the girl tries to associate him. Plath also accentuates linguistically the speaker's reliving of her childhood. Using the heavy cadences of nursery rhyme and baby words such as "Chuffing," "Achoo," and "gobbledygoo," she employs a technical device similar to Joyce's in *A Portrait of the Artist as a Young Man*, where the child's simple perspective is reflected through language. Like Joyce, Plath wants to recreate with immediacy the child's view. But whereas Joyce evolves his Stephen Dedalus from the "baby tuckoo" and the "moocow" stage into maturity, she has her speaker psychically regress to her childhood fantasies, where every German is potentially her father and the German language seems to be an engine "chuffing" her off to Dachau. Because the persona's past is pathologically connected to her present, this regression requires minimal distance for the adult woman who has been unable to relinquish the childish perspective.

The tough, even brutal, language to which Alvarez reacted provides an ironic contrast to the language associated with a child's vision of "daddy." This juxtaposition is most evident in the early lines:

> Barely daring to breathe or Achoo.
> Daddy, I have had to kill you.

It is inaccurate to see this last statement entirely as a suggestion of patricide, for the persona's threat is against the infantile version of the father which the word "daddy" connotes. These lines accentuate the irony of the impotent little girl's directing her rage at a monumental fantasy father.

As the language of the poem begins to exclude baby talk and to develop more exclusively the vocabulary of venom, it signals a change in the persona's method of dealing with this image of the father. She moves from confrontation with her childhood projections to an abjuration of the total psychic picture of the father in an attempt at exorcism. Sounding more like Clytemnestra than a little girl playing Electra, she renounces the deity turned demon with a vengeance in the declaration, "Daddy, daddy, you bastard, I'm through." The virulence of this and the statements immediately preceding it indicates a ritualistic attempt to transform the little girl's love into the adult's hatred and thereby kill the image which has preyed upon her.

The turning point in the poem and in the speaker's efforts to purge herself of the psychological significance of the father image occurs in the following stanza:

> But they pulled me out of the sack.
> And they stuck me together with glue.

> And then I knew what to do.
> I made a model of you.

The statement, "I made a model of you," suggests several levels of meaning. On the most obvious level, the speaker implies that she made of her father a prototype of all men; and this is borne out in the merging of the father with the man to whom she says "I do, I do." Her image of the "man in black with a Meinkampf look" is superimposed upon the husband so that instead of having one unreality to destroy, she has two — the prototypic father and the husband who is fashioned in his likeness. The poem "Stings" establishes a similar relationship between the dead-imaginary father and the living but spectral husband:

> A third person is watching.
> He has nothing to do with the bee-seller or me.
> Now he is gone
>
> In eight great bounds, a great scapegoat.

A more complicated implication of the speaker's action in making a model of the father, but one which is also consonant with the allusions to folklore in the later references to vampirism, concerns the persona's use of magic to rid herself of the mental impressions associated with her father. The making of a model, image, or effigy suggests symbolically a reaction not so much to the real father but to the *imago*, or projection of his image in the mind of the persona. She employs what Frazer in *The Golden Bough* refers to as "sympathetic magic" — a generic term for various forms of magic which are based on the premise that a correspondence exists between animate and inanimate objects. One form, homeopathic magic, is predicated on the belief that any representation may affect what it depicts. For example, a picture of a person, a voodoo doll, or any other sort of portrayal can, when acted upon, influence its prototype.[8] In "Daddy," it is the model of the father that the persona destroys; and the solution suggested in the making of the model seems to occur as a consequence of its association with the speaker's own reconstruction after her attempted suicide, when she is "stuck . . . together with glue." Her remodeling, described in a way that recalls the assembling of a collage, seems to be the associative stimulus for the idea of constructing the model through which to effect her dispossession. It is this model, a fabricated representation of a distorted vision of the father — a patchwork mental impression of him — that she seeks to destroy.

Ironically, of course, she is also destroying a portion of her own psychological constitution with which she has lived, however detrimentally, all of her life. With the special significance which Carl Jung gives to the the idea of "image" as a "concentrated expression of the *total psychic situation*,"[9] it is obvious that in attempting to destroy her image of the father, the persona risks total psychic destruction for herself. The final words of the poem, "I'm through," which have been so variously interpreted, imply both that the magic has worked its power of dispossession and also that the speaker is left with nothing. Dispossessed of the *imago* which has defined her own identity and with which she has been obsessed, she is psychically finished, depleted. The villagers, in a kind of ritual death dance, demolish the model of the father, both as it is representative of daddy and of the shadowy vampire-husband behind whose mask that image lurks; and in a final excoriation reminiscent of exorcism rites in which the pride of Satan is attacked by calling him vile names,[10] the daughter declares, "Daddy, daddy, you bastard, I'm through." The ambiguity which Plath creates here in the multiple meanings of "through" indicates the irony of the persona's finishment. Her freedom from the father image which she has created leaves her psychologically void, done in.

Other poems in the *Ariel* volume culminate in a similarly erotic frenzy of rebirth and destruction. As "Stings," "Ariel," and "Lady Lazarus" end, an instant of magical release transforms into destruction or annihilation. These poems are even more specific than "Daddy" in portraying the immediate snuffing out of a momentary burst of resurrecting fire. In "Lady Lazarus," the persona, instead of "coming forth" to life and the glory of God like Lazarus rising from the grave, thrusts herself up with a rush of self-destructive hatred to "eat men like air." She rises to destroy and be destroyed. In "Stings" the speaker is apparently making a positive and energetic statement of her refusal to be like other women, "honey-drudgers" and sex machines; she has "a self to recover, a queen." As in "Daddy," the struggle in these poems is the poet's struggle to reclaim her self. But in all the Ariel poems, the very act of escaping old selves seems to obliterate the very possibility of newness that she is seeking. In expelling the hurtful images rooted in her past, she annihilates her total situation, and the process produces a vacuum. In "Stings" she escapes over "the mausoleum, the wax house," that had constrained the queen; but the escape is to violent flame-colored death:

> Now she is flying
> More terrible than she ever was, red
> Scar in the sky, red comet
> Over the engine that killed her—

Likewise, the creative sexual energy of "Ariel" ends with a suicidal flight into the "red eye, the cauldron of morning." "Lady Lazarus," "Ariel," "Stings," and "Poppies in July" all couple violence with the color red ("I rise with my red hair and I eat men like air"; "drive into the red eye, the cauldron of morning"; "a queen . . . is flying . . . More terrible than she ever was, red Scar in the sky, red comet"; "Little poppies, like hell flames"), suggesting perhaps an intolerable ambivalence toward passion and even life itself. Consistently, these poems present a transitory exorcism of the imprisoning force, only to catapult the persona (and the reader) into a bloody vacuum. They establish a pattern of paradox in which the persona is reborn—but into nothingness.

The tension between rebirth and annihilation pervades the Ariel poems and seems to be a consequence of unreconciled relationships. Plath recognizes her Nazis and vampires to be mental images of her own creation, but she persists in relating to them as if they were real. Here, as in the other poems, when she lets go of the image, there is nothing left and she is finished, "through."

Paradoxically, the problem with the exorcism in "Daddy" is not that it fails to work, but that it does work. In "A Life," from her earlier volume, *Crossing the Water,* Plath imagines a woman with "too many dimensions to enter":

> Grief and anger exorcised,
> Leave her alone now
>
> The future is a grey seagull
> Tattling in its cat-voice of departure, departure.
> Age and terror, like nurses, attend her,
> And a drowned man, complaining of the great cold,
> Crawls up out of the sea.[11]

Here she fails to divest herself of daddy and goes on living. After the successful exorcisms of Ariel she cannot. She roots out the old fixations, but without them she is psychically empty, effaced — as many of the late poems suggest. David Holbrook is astute in saying: "What she wanted was to bring her real self to birth. What she did was destroy everything."[12]

Sylvia Plath may be one of those inexplicable suicides described by R.D. Laing in *The Politics of Experience.* For Laing "both experience and behavior are always in relation to someone or something other than self."[13] If somehow "we are stripped of experience, we are stripped of our deeds," and thus are "bereft of our humanity."[14] In the Ariel poems, Plath strips herself of her own experience in an attempt to find freedom from the painful, constricting nature of that experience. In doing so, she approaches what Laing calls the "fathomless and bottomless groundlessness of everything . . . the ultimate terror."[15] She is left on that borderline between being and nonbeing which Laing calls hell and which, if not carefully negotiated, may result in suicide. He suggests that "there are sudden apparently inexplicable suicides that must be understood as the dawn of a hope so horrible and harrowing that it is unendurable."[16] In Laingian terms, the Ariel poems thrust Sylvia Plath into the borderland between unbearable nothingness and the threatening possibility of an unknown, horrible, harrowing hope.

Notes

1. A. Alvarez, *The Savage God: A Study of Suicide* (New York: Random House, 1970), p. 16.

2. Alvarez, p. 17.

3. Robet Boyers, "Sylvia Plath: The Trepanned Veteran," *Centennial Review,* 13 (1969),

138–53. Boyers identifies the persona's victimization in "Daddy" with universal oppression and locates its source in the "history of Western Culture." He reads the particular act of violence in the poem, however, as a symbolic murder. See also Peter Cooley in "Autism, Autoeroticism, Auto-da-fe: The Tragic Poetry of Sylvia Plath," *The Hollins Critic*, 10 (1973), 1–13. Cooley sees the poem as the incantation "whose every performance by the reader raises and re-murders the father." Judith Wells calls the poem a "voodoo murder" in "Daddy's Girl," *Libera* 1 (1972), 43–45.

4. Quoted by A. Alverez in "Sylvia Plath," *The Art of Sylvia Plath*, ed. Charles Newman (Bloomington and London: Indiana University Press, 1970), p. 65.

5. Sylvia Plath, *Ariel* (London: Faber and Faber, 1965), p. 54. All quotations are from this edition of *Ariel*.

6. Anthony Libby, "God's Lioness and the Priest of Sycorax: Plath and Hughes," *Contemporary Poetry*, 15 (1974), 388.

7. Quoted in Newman, p. 65.

8. Sir James George Frazer, *The Golden Bough: A Study in Magic and Religion*, Abridged Ed. (1922, rpt. New York: Macmillan, 1963), p. 12–55.

9. Carl Jung, *The Basic Writings of C. G. Jung*, ed. Violet Staub de Laszlo (New York: The Modern Library, 1959), p. 256.

10. St. Elmo Nauman, Jr. "Exorcism and Satanism in Medieval Germany," in *Exorcism through the Ages*, ed. St. Elmo Nauman, Jr. (Secaucus, New Jersey: The Citadel Press, 1974), p. 82.

11. Sylvia Plath, *Crossing the Water* (New York: Harper & Row, 1971), p. 55.

12. David Holbrook, "R.D. Laing & the Death Circuit," *Encounter* (August, 1968), p. 38.

13. R.D. Laing, *The Politics of Experience* (New York: Ballantine Books, 1967), p. 25.

14. Laing, p. 29.

15. Laing, p. 38.

16. Laing, p. 43.

The Self in the World: The Social Context of Sylvia Plath's Late Poems

Pamela J. Annas*

> For surely it is time that the effect of disencouragement upon the mind of the artist should be measured, as I have seen a dairy company measure the effect of ordinary milk and Grade A milk upon the body of the rat. They set two rats in cages side by side, and of the two one was furtive, timid and small, and the other was glossy, bold and big. Now what food do we feed women as artists upon?
>
> VIRGINIA WOOLF
> *A Room of One's Own*

The dialectical tension between self and world is the location of meaning in Sylvia Plath's late poems. Characterized by a conflict between stasis

*Reprinted with permission from *Women's Studies*, 7 (1980), 171–83.

and movement, isolation and engagement, these poems are largely about what stands in the way of the possibility of rebirth for the self. In "Totem," she writes: "There is no terminus, only suitcases / Out of which the same self unfolds like a suit / Bald and shiny, with pockets of wishes / Notions and tickets, short circuits and folding mirrors." While in the early poems the self was often imaged in terms of its own possibilities for transformation, in the post-*Colossus* poems the self is more often seen as trapped within a closed cycle. One moves—but only in a circle and continuously back to the same starting point. Rather than the self *and* the world, the *Ariel* poems record the self *in* the world. The self can change and develop, transform and be reborn, only if the world in which it exists does; the possibilities of the self are intimately and inextricably bound up with those of the world.

Sylvia Plath's sense of entrapment, her sense that her choices are profoundly limited, is directly connected to the particular time and place in which she wrote her poetry. Betty Friedan describes the late fifties and early sixties for American women as a "comfortable concentration camp"—physically luxurious, mentally oppressive and impoverished.[1] The recurring metaphors of fragmentation and reification—the abstraction of the individual—in Plath's late poetry are socially and historically based. They are images of Nazi concentration camps, of "fire and bombs through the roof" ("The Applicant"), of cannons, of trains, of "wars, wars, wars" ("Daddy"). And they are images of kitchens, iceboxes, adding machines, typewriters, and the depersonalization of hospitals. The sea and the moon are still important images for Plath, but in the *Ariel* poems they have taken on a harsher quality. "The moon, also, is merciless," she writes in "Elm." While a painfully acute sense of the depersonalization and fragmentation of 1950's America is characteristic of *Ariel*, three poems describe particularly well the social landscape within which the "I" of Sylvia Plath's poems is trapped: "The Applicant," "Cut," and "The Munich Mannequins."

"The Applicant" is explicitly a portrait of marriage in contemporary Western culture. However, the "courtship" and "wedding" in the poem represent not only male / female relations but human relations in general. That job seeking is the central metaphor in "The Applicant" suggests a close connection between the capitalist economic system, the patriarchal family structure, and the general depersonalization of human relations. Somehow all interaction between people, and especially that between men and women, given the history of the use of women as items of barter, seems here to be conditioned by the ideology of a bureaucratized market place. However this system got started, both men and women are implicated in its perpetuation. As in many of Plath's poems, one feels in reading "The Applicant" that Plath sees herself and her imaged *personae* as not merely caught in—victims of—this situation, but in some sense culpable as well. In "The Applicant," the poet is speaking directly to the reader, addressed as "you" throughout. We too are implicated, for we too are potential "applicants."

People are described as crippled and as dismembered pieces of bodies in the first stanza of "The Applicant." Thus imagery of dehumanization begins the poem. Moreover, the pieces described here are not even flesh, but "a glass eye, false teeth or a crutch, / A brace or a hook, / Rubber breasts or a rubber crotch." We are already so involved in a sterile and machine-dominated culture that we are likely part artifact and sterile ourselves. One is reminded not only of the imagery of other Plath poems, but also of the controlling metaphor of Ken Kesey's *One Flew Over the Cuckoo's Nest*, written at about the same time as "The Applicant"—in 1962—, and Chief Bromden's conviction that those people who are integrated into society are just collections of wheels and cogs, smaller replicas of a smoothly functioning larger social machine. "The ward is a factory for the Combine," Bromden thinks. "Something that came all twisted different is now a functioning, adjusted component, a credit to the whole outfit and a marvel to behold. Watch him sliding across the land with a welded grin . . ."[2]

In stanza two of "The Applicant," Plath describes the emptiness which characterizes the applicant and which is a variant on the roboticized activity of Kesey's Adjusted Man. Are there "stitches to show something's missing?" she asks. The applicant's hand is empty, so she provides "a hand"

> To fill it and willing
> To bring teacups and roll away headaches
> And do whatever you tell it
> Will you marry it?

Throughout the poem, people are talked about as parts and surfaces. The suit introduced in stanza three is at least as alive as the hollow man and mechanical doll woman of the poem. In fact, the suit, an artifact, has more substance and certainly more durability than the person to whom it is offered "in marriage." Ultimately, it is the suit which gives shape to the applicant where before he was shapeless, a junk heap of fragmented parts.

> I notice you are stark naked.
> How about this suit—
>
> Black and stiff, but not a bad fit.
> Will you marry it?
> It is waterproof, shatterproof, proof
> Against fire and bombs through the roof.
> Believe me, they'll bury you in it.

The man in the poem is finally defined by the black suit he puts on, but the definition of the woman shows her to be even more alienated and dehumanized. While the man is a junk heap of miscellaneous parts given shape by a suit of clothes, the woman is a wind-up toy, a puppet of that black suit. She doesn't even exist unless the black suit needs and wills her to.

> Will you marry it?
> It is guaranteed

> To thumb shut your eyes at the end
> And dissolve of sorrow.
> We make new stock from the salt.

The woman in the poem is referred to as "it." Like the man, she has no individuality, but where his suit gives him form, standing for the role he plays in a bureaucratic society, for the work he does, the only thing that gives the woman form is the institution of marriage. She does not exist before it and dissolves back into nothingness after it. In "The Applicant" there is at least an implication that something exists underneath the man's black suit; that however fragmented he is, he at least *marries* the suit and he at least has a choice. In contrast, the woman *is* the role she plays; she does not exist apart from it. "Naked as paper to start," Plath writes,

> But in twenty-five years she'll be silver,
> In fifty, gold.
> A living doll, everywhere you look.
> It can sew, it can cook.
> It can talk, talk, talk.

The man, the type of a standard issue corporation junior executive, is also alienated. He has freedom of choice only in comparison to the much more limited situation of the woman. That is to say, he has relative freedom of choice in direct proportion to his role as recognized worker in the economic structure of his society. This should not imply, however, that this man is in any kind of satisfying and meaningful relation to his work. The emphasis in "The Applicant" upon the man's surface—his black suit—together with the opening question of the poem ("First, are you our sort of person?") suggests that even his relationship to his work is not going to be in any sense direct or satisfying. It will be filtered first through the suit of clothes, then through the glass eye and rubber crotch before it can reach the real human being, assuming there is anything left of him.

The woman in the poem is seen as an appendage; she works, but she works in a realm outside socially recognized labor. She works for the man in the black suit. She is seen as making contact with the world only through the medium of the man, who is already twice removed. This buffering effect is exacerbated by the fact that the man is probably not engaged in work that would allow him to feel a relationship to the product of his labor. He is probably a bureaucrat of some kind, and therefore his relationship is to pieces of paper, successive and fragmented paradigms of the product (whatever it is, chamberpots or wooden tables) rather than to the product itself. And of course, the more buffered the man is, the more buffered the woman is, for in a sense her real relationship to the world of labor is that of consumer rather than producer. Therefore, her only relationship to socially acceptable production—as opposed to consumption—is through the man.

In another sense, however, the woman is not a consumer, but a commodity. Certainly she is seen as a commodity in this poem, as a reward only slightly less important than his black suit, which the man receives for being "our sort of person." It can be argued that the man is to some extent also a commodity; yet just as he is in a sense more a laborer and less a consumer than the woman — at least in terms of the social recognition of his position — so in a second sense he is more a consumer and less a commodity than the woman. And when we move out from the particularly flat, paper-like image of the woman in the poem to the consciousness which speaks the poem in a tone of bitter irony, then the situation of the woman as unrecognized worker / recognized commodity becomes clearer. The man in "The Applicant," because of the middle class bureaucratic nature of his work (one does not wear a new black suit to work in a steel mill or to handcraft a cabinet) and because of his position vis-a-vis the woman (her social existence depends upon his recognition), is more a member of an exploiting class than one which is exploited.[3] There are some parts of his world, specifically those involving the woman, in which he can feel himself relatively in control and therefore able to understand his relationship to this world in a contemplative way. Thus, whatever we may think of the system he has bought into, he himself can see it as comparatively stable, a paradigm with certain static features which nevertheless allows *him* to move upward in an orderly fashion.

Within the context of this poem, then, and within the context of the woman's relationship to the man in the black suit, she is finally both worker and commodity while he is consumer.[4] Her position is close to that of the Marxist conception of the proletariat. Fredric Jameson, in *Marxism and Form*, defines the perception of external objects and events which arises naturally in the consciousness of an individual who is simultaneously worker and commodity.

> Even before [the worker] posits elements of the outside world as *objects* of his thought, he feels *himself* to be an object, and this initial alienation within himself takes precedence over everything else. Yet precisely in this terrible alienation lies the strength of the worker's position: his first movement is not toward knowledge of the work but toward knowledge of himself as an object, toward self-consciousness. Yet this self-consciousness, because it is initially knowledge of an object (himself, his own labor as a commodity, his life force which he is under obligation to sell), permits him more genuine knowledge of the commodity nature of the outside world than is granted to middle-class "objectivity." For [and here Jameson quotes Georg Lukács in *The History of Class Consciousness*] "his consciousness is the self-consciousness of merchandise itself . . ."[5]

This dual consciousness of self as both subject and object is characteristic of the literature of minority and / or oppressed classes. It is characteristic of the proletarian writer in his (admittedly often dogmatic) perception of his relation to a decadent past, a dispossessed present, and a utopian future.

It is characteristic of black American writers; W. E. B. DuBois makes a statement very similar in substance to Jameson's in *The Souls of Black Folk*, and certainly the basic existential condition of Ellison's invisible man is his dual consciousness which only toward the end of that novel becomes a means to freedom of action rather than paralysis.[6] It is true of contemporary women writers, of novelists like Doris Lessing, Margaret Atwood, and Rita Mae Brown, and of poets like Denise Levertov, Adrienne Rich, and Marge Piercy. In a sense, it is more characteristic of American literature than of any other major world literature, for each immigrant group, however great its desire for assimilation into the American power structure, initially possessed this dual consciousness. Finally, a dialectical perception of self as both subject and object, both worker and commodity, in relation to past and future as well as present, is characteristic of revolutionary literature, whether the revolution is political or cultural.

Sylvia Plath has this dialectical awareness of self as both subject and object in particular relation to the society in which she lived. The problem for her, and perhaps the main problem of Cold War America, is in the second aspect of a dialectical consciousness — an awareness of oneself in significant relation to past and future. The first person narrator of what is probably Plath's best short story, "Johnny Panic and the Bible of Dreams," is a clerk / typist in a psychiatric clinic, a self-described "dream connoisseur" who keeps her own personal record of all the dreams which pass through her office, and who longs to look at the oldest record book the Psychoanalytic Institute possesses. "This dream book was spanking new the day I was born," she says, and elsewhere makes the connection even clearer: "The clinic started thirty-three years ago — the year of my birth, oddly enough."[7] This connection suggests the way in which Plath uses history and views herself in relation to it. The landscape of her late work is a contemporary social landscape. It goes back in time to encompass such significant historical events as the Rosenberg trial and execution — the opening chapter of *The Bell Jar* alludes dramatically to these events — and of course it encompasses, is perhaps obsessed with, the major historical event of Plath's time, the second world war. But social history seems to stop for Plath where her own life starts, and it is replaced at that point by a mythic timeless past populated by creatures from folk tale and classical mythology. This is not surprising, since as a woman this poet had little part in shaping history. Why should she feel any relation to it? But more crucially, there is no imagination of the future in Sylvia Plath's work, no utopian or even antiutopian consciousness. In her poetry there is a dialectical consciousness of the self as simultaneously object and subject, but in her particular social context she was unable to develop a consciousness of herself in relation to a past and future beyond her own lifetime. This foreshortening of a historical consciousness affects in turn the dual consciousness of self in relation to itself (as subject) and in relation to the world (as object). It raises the question of how one accounts objectively for oneself. For instance, if I am involved in everything I see, can I still be objective and empirical in my perception, free from myth and language? Finally, this foreshortening of historical consciousness affects the question of whether the subject is a function of the object or *vice versa*. Since the two seem to have equal possibilities, this last question is never resolved. As a result, the individual feels trapped; and in Sylvia Plath's poetry one senses a continual struggle to be reborn into some new present which causes the perceiving consciousness, when it opens its eyes, to discover that it has instead (as in "Lady Lazarus") made a "theatrical / Comeback in broad day / To the same place, the same face, the same brute / Amused shout: 'A miracle!' "

This difficulty in locating the self and the concomitant suspicion that as a result the self may be unreal are clear in poems like "Cut," which describe the self-image of the poet as paper. The ostensible occasion of "Cut" is slicing one's finger instead of an onion; the first two stanzas of the poem describe the cut finger in minute and almost naturalistic detail. There is a suppressed hysteria here which is only discernible in the poem's curious mixture of surrealism and objectivity. The images of the poem are predominantly images of terrorism and war, immediately suggested to the poet by the sight of her bleeding finger: "out of a gap / A million soldiers run," "Saboteur / Kamikaze man — ," and finally, "trepanned veteran." The metaphors of war are extensive, and, though suggested by the actual experience, they are removed from it.

In the one place in the poem where the speaker mentions her own feelings as a complete entity (apart from but including her cut finger) the image is of paper. She says,

> O my
> Homunculus, I am ill.
> I have taken a pill to kill
> The thin
> Papery feeling.

Paper often stands for the self-image of the poet in the post-*Colossus* poems. It is used in the title poem of *Crossing the Water*, where the "two black cut-paper people" appear less substantial and less real than the solidity and immensity of the natural world surrounding them. In the play *Three Women*, the Secretary says of the men in her office: "there was something about them like cardboard, and now I had caught it." She sees her own infertility as indirectly related to her complicity in a bureaucratic, impersonal, male-dominated society. Paper is symbolic of our particular socioeconomic condition and its characteristic bureaucratic labor. It stands for insubstantiality; the paper model of something is clearly less real than the thing itself, even though in "developed" economies the machines, accoutrements, and objects appear to have vitality, purpose, and emotion, while the people are literally colorless, objectified, and atrophied.

The paper self is therefore part of Plath's portrait of a depersonalized society, a bureaucracy, a paper world. In "A Life" (*Crossing the Water*), she writes: "A woman is dragging her shadow in a circle / About a bald hospital saucer. / It resembles the moon, or a sheet of blank paper / And appears to have suffered a private blitzkrieg." In "Tulips" the speaker of the poem, also a hospital patient, describes herself as "flat, ridiculous, a cut-paper shadow / Between the eye of the sun and the eyes of the tulips." In "The Applicant," the woman is again described as paper: "Naked as paper to start / But in twenty-five years she'll be silver, / In fifty, gold." Here in "Cut," the "thin, / Papery feeling" juxtaposes her emotional dissociation from the wound to the horrific detail of the cut and the bloody images of conflict it suggests. It stands for her sense of depersonalization, for the separation of self from self, and is juxtaposed to that devaluation of human life which is a necessary precondition to war, the separation of society from itself. In this context, it is significant that one would take a pill to kill a feeling of substancelessness and depersonalization. Writing about American women in the 1950's, Betty Friedan asks, "Just what was the problem that had no name? What were the words women used when they tried to express it? Sometimes a woman would say, 'I feel empty somehow . . . incomplete.' Or she would say, 'I feel as if I don't exist.' Sometimes she blotted out the feeling with a tranquilizer."[8]

A papery world is a sterile world; this equation recurs throughout the *Ariel* poems. For Sylvia Plath, stasis and perfection are always associated with sterility, while fertility is associated with movement and process. The opening lines of "The Munich Mannequins" introduce this equation. "Perfection is terrible," Plath writes, "it cannot have children. / Cold as snow breath, it tamps the womb / Where the yew trees blow like hydras." The setting of "The Munich Mannequins" is a city in winter. Often, Plath's poems have imaged winter as a time of rest preceeding rebirth ("Wintering," "Frog Autumn"), but only when the reference point is nature. The natural world is characterized in Sylvia Plath's poems by process, by the ebb and flow of months and seasons, by a continual dying and rebirth. The moon is a symbol for the monthly ebb and flow of the tides and of a woman's body. The social world, however, the world of the city, is both male defined and separated from this process. In the city, winter has more sinister connotations; it suggests death rather than hibernation. Here the cold is equated with the perfection and sterility to which the poem's opening lines refer. Perfection stands in "The Munich Mannequins" for something artifically created and part of the social world.

The poem follows the male quest for perfection to its logical end — mannequins in a store window — lifeless and mindless "in their sulphur loveliness, in their smiles." The mannequins contrast with the real woman in the same way that the city contrasts with the moon. The real woman is not static but complicated:

> The tree of life and the tree of life

Unloosing their moons, month after month, to no purpose.
The blood flood is the flood of love,

The absolute sacrifice

However, in Munich, "morgue between Paris and Rome," the artificial has somehow triumphed. Women have become mannequins or have been replaced by mannequins, or at least mannequins seem to have a greater reality because they are more ordered and comprehensible than real women.

It is appropriate that Plath should focus on the middle class of a German city, in a country where fascism was a middle class movement and women allowed themselves to be idealized, to be perfected, to be made, essentially, into mannequins. In "The Munich Mannequins," as in "The Applicant," Plath points out the deadening of human beings, their disappearance and fragmentation and accretion into the objects that surround them. In "The Applicant" the woman is a paper doll; here she has been replaced by a store window dummy. In "The Applicant" all that is left of her at the end is a kind of saline solution; in "The Munich Mannequins" the only remaining sign of her presence is "the domesticity of these windows / The baby   lace,   and   green-leaved   confectionery." And   where the man in "The Applicant" is described in terms of his black suit, here the men are described in terms of their shoes, present in the anonymity of hotel corridors, where

Hands will be opening doors and setting

Down shoes for a polish of carbon
Into which broad toes will go tomorrow.

People accrete to their things, are absorbed into their artifacts. Finally, they lose all sense of a whole self and become atomized. Parts of them connect to their shoes, parts to their suits, parts to their lace curtains, parts to their iceboxes, and so on. There is nothing left; people have become reified and dispersed into a cluttered artificial landscape of their own production.

Because the world she describes is a place created by men rather than women (since men are in control of the forces of production), Plath sees men as having ultimate culpability for this state of affairs which affects both men and women. But men have gone further than this in their desire to change and control the world around them. In "The Munich Mannequins" man has finally transformed woman into a puppet, a mannequin, something that reflects both his disgust with and his fear of women. A mannequin cannot have children, but neither does it have that messy, terrifying, and incomprehensible blood flow each month. Mannequins entirely do away with the problems of female creativity and self-determination. Trapped inside this vision, therefore, the speaker of the *Ariel* poems sees herself caught between nature and society, biology and intellect, Dionysus and Apollo, her self definition and the expectations of others, as between two mirrors.

Discussion of the *Ariel* poems has often centered around Sylvia Plath's most shocking images. Yet her images of wars and concentration camps, of mass and individual violence, are only the end result of an underlying depersonalization, an abdication of people to their artifacts, and an economic and social structure that equates people and objects. Like the paper doll woman in "The Applicant," Sylvia Plath was doubly alienated from such a world, doubly objectified by it, and as a woman artist, doubly isolated within it. Isolated both from a past tradition and a present community, she found it difficult to structure new alternatives for the future. No wonder her individual quest for rebirth failed as it led her continuously in a circle back to the same self in the same world. Finally, what Sylvia Plath has bequeathed us in her poems is a brilliant narrative of the struggle to survive.

Notes

1. Betty Friedan, *The Feminine Mystique* (New York: Dell, 1963). See Chapter 12, "Progressive Dehumanization: The Comfortable Concentration Camp," 271–98.

2. Ken Kesey, *One Flew Over the Cuckoo's Nest* (New York: Viking, 1962), 38.

3. Frederick Engels, *The Origin of the Family, Private Property and the State* (New York: International Publishers, 1942). "The modern individual family is founded on the open or concealed domestic slavery of the wife, and modern society is a mass composed of these individual families as its molecules.

"In the great majority of cases today, at least in the possessing classes, the husband is obliged to earn a living and support his family, and that in itself gives him a position of supremacy without any need for special legal titles and privileges. *Within the Family he is the bourgeois, and the wife represents the proletariat.*" (p. 37, italics mine).

4. The progress of monopoly capitalism in the twentieth century has, however, served to proletarianize people who thought (or whose parents thought) they had escaped from the working class — clericals, sales, and lower and middle management — and is now beginning to make workers, in the traditional sense of people who have to sell their labor piecemeal and who have no relation to or control over the product of their labor, out of the professional classes. See especially Parts IV and V, "The Growing Working Class Occupations" and "The Working Class" in *Labor and Monopoly Capital: The Degradation of Work in the Twentieth Century*, by Harry Braverman (New York: Monthly Review Press, 1974), 293–449.

5. Fredric Jameson, *Marxism and Form* (Princeton, N.J.: Princeton Univ. Press, 1971), 186–87.

6. W. E. B. Dubois, "The Souls of Black Folk" in *Three Negro Classics* (1903; rpt. New York: Avon, 1965), 214–15.

7. Sylvia Plath, "Johnny Panic and the Bible of Dreams," *The Manufacture of Madness*, ed. Thomas Szasz (New York: Doubleday, 1973), 313, 308. First published in *Atlantic*, Sept. 1968, 54–60.

8. Friedan, *Feminine Mystique*, 16.

Sylvia Plath's Traditionalism   Frederick Buell*

Sylvia Plath's characterization of *The Bell Jar* as a potboiler is certainly too harsh; its sensationalism and its topicality, along with its thinly veiled autobiographical reference, have, however, contributed to a surprising delay in thorough critical appreciation of her finest poetry. Now that *Letters Home* has been published, the tendency to look at her work solely or primarily in terms of topical and autobiographical contexts will surely be reinforced. A judicious reading of *The Bell Jar* and a careful use of *Letters Home* can, I believe, reveal much that is important about her poetry, if, however, primary attention is given to her dialogue, as poet, with the central tradition of literary modernism, the tradition of post-Romantic, symbolist writing. It is in this context that I would like to make some comments first about *The Bell Jar* and *Letters Home;* my main concern is to show how Plath, in her finest poetry, managed to re-enliven post-Romantic, symbolist assumptions about art at the same time that she brought them to some of their furthest conceivable limits.

What seems to me to be the real center of power of *The Bell Jar* is less its explicit plot than it is the consciousness and the narrative voice of the novel. As with Plath's best poems (in which her representation of anxiety and lucid horror attains a far greater maturity and universality), one feels that the opening sentences contain, if only in their tone, the fatality and stasis that will thereafter be made explicit:

> it was a queer, sultry summer, the summer they electrocuted the Rosenbergs, and I didn't know what I was doing in New York. I'm stupid about executions. The idea of being electrocuted makes me sick, and that's all there was to read about in the papers — goggle-eyed headlines staring up at me on every street corner and at the fusty, peanut-smelling mouth of every subway. It had nothing to do with me, but I couldn't help wondering what it would be like, being burned alive all along your nerves.[1]

In this passage, as in the most intense moments throughout the novel, Esther reveals herself as vulnerably, anxiously, and obsessively self-conscious, yet with a frightening lack of an inner, stable "self"; external events are caught in the web of an intense and ruthlessly analytic self-awareness, one which is anxiously preoccupied with an insufficiency or a vacancy where a self should be. One feels that Esther is constantly on the verge of being spiritually annihilated by the disparate pressures of the unstable world around her; as the novel progresses, it becomes clear that these outside pressures are far less intense than the way in which her self-consciousness turns them inward upon herself. She lives, save in the scenes with Dr. Nolan, in complete emotional isolation, unable to find or realize herself within any of the surrounding social contexts; at best, she tries to cope with

*Reprinted with permission from *Boundary 2*, 5 (Fall, 1976), 195–211.

this introspective anxiety and isolation by means of the American myth of solitarily-won success, but the more intelligently analytical she becomes about her own fierce, injured ambition, the more painfully she returns to her own insufficiency and nothingness.

While at college, Esther could cope, albeit precariously, with pressures that, in contrast to those surrounding her in New York, were more reified in the demands of a cloistered and tightly structured environment; here, she could "succeed" so brilliantly as to establish herself in others' eyes, if not — as was the case with her success, and the resultant anxiety and guilt, at escaping Chemistry — in her own. In New York, however, she encountered such a multiplicity of standards for success — none of which was absolute, and all of which were in large part sham — and people with such a multiplicity of talents, that the experience became spiritually nauseating.[2] She could find no social structure which was central, no one achievement which was *the* one thing to attain, as good marks were for her in college; she could find no way to master her environment and her own inner anxiety about her identity by dint of the dehumanizing ascetic labor she required of herself in college. She realized in New York that all her preparatory labors did not ready her for competing in the larger, more chaotically uncentered "real" world. She felt suddenly how completely unprepared for it she was; indeed, her laborious preparations had only made things more difficult for her.

Her agony of self-consciousness and self-appraisal was based, however, on something far more demanding than mere ambition — the attainment of some admired position for purposes of self-exaltation — not because she was more selfless than this, but because she was incomparably more anxiously preoccupied with herself. Behind her drive to success was a more-than-worldly drive to self-perfection: perfection both in her experience of all (particularly the extremes) in life and in the invulnerability of an attained mastery of that experience. Short of this, whatever she achieved would be quickly annihilated by a new awareness of still more beyond her reach — as if an intensely puritanic consciousness had to redeem itself, alone, without help, from time and multiplicity. The aloneness, the solipsism, of this attempt was well imaged in the book's central symbol and title.

This pattern is presented more poignantly and naively in Sylvia Plath's *Letters Home.* The letters reveal the willfulness with which the novel was written: the novel (its first part, at least) was an exercise in systematic disillusionment, an almost point by point reevaluation and rejection of the yearnings, hopes, and values that had, in enthusiasm and dejection alike, guided her life as a student in high school and college and as a young married woman. The letters are an essential document of what is now called *the* fifties — or what, more exactly, would be middle class white, especially WASP, America, seen through the eyes of its young people, during the fifties — written by someone who gradually was forced to understand and undergo the demands of her uncommonly intense spirituality, a spirituality that was internally torn and compromised by the society that placed such homely and excruciatingly secular limitations on it.

Always behind the painfully homely fifties Americana of the letters lay an impulse to self-perfection that was — if only in the unexamined intensity with which "Sivvy" attempted to meet and transform the values of her time — the troubled indication of her later understandings. Success, popularity, and marriage, and the frequently expressed desire for a rich, full, well-rounded life were the terms that her society and her environment gave her to understand and guide her yearnings; these goals were finally unable to contain the energy of will that lay behind them. Plath bitterly experienced the paradox of the ideal of the well-rounded, the cheerily happy, and the successful person who, however, had to earn these qualities by dint of lonely and self-denying self-conscious labor in a host of different (and trivial) fields — clothing, poise, friendliness, etc. This paradox was particularly vivid to anyone from a socially marginal background — just to be a scholarship girl at Smith put one in that agony of hopefulness and struggle; or to anyone at all unusual in physical appearance — at fifteen Plath had grown to the unusual height of five feet nine inches; or to anyone, particularly a woman, with ambitions out of the ordinary — from a very early age Plath was committed to becoming a writer. Perhaps the most terse and absolute way of putting this paradox is that one had to appear, more, to *be* perfectly natural, a perfection of naturalness. One had to strike always just the right casual tone, one had to have the right boyfriend without visibly struggling to get him; those who struggled in society — those trying to overcome disadvantages and "inferiority complexes" — and those who struggled in schoolwork (the grinds) were excluded on sight. In terms of Western religiosity, this paradox is intolerable; the human will, and the realm of moral activity it occasions, is meant to direct itself toward something higher than and prior to nature, especially the "nature" conceived in the fifties as smiling, optimistic, materially successful happiness. Plath was under especially great strain by virtue of her intensity; she went after these all too secular and limited goals with an energy and desire that only a more than natural world could contain. Her cry upon being rescued from her attempted suicide — "Oh, if I only could be a freshman again. I so wanted to be a *Smith* woman" — contains a poignancy that is also excruciating in the extreme poverty and worldliness of the thing to which she attached her intense desire (LH, 126). Equally excruciating and poignant are the expressions of painfully hopeful enthusiasm with which her letters abound; one feels behind them a will and ambition — a force that Yeats would call antithetical — that no natural goal could contain. More ominously, one begins to feel that these desires not only threaten to explode traumatically beyond nature, but also that the more they focus blindly upon natural good — happiness, brought about through success — the more unnatural, even perverse, they become in themselves. Behind the American myth of success that produces natural happiness is concealed the reality of the bell jar: an utter solipsism, a capacity for extreme self-laceration in failure, and even a certain demonic tincture to the will occasioned by both success and failure. The epithet "self-made" is revelatory of these things: to a religious understanding, it is an extreme of blasphemy. Its pathetic side is its loneliness—particularly in the self-conscious, mutually inspecting, conformist America of the fifties; its demonic side is its willful solipsism and its pride of self-causation, available in both failure and success.[3]

Within these paradoxical fifties values, Plath sought what she articulated often as success and therefore happiness and what, in moments of greater self-knowledge, she articulated as self-perfection. Whether by chance or by design, the crises in her life revealed to her the incompatibility of these two goals. Her letters, filled with resurgent beginnings, enthusiasms, visions of new programs of action that would complete and perfect her and also bring success and happiness of a kind yet untasted, a kind at last real and permanent, show how the two goals were able to remain uneasily compatible as long as she felt her life lay before her in prospectiveness, that somewhere soon doors would be unlocked, that she had just found out at last the way to begin ordering her life so as to be fruitful in natural life as well as in ambition: as long as she could retain this prospectiveness—at the cost, to be sure, of assuming her own naivete and immaturity—she had the resilience to withstand the disillusionment that followed upon the heels of enthusiasm.[4] The moments in her life when she lost this resilience occurred when the shock of a disillusionment was too encompassing; first, when her shock at discovering the unencompassable multiplicity of New York City coincided with a number of other frustrations, and second, when her marriage to Ted Hughes, a marriage that seemed at last to reconcile will and nature, ambition for self-perfection, success, and life, collapsed. That this aspect of her marriage exhilarated her is clear from the letters; magically, their relationship touched off in both of them a burst of creativity deeper than before, and they seemed to be able to lead each other into artistic as well as human fulfillment. Revelatory of this and the strain it could also cause was the letter in which Plath announced to her mother that at last she had written happy poems and that some new acceptances were examples of "what true love can produce"; equally double-edged was the later letter in which Plath justified her (by contemporary standards) mildly atypical lifestyle: "when we are both wealthy and famous, our work will justify our lives, but now our lives and faith must justify themselves" (LH, 274, 343).

What happened in Plath's moments of breakdown was that life, natural existence, lost all radiance and became the maze of dislocated sensations and sensationalisms into which a haunted Esther found herself placed—or, more profoundly, a Belsen in which a full, conscious being was imprisoned fully aware, a state Plath depicted in the later, extreme poems.[5] In this torment, Plath was left alone with her conscious will, which now fully apprehended itself as unnatural. The terms for this unnaturalness broadened immensely: they grew out of the fifties social horror of failure. In it, failure meant that "no one would find me interesting or valuable" and that, like a piece the *Ladies' Home Journal* had rejected, "I begin to feel that *I* lack that 'indefinable something' that makes a winner" (LH, 133, 156).[6] One would be, to expand the terms beyond these contexts, absolutely isolated from human community and nature, left alone in self-consciousness of this unnatural isolation; the sensation of knowledge self-consciousness brings would be a product and a symptom, perhaps also a cause, of this unnaturalness. The rest of the world — save for the anti-community of aware victims — would be stupidly happy; the conscious would be intelligent, but damned and tormented. A bitter exaltation would be possible in this knowledge: in so far as the knowledge was of failure, a perverse remorse and even pride, which claimed a perfection of its own failure and therefore negatively overcame all mere nature within oneself (spontaneity) and without (external accident), would be available, and, in so far as the knowledge was purified of personal failure and transformed into a realization of the unnaturalness of all human consciousness, it would have the perverse power of a vision from the underworld, the real fallen state of humankind, a vision others were too fearfully or stupidly naive to see. A negative kind of perfection would be possible: a perfection of anti-natural consciousness. In this state, consummately realized in Plath's later poetry, the possessor of such knowledge would become a visionary with a gnostic hatred of nature combined, however, with the equally strong awareness that there was no saving gnosis. Examples of Plath's gnosticism abound in the later poetry; to pick one of the more straightforward, in "A Birthday Present," nature, imaged as clouds, becomes "veils" that are "killing my days," although "To you they are only transparencies, clear air."[7] At best, nature, described in rhetoric that is a conscious echoing and inversion of D. H. Lawrence's, is imaged as a barbarous, in itself beautiful, vitality from which human consciousness is isolated and by which it is threatened (examples are "Tulips" and "Poppies in July"). The awareness in Plath that there is no saving gnosis (even in suicide, contrary to the beliefs of extreme dualists — from those of the East, such as the Jains, to those of the West, such as the thirteenth-century Catharists — who legitimized voluntary death as a religious act) reveals itself most completely in the poems of greatest extremity, such as "Lady Lazarus"; in them, anti-natural perfection is shown to be a sterile, solipsistic ideal, located nowhere, and visible only in the totality with which the visionary willfully dehumanizes and annihilates the natural. The final twist of the knife is that Plath makes a matter-of-fact and clear-sighted moral appraisal of this process: the process of revelation is judged as ethically abhorrent — not only because it is destructive but also because it is anti-natural, and thus forever inauthentic, falsely posturing — as the revelation itself is cynical in its message. The secularity of will in the America of the fifties, the decay of all supernatural focus for its energies, thus gave Plath's idealism no locus in scripture or human tradition.

Especially for a woman with desires larger than the allowed social ob-

jectives, the experience of unnaturalness would be thorough-going and intense. Insofar as womanhood was identified with natural richness, the
experience of an opposite force within would be terrible. This is what looms
ominously behind one of the hopeful comments Plath, trying to temporize
her imagination, made in her letters:

> I cannot draw well or write exceptionally, but I feel now so far beyond that
> perfectionist streak which would be flawless or nothing—now I go on in
> my happy-go-lucky way and make my little imperfect worlds in pen and
> typewriter and share them with those I love. (LH, 228)

Imperfection, sharing, love—these are linked with brittle cheerful acceptance by someone who would later be driven, or liberated, into willful attainment, in poetry, of their opposites. Her old problem of perfectionism,
which she recognized as one of the causes of her first breakdown, was closely
allied with the terrifying fulfillment of her vocation as an imaginative
writer, a vocation that revealed itself more absolutely and monomaniacally
when her life fell to pieces around her. Formal perfection in poetry appeared to be the willed attainment of conscious unnaturalness, a flawless
and dehumanized perfection that revealed itself in the completeness with
which—in the world without and within—it terrorized the natural.

We can now return briefly to *The Bell Jar* to look at the two figures who
flank Esther at the beginning of her stay in New York: they represent opposed possibilities, and it would not be forcing the issue too much to read
them as emblems for two kinds of creativity. Though attracted to "Pollyanna Cowgirl" as a kind of lost hope for innocence, she could not hope as a
self-conscious writer to remain in that state. In New York, the naturalness
of Pollyanna Cowgirl was only a public-relations image, manipulated cynically by urban advertising men; even her writing teacher would have called
it factitious. As with the world of suburban normality in the book, the superficial, apparently innocent image was a trivializing deception, cynically
manipulated, hiding a nausea and terror behind it; once that reality had
become known, Esther could find no way to return to whatever innocence—or better, nostalgia for innocence—she may have had.

One might look to Doreen as an emblem of an alternate possibility for
poetry: a poetry of sophisticated decadence as opposed to graceful, trivial,
inauthentically naive verse. But this decadence, with its cultivation of a
fallen, inauthentic world of manipulated form, in which the word "factitious" would indicate superiority rather than inadequacy, was impossible
for Esther, even though it attracted her strongly; it was morally nauseating
as well as practically unattainable. Against the decadence of Doreen we
must place the voice of cynicism in Plath's later poetry, a voice resonant
with the superiority of someone who is willfully unnatural and therefore
knowing, yet also familiarly aware of such superiority as self-destructive
and even cheap, a mere pose. If Esther is still too afraid, naive, and awk-
ward to become another Doreen, Plath is in her later poetry too accom-

plished and too knowing; decadence fails to satisfy the demands not just of her conscience but also of her withering judgment about the cultivated impotence of merely aesthetic gestures—that is, her demand that poetry satisfy a reality-hunger, even when the reality is conscious annihilation. From this standpoint, the world of advertising is perverted not in its falsification of experience, but in the blandness and tameness with which it falsifies: it is simply not perverted with enough conscious intensity and intelligence to be truly powerful. Consider how much more powerful an understanding of the unnatural a failed suicide attempt gives; one returns from it with an increased consciousness of isolation and a frightening power over oneself which arises from the fact that one has been capable of one of the most extreme anti-natural acts. Consider then how such knowledge might be expressed in a dehumanized aesthetic such as the one that Esther wished she had voiced to Buddy, a belief that the immortality of poems can make them perfect, unlike natural men, who, though temporarily curable by supposedly humanistic doctors, are really only dust. Poetic form would be, in this aesthetic, more than inorganic; it would be anti-organic.

In *The Bell Jar*, Esther's attempted suicide does not produce an extreme of fallen self-control and self-knowledge. Insofar as she is a diminished projection of Sylvia Plath, far more naive than one feels her author is, she cannot. One reason for this is that the novel represents, as the later poetry does not, a desire to avoid this self-recognition and to attain a conditionally happy end. It also means that the novel was still written out of self-therapeutic hopefulness, in a way that the later poetry will explicitly negate. The shock of the most extreme later poetry is that of encountering a person—better, a persona, if one uses that word with a reserve of contempt for the unnaturalness of critical jargon—who has irremediably decided on things: one for whom consciousness is unnatural, and will and rational intelligence are the capacity to heighten such awareness, to act it out to its fullest.

In its fullest, most fallen form, such consciousness would approach the absolute poetry Plath came to write. It would create the illusion of having attained a sort of total knowledge: that there was no kind of experience—even despair—that it had not had, as in "Elm" ("I know the bottom, she says. I know it with my great tap root: / It is what you fear. / I do not fear it: I have been there"), or had and thereby finished with, as in "Cut" ("What a thrill— / My thumb instead of an onion") (A, 15, 13). The late poems of W. B. Yeats seem humane by comparison: behind their stoic fatalism is an affirmation of the wheel of time, however inexorably repetitive it is. Yeats has a gnosis, however grim; Plath has none, and her will is just as powerful and intact in destructive knowledge as Yeats's is in fatalism. This fallen consciousness would contain no capacity for hopeful growth: either there would be terrible stasis or intensification (as at the end of "Lady Lazarus" and "Stings"). Spontaneity would be impossible; it would be shunned as the superficial innocence of "Pollyanna Cowgirl" was. Likewise, benign contentment, harmony with self, and all mere naturalness would be impossible; to live thus would be to live like Dodo Conway, the most contemptuously treated character in *The Bell Jar*. Instead, the self-tyranny implicit in fallen self-knowledge would have to be made absolute: by tyrannizing her ordinary, flawed, natural self, she would achieve a dehumanized poetic voice and lyrical "I" that would fix, freeze, and ultimately annihilate her natural self, and would take into its active energy by virtue of its finer, prouder, consciously unnatural tyranny all the inhumanity of fallen, determined life. It would self-destructively transcend fate by wreaking for itself a more powerful internalized fatality.

Plath's major work, then, seems to vacillate reliably between two kinds of extreme images, one kind relating to herself as formed, fixed subject matter, and one kind relating to herself as demonic creator. Either she will image herself (even yearningly) in terms of a frighteningly stupefied, static, insensate object, something utterly determined and therefore almost peaceful—examples are "Edge" and "Paralytic"—or she will image herself as the destructively powerful phoenix-witch-bitch-goddess—the best example being the triumphant horror at the end of "Lady Lazarus." The former type of image may be either a regressive return to purity or the accomplishment that comes on the other side of sensational or psychological violence; the latter image may be seen either in terms of a demonic virginity (as with the hive in "The Bee Meeting" or the "pure acetylene / Virgin" of "Fever 103°") or in terms of a castrating, self-terrorizing creature of experience (as in "Years" and the ends of "Lady Lazarus" and "Stings").[8] Between these two extremes, we frequently hear the voice of a vacillating consciousness, nervous or desperately naive, tormented without understanding by impinging forces, or even numbed, a consciousness that hopes only for neutrality, invisibility, or even insensibility (as in "Getting There," much of "A Birthday Present," "Tulips," and "The Arrival of the Bee Box"): it is a precarious wavering between the stasis of insensibility and the kinetic stasis of full consciousness.

On the aesthetic level, Plath's poems, at their most intense and therefore absolute, represent the fusion of these extremes: a perfect work of art is one that is dehumanized, antithetical to the suffering natural self, yet created willfully out of and imaginatively destructive of that self. At their best, they represent a dying—better, an annihilation of the "trash" of multiplicity—so conscious that it "feels real," and they arise out of the blasphemous "call" of suicidal art (A, 7). For their material, they return, obsessively, to Plath's (often early) personal past, seeking out the most determined data of her natural self, trying to finalize and absolutize these private torments—to render them as impersonal as fate. At their greatest, as in "Lady Lazarus," these private experiences have been so completely absolutized that personal vision becomes also cosmic: Plath is very serious, I think, when, at the end of the poem, she refers to "Herr God, Herr Lucifer." The cosmic force that has created matter and consciousness is a totalitarian and destructive one;[9] human life is a concentration camp; the only victory possible is to become as dehumanized as fate and therefore as divine, to "rise with my red hair / And . . . eat men like air" (A, 9). To triumph over these forces, they must be destructively internalized, made a part of her active will. Such poems are far from confessional in any therapeutic sense: all possible relief is excluded by the completeness of the sarcastic self-knowledge — self-knowledge so certain and familiar it cannot even be expressed with shock and horror, as if it were something new, but only with sarcasm, as something that has become contemptible with familiarity.

II

By now it should be clear that Plath's work cannot be seen in a literary vacuum, as something unconnected with literary and intellectual trends. Plath's work must be examined in the context of post-Romantic and symbolist literary tradition, a heterogenous tradition that has, since the classic era of "modern" literature, become so recognizable as to be clichéd. I would argue that it is Plath's acceptance, conscious or unconscious, of what is most extreme in literary modernism in the late nineteenth and early twentieth centuries that allowed her so devastatingly to generalize her private torments into poetry.

Clearly, Plath's work stands as a variant of the omnipresent alienation and anxiety felt by modern poets face to face with a world that seemed increasingly dehumanized; this was not just an imaginative reaction to the shock of urbanization and industrialization in the West, but more significantly it was a reaction to a large number of new determinisms — from Darwin, to Marx, to Freud — that man had come to see as controlling not only his behavior but his consciousness as well. The realm of nature, subject to outside determinisms, was extended into man's inner sanctuary, his consciousness; the risk was that this sanctuary would become dehumanized in the process, would appear as something alien to the self-conscious person. In a consummate irony, human reason succeeded in dehumanizing itself: the new sciences, as well as new technological achievement, had, in promising increased control over environment and self, simultaneously reduced the individual's experience of freedom and control by uncovering a plurality of social, psychological, political, economic, and physical determinisms. The brunt of this was, on the one hand, to isolate and trivialize sensibility, to alienate man's consciousness from himself and his world; the result was a character like Eliot's Prufrock — solipsistic, anxiety-ridden, and spiritually empty. On the other hand, it revealed a vision of the potential of human rationality to produce something inhuman; if one dehumanized oneself, rid oneself of sensibility, moral scruple, and became pure reasoner and controller, then one could produce the inhumanity of modern warfare or the masterful techniques of dehumanization of the concentration camps.[10]

One can see in Plath many echoes of the Prufrock self-consciousness, the excruciating self-awareness that surrounds an inner void in Esther and the vacillating lyric voice that yearns for neutrality in the poems; much more prevalent is the latter problem, an analytic rationality that is not only an alienation from self but also a willed dehumanization of self. The grim portrayal of dehumanizing science that one finds in writers like Edgar Allan Poe, Gottfried Benn, and William Butler Yeats is one of Plath's important preoccupations, just as the Third Reich and concentration camps are the source of her most extreme imagery. Plath's obsession with the demonic side of medical science and the kind of disgusted attention to fleshly physical processes it is capable of producing is one that, because it deals with the human body, makes her absorption of scientific rationality both uniquely lyrical and inhuman. Closest to her in this respect would be the Gottfried Benn of *Morgue;* the capacity of scientifically objective vision to observe the most disgusting details of physical process reveals itself in "Two Views of the Cadaver Room" and "Mann und Frau gehen durch die Krebsbaracke" alike. With Plath, though, the potential for dehumanization is, if anything, greater than in Benn; for Benn, women still held potential for celebration in that they released men from their self-consciousness, even if into the "bestial transcendence" of organic nature.[11] Plath — to whom the myth of woman as natural creature and of sexual intercourse as renaturalization of the imagination was not so available — was far more frighteningly alone with this vision of an objectivity that murders to dissect nature and which itself is perceived with distaste as completely amoral, inhuman. Even more frightening is the fact that Plath, unlike Benn, pictures herself instinctively as the patient as well as the medical observer-manipulator; this fated choice stems not only from the fact that most doctors are men, while women are identified with the spontaneous nature that is to be operated upon, but also from the traditional identification of men as the recipients of the highest knowledge, whether this is, as in Eden, something glorious, or, as in the modern *Weltanschauung,* in which revelation is no longer believed in, the agony of objective knowledge and self-consciousness. Plath, moreover, in her refusal to allow any area of experience, especially the darkest, to go unexplored, attained for herself the facility and demonic power of the knower with a caustic completeness; she became both patient and doctor, violated known and violating knower. Her ruthless observations of herself — "What a thrill — / My thumb instead of an onion" — represent a willed objectivity and dehumanization more conscious than Buddy Willard's colleagues' manipulation of women in the obstetric ward. She did not divide her human self from her inhuman knowledge, her sensitivity from her rationality; she worked to fuse the two into a self-destructive unity.

Closely related to this vision of science is an aesthetic that stems from Edgar Allan Poe, one that is easily traceable through such writers as Baudelaire, Valéry, Benn, and T. S. Eliot. Just as the sensation of an absolute, inhuman knowledge is attainable through dehumanization of and alienation from oneself, so absolute poetry, a poetry laden with Satanic, Promethean, and Faustian overtones, is attainable through a dehumanization of the creator and alienation from the creator's work and audience. The myth of creation in Poe's pseudoscientific "The Philosophy of Composition" is that of a creator in complete, conscious control over his medium, allowing no accident (or even spontaneity) to interfere with his careful construction of a pure, verbal machine. The poet is, on the one hand, in absolute control of his composition; he is, on the other hand, alienated from the result and solipsistically isolated within his own impersonal consciousness. Moreover, such a poet is, as Gottfried Benn makes clear, alienated from his audience as well: he seeks to write "the absolute poem, the poem without faith. The poem without hope, the poem addressed to no one, the poem made out of words which you assemble in a fascinating way."[12]

Much of what this implies — that the formal perfection of a poem is alien, even hostile to life and nature — I have already discussed with regard to Plath. It is noticeable in such diverse areas as Plath's ability to force herself to live at times — as it appeared to others — flawlessly in the assigned social roles; it is behind Plath's comment to her husband, when he expressed dismay at the pessimism of "The Moon and the Yew Tree," that the poem was "an exercise on . . . [a] theme";[13] and it lies behind the fearful self-control in the closing lines of "The Disquieting Muses": "But no frown of mine / Will betray the company I keep."[14]

Against the background of the tradition of "absolute" poetry, however, Plath's work stands out as a remarkable intensification. Unlike T. S. Eliot, for whom the doctrine of impersonality served the ultimately humane goal of integrating the private sensibility into something, a tradition, larger than any individual talent, Sylvia Plath's willed dehumanization of voice in her late poetry sought an absoluteness of inhuman solipsism. Like that of the Byzantine art described by T. E. Hulme, form for Plath was ultimately based upon antipathy to the natural world; T. E. Hulme's description of it is extremely suggestive in this context:

> Renaissance art we may call a "vital" art in that it depends on pleasure in the reproduction of human and natural forms. Byzantine art is the exact contrary of this. There is nothing vital in it; the emotion you get from it is not a pleasure in the reproduction of natural or human life. The disgust with the trivial and accidental characteristics of living shapes, the searching after an austerity, a *perfection* and rigidity which vital things can never have, lead here to the use of forms which can almost be called geometrical. Man is subordinate to certain absolute values: there is no delight in human form, leading to its natural reproduction; it is always distorted to fit into the more abstract forms which convey an intense religious emotion.[15]

In Plath's most extreme work, the disgust with the "trivial or accidental characteristics of living shapes" is the main thematic concern; the perfection she seeks, however, is not of a realm separate from and superior to nature, but a perfection of disgust at nature, a scathingly matter-of-fact and clear-sighted intellectual satanism, not a religious emotion.

Unlike Poe, who, in his aesthetic theory, separated the provinces of aesthetics and ethics and who thus showed his kinship with "art for art's sake,"[16] Plath not only refuses to avoid moral self-analysis but also submits herself fully and willfully to it. She does not, like Benn, resort to the formulation of a permanently split identity, a *Doppelleben*, a complete separation of her natural and artistic selves, in order to survive as artist and person; her art grows out of and is enacted upon her natural self. She makes her suicide attempts, in the consciousness and intentionality with which she portrays them as having been done, become, like her poems, works of absolute poetry: "Dying is an art," a work that is performed with conscious, dehumanized, scientific precision and is, obviously, as a finished act, alienated from its creator. She does not perform suicide for suicide's sake, as a form abstracted from reality; her suicides are rich in both formal perfection and content, be it moral, emotional, or realistic-situational content: "I do it so it feels like hell. / I do it so it feels real" (A, 7).

The alienation of poet from audience made explicit in the comment by Benn cited above is something that "Lady Lazarus" also intensifies. While many of Plath's poems can be seen as written from a self absorption that is indifferent to its audience, "Lady Lazarus" reveals a further possibility, one that comes from her attempt to negate all gratification from the confessional element in her poetry. Since Poe and Baudelaire, the poet's relationship to his audience had become increasingly problematic; vis-à-vis a bourgeois readership, the artist was tempted to see himself alternatively in exalted terms — whether as aristocrat or hermetic poet — and in self-abasing terms — as outcast and contemptible poet, misfit and sterile prophet.[17] The image of the poet as representative man, one of the great achievements of Romantic literature, had turned sour; at best, this status was held onto in a strangely negative way, in that the dilemma of the poet — vacillating between extremes, alienated from society — was an extreme rendering of the common experience of man in a dehumanized twentieth-century society. In Baudelaire's "La muse venale," we find a rendering of the dilemma of the modern poet as representative outcast that is close to an image in "Lady Lazarus." In it, the poet is pictured as a starving acrobat or clown who must stifle his own tears with laughter in order to amuse a vulgar crowd; he must repress his feelings and prostitute his art for the sake of the mob in order to be their entertainer and victim simultaneously, thereby revealing to the poem's reader, in so far as he resists identification with the mob, what has happened to the sensitive person. In Plath's "Lady Lazarus," she too pictures herself as a circus figure performing for a brutalized crowd. She is, however, a freak as much as she is an acrobat; her performance stems less from external causes — hunger and the social position of the artist — than it does from self-destructive inner demands; there is absolutely no pity in her self-portrayal; and she allows the reader less room to distance himself from identification with the mob, those who search confessional poetry for the "word or a touch / or a bit of blood" (A, 8). As the poem makes clear, there is

a "large charge" for this: the mob pays the price of unconscious self-brutali-
zation, and the reader, in so far as he resists identification with the mob,
pays the price of knowledge that the pride, isolation, and ferocious blasphemy and self-desecration of the sarcastic speaker, then, seems more completely willed and final than it does in Baudelaire; the reader faces either
the speaker's loathing or at best the pitiless and isolated knowledge of an
extreme he has not imagined before.[18]

In outlining what I see as the literary background of Plath's work — by
which I mean a context of widely shared assumptions about poetry and not
a set of specific influences — I have been presenting her as someone who attained a more complete realization of elements than had previously been
achieved in poetry. By this I do not mean to argue that Plath's work is superior to that of all her forerunners; certainly, compared to Baudelaire's, it is
narrower, and the almost complete exclusion of empathy for anything or
anyone apart from her process of self-examination and self-domination contributes to that narrowness. What I do wish to argue is that it represents a
genuine renewal of and achievement within post-Romantic and symbolist
literary tradition, and that exactly here is where Plath's status as a representative of a new self-consciousness in women becomes most important to
her poetry. At every point, her poetic traditionalism is vitalized by the fact
that she is writing as a contemporary woman; and in her doing so, postures
which sometimes had remained merely theatrical or fictionalized poses became realized with the power and matter-of-factness of a sustained, personally experienced crisis. I have already suggested how this is the case with her
absorption of an explicitly dehumanized rationality and scientific objectivity: she takes into herself the hitherto male agony of rationality and self-
consciousness without the possibility of there being, somewhere, a womb or
a natural vitalism, however strident, to expunge itself in a kind of renatura-
lizing marriage. Morover, her assumption of these powers divides her radically against herself as a natural being. It is impossible, I believe, to read the
end of "Tulips" as a moment of attained harmony between consciousness
and natural process: the lines "it [her heart] opens and closes / Its bowl of
red blooms out of sheer love of me" (A, 12) are one of the most chilling moments of sarcastic irony in her work. Similarly, the fact that Plath was a
woman writing in the tradition of "absolute" poetry reappraises and renews
that tradition. For a woman to be so self-conscious, unspontaneous, and
alienated an artificer is, in traditional terms, so extreme a fusion of opposites that no merely decorative cult of artifice and unnaturalness would
seem to be possible; both the experience of the unnatural and the dehumanization of the artificer must take on a full weight of moral and experiential
horror. Alongside Plath's self-presentations, Yeats's antithetical descriptions
of women seem more than just decades out of date. The intelligent woman
who set about attaining the authority of such alienation would draw upon
her unique experience of having lived at the center of, and seen through,
bourgeois social and cultural illusions, her experience of extreme isolation

within society, and her experience of the uncommon psychological violence she faced whenever she deviated from her assigned roles. I believe Plath achieved this authority in her best work, and that her readers are now vividly aware of it: they see her as someone whose intelligence was so complete and self-annihilating as to give them a new and terrifying vision of the extremes of consciousness and fate.

Notes

1. Sylvia Plath, *The Bell Jar* (New York: Harper and Row, 1971), p. 1.

2. In a letter to her brother Warren, Plath concludes her excited description of the multitude of her activities in New York with the following statement: "oh, God, it is unbelievable to think of all this at once — my mind will split open." *Letters Home* (New York: Harper and Row, 1975), p. 120. Further references to this book will be abbreviated LH.

3. Being self-reliant is, of course, kin to but qualitatively different from being self-made. The idea of the self-made man can be seen as a grotesque simplification or a sinister caricature of Emerson's ideal.

4. At times, Plath spoke in her letters of life as a continuous struggle, a succession of successes and disappointments; the letters' dominant tone, however, is enthusiasm, interspersed with moments of despair, that has no such perspective on itself. Instances of it can be found on almost any page of the *Letters*.

5. A letter written after her separation from Ted Hughes must be cited here:

> I am even enjoying my rather frustrating (culturally and humanly) exile now. I am doing a poem a morning, great things, and as soon as the nurse settles, shall try to draft this terrific second . . . novel that I'm dying to do. Don't talk to me about the world needing cheerful stuff! What the person out of Belsen — physical or psychological — wants is nobody saying the birdies still go tweet-tweet, but the full knowledge that somebody else has been there and knows the *worst*, just what it has been like. It is much more help for me, for example, to know that people are divorced and go through hell, than to hear about happy marriages. Let the *Ladies' Home Journal* blither about *those*. (LH, 473)

6. The latter comment is, of course, stated with light self-irony. The same feeling in a more desperate time could be torment.

7. Sylvia Plath, *Ariel* (New York: Harper and Row, 1966), p. 43. Further references to this book will be abbreviated A.

8. My formulation of these two extremes is clearly indebted to George Stade's fine introduction to Nancy Hunter Steiner's *A Closer Look at Ariel* (New York: Popular Library, 1973), pp. 11–17; there, Stade draws on the poem "In Plaster" for a dichotomy between "the plaster saint" or "the outer shell of consciousness" and the "old yellow," the "chthonic presence within." I would alter the emphasis somewhat, in seeing these not only in terms of a given psychological duality, but also as two extreme resorts for her dehumanizing form-consciousness, two extreme kinds of attainment. The term "old yellow" in particular needs expansion: in "In Plaster," it is still something buried, making the thought of liberation — or, as Stade puts it, rushing "past the boundaries of selfhood" (p. 41) — seem still a creative possibility; in "Ariel," it is in the suicidal process of that liberation, borne on the power of Ariel, her horse and the spirit of poetry, a power still not subject to her will and thus causing the possibility of suicide to seem a genuine ecstasy; in "Lady Lazarus" and "Stings," it has achieved its maturity, its full, willed, dehumanized self-control and solipsistic kinetic stasis, and, thus, in its completed attainment, is as much a perfection of self-entrapment as it is one of revolt and liberation.__

9. Annette Lavers' compressed formulation in "The World as Icon," in *The Art of Sylvia*

Plath, ed. Charles Newman (Bloomington: University of Indiana Press, 1973), is relevant here: "This 'reification' which alienates the living self (and is a frequent theme in Existentialist literature) fits into the neo-platonic schema . . . whereby degeneration into matter is the sign of an irreversible degeneration" (p. 127).

10. Hannah Arendt's analysis of the concentration camps in *The Origins of Totalitarianism* (New York: World Publishing Co., 1958), pp 444 ff., vividly portrays them as the product of a dehumanized rationality. One only needs to accept the Nazi's premises; the rest is logic.

11. Michael Hamburger quotes Gottfried Benn in *The Truth of Poetry* (New York: Harcourt Brace Jovanovich, 1969), p. 133. My discussion of post-Romantic and symbolist tradition owes a general debt to Hamburger's book despite his sceptical critique of the ideal of a dehumanized literary form in symbolist literature.

12. Cited in *The Truth of Poetry*, p. 16.

13. Ted Hughes, "Notes on the Chronological Order of Sylvia Plath's Poems," in *The Art of Sylvia Plath*, p. 194.

14. Sylvia Plath, *The Colossus* (New York: Random House, 1968), p. 60.

15. T. E. Hulme, as quoted in William V. Spanos, "Modern Literary Criticism and the Spatialization of Time: An Existential Critique," *JAAC*, 29 (Fall 1970), 94. Spanos' discussion of the aesthetics of Worringer and Hulme and his comments on the modern "angelists" provide an excellent background for understanding Plath's assumptions about poetic form.

16. I am referring to Poe's theory and practice of poetry, not prose.

17. See Hamburger's commentaries of Baudelaire in *The Truth of Poetry*.

18. Another way in which Plath aggressively and chillingly alienates the reader is to use a tone of voice that can only be called sneering. "The Applicant" is written completely in this voice; the end of "Getting There," where the speaker of the poem pictures herself stepping "to you from the black car of Lethe, / Pure as a baby," contains a sneer directed inwards—the sarcasm of "pure as a baby," and perhaps horror at the possibility of a solipsism so complete that one could have gone through the surreal dream experience in the poem while remaining untouched—and outwards—a snide implication that "you," the reader, naive and unknowing, would also, if he so encountered this woman, suppose her healthy, "normal."

"More Terrible Than She Ever Was": The Manuscripts of Sylvia Plath's Bee Poems   Susan R. Van Dyne*

In less than a week early in October of 1962, Sylvia Plath completed a sequence of five poems about keeping bees at her cottage in Devon where she'd lived with her poet husband, Ted Hughes. Around Christmas, she gathered and ordered poems for her second collection of poetry and set these poems last. Why Plath chose the bee poems as a fitting close to this stage of her work is fully clear only now that we have the poet's worksheets for this period. We've known from Hughes and from Plath's own account that the poems in the last months of her life came with phenomenal speed; in the month of

*Reprinted with permission from *Sylvia Plath, Stings, Original Drafts of the Poem in Facsimile*, Reproduced from the Sylvia Plath Collection at Smith College (Northampton, Massachusetts: Smith College Library Rare Book Room, 1982).

October alone she produced over thirty in a voice that speaks with new urgency and authority. The impression given by such productivity is of a young woman romantically driven to glean her teeming brain before she ceased to be. Not until we examine the drafts of these poems do we recognize Plath's calculated choices to emend and, more often, to delete. Now available to scholars through the Sylvia Plath Collection at Smith College (which also includes her journals and books from her library), the manuscripts for the bee poems of the *Ariel* volume refute any expectation that her poems have a simple correspondence to the events of her life.

Rather, the worksheets allow us to see how a number of related narratives are superimposed on each other. Establishing the relationships among the other texts directly echoed or obliquely evoked in these poems is as critical to our understanding as recovering a fuller awareness of the relation of the text to the autobiographical events of this period. What the poet chose to emphasize as she moved from first draft to finished poem tells us more about the identity she intended to will for herself through the self-conscious act of poetic expression than about the immediate historical circumstances she may have wished to disguise or deny.

The bee poems represent a pivotal moment in Plath's career, when she attempted to articulate who she was in terms of her emotional and artistic past and to imagine who she would become. This second story, of primary importance to the poet and the critic, informs Plath's observations of the bees she bought and kept in Devon during the summer and fall of 1962. The worksheets recall other stories Plath had told about herself. The newest bee poems reword an extended narrative motif that appears in the fictional self-presentation of poems composed earlier, such as "Electra on Azalea Path" (*CP*, p. 116), the already published "The Beekeeper's Daughter" (*CP*. p. 118), and in her undergraduate verse (now available in the Plath Collection) in a poem called "Lament."[1] These worksheets also respond, for reasons that are probably both practical and psychological that I'll speculate about later, to Plath's autobiographical novel, *The Bell Jar*.

The manuscripts from this single week show evidence of considerable cross-fertilization. These texts refer to each other repeatedly during their period of gestation. An emotionally laden word or image from one poem will reappear in the drafts for several others suggesting a network of symbolic relationships that are less directly implied in the completed poems. The poems are also embedded in another contemporary narrative, the less obviously fictional story the poet told in letters to her mother during the summer and fall of 1962. Finally, the archetypal resonance of certain characters and events in "Stings," the central poem of the sequence, reminds us that Plath's personal history was enmeshed in an inherited cultural story about a poor girl whose beauty and wit provoke the hatred of her sisters, but whose merit is finally rewarded by marriage to the prince. Out of all these narratives, Plath worked to reconstruct and, more critical, to invent her history. If the events of Plath's outward life seemed to imitate the received

American fairy tales of female success, the inward workings of her poetic genius in her late art as often questioned and subverted these stories.

Plath's worksheets for the bee poems represent, I believe, Plath's search for an authentic and autonomous self. In telling the story of the queen, Plath sought to give shape to her experience as a woman and a poet. Their correspondence to outward events, the psychic dream-work of the poems in which emotions and roles are rearranged, and the poet's conscious choices for the final text of these poems all indicate Plath's violent need to appropriate the queen's story in order to believe in a sustaining fiction for her own.

During the same summer she began to keep bees, Plath became aware of Hughes' affair with the wife of another poet. In September, Plath and her husband separated. In early October the poet's fury at Hughes' betrayal was still incandescent; as the summer waned, her fear of being imprisoned in the isolated Devon cottage through a country winter with two-year old Frieda and infant Nicholas intensified. Plath looked forward to her thirtieth birthday in late October with intuitions of a premature burial. Things seemed out of her control. In short-range terms, Ted's desertion meant Sylvia was denied the relief of a vacation in Ireland exclusively devoted to their writing: more frightening, she might also be denied access to his publishing contacts for her future work. The time and energy to write — always the resources Plath had most jealously hoarded — would inevitably be consumed now in childcare. Her letters in this period worry obsessively about domestic help. With characteristic hyperbole, Plath represented her state to her mother and friends as impoverished and exhausted. She felt herself poorer than she actually was and she reported more ill health, sleeplessness, and physical incapacity than the level of her productivity during these months would seem to confirm.

Not surprisingly, central to the bee poems are issues of control, ownership, and power. The sequence includes fantasies of oppression, martyrdom or ritual sacrifice (in "The Bee Meeting" and "The Swarm") as well as dreams of terrible power (in "The Arrival of the Bee Box" and "Stings"). The drafts for the sequence reveal quite a few wishes for vengeance. Abandoned as a wife and mother, Plath tried to imagine in these poems an autonomous, potent identity as a poet. The power most essential to her survival, these poems testify, was authentic, articulate expression.

When Plath chose to conclude *Ariel* with this group of poems (an order Hughes didn't observe in publishing it posthumously), she recognized that the series pointed toward survival. She remarked that her selection "began with the word 'Love' and ended with the word 'Spring.' "[2] Nevertheless, the bee poems look backward to the unfinished emotional business of childhood and her relationship to her father as much as they optimistically claim a certain future. In the earliest versions, Plath's notations indicate that she knew the material deserved extended treatment and that she conceived of the group as an ordered sequence. Each of the handwritten drafts of the five poems is numbered consecutively, beginning with the draft of "The Bee

Meeting" and concluding with "Wintering" five days later. The first typed draft of "The Bee Meeting" is dated October 3, 1962. "The Arrival of the Bee Box" came the next day. "Stings," "The Swarm," and "Wintering" arrived at one-day intervals on October 6, 7, and 8. All but "Stings" seemed to evolve from first draft to a clean typescript of what would become the final published version within a single day. During the week of composition, Plath tried out several working titles for the group. "The Beekeeper" was her initial choice, self-consciously echoing a change in her role since the poem "The Beekeeper's Daughter" in *The Colossus*. By the time of "The Arrival of the Bee Box" on the following day, Plath had substituted "The Beekeeper's Daybook," and by the time she was typing "Stings" midway in the cycle, she settled simply for the running title "Bees." None of the publications of these poems observes her numbering of the parts of the series or any of her titles for the sequence. During the process of composition, Plath reinforced her sense of the integrity of the sequence. Her handwritten additions to the typescript of the earliest poem, "The Bee Meeting," show her correcting the running title several times. She also calculated the total number of lines in the group (266) here. Clearly she felt the five-line stanza, despite dramatic differences in line length in individual poems, was a unifying feature of the sequence. Her tabulations show the length of each poem as multiples of five; they are roughly equal, between 50 to 65 lines apiece.[3] "The Arrival of the Bee Box" (with 36 lines) is an exception. The poem seems to have been miraculously given in nearly its finished form; Plath tinkered with a few words, but did nothing to alter or extend its original articulation.

The unerring drive with which Plath composed the sequence is further substantiated by her habit of drafting her first handwritten copies and earliest typescripts of each poem on used paper. Plath worked out the first stages of these poems on the back of a typed draft of *The Bell Jar*. Whether it was frugality, a rage for order, or the dictate of her headlong muse, Plath's earliest drafts are recorded on the reserve of *The Bell Jar* papers with hardly a page skipped or used out of its numbered sequence. So consistently and carefully does Plath re-use the novel manuscript for her poems throughout this sequence that the rare occasions she uses pages out of sequence seem peculiarly resonant. Thus I'm tempted to attach special meaning to the fact that within consecutive drafts for "The Bee Meeting," "The Arrival of the Bee Box," and "Stings" several pages from the novel turn up in unexpected places. These disordered, or consciously chosen, pages include evocative material about birth, poetry, and sexual infidelity.

Likewise the few missing pages from *The Bell Jar* would lead me to speculate that we may lack intermediate versions of some of the poems. A late draft of the poem "Stings," possibly the penultimate version, has already turned up elsewhere in the Collection because Plath re-used it in writing "Winter Trees" a month afterward. However, almost without interruption, Plath worked her way through a stack of the novel's pages from back to front. Her worksheets begin with the conclusion of Chapter 6; by the time she types "Wintering" she's worked down to within five pages of the beginning of Chapter 4. About half the total of what Plath and then Hughes preserved, some 26 out of 57 pages of manuscript, appears on *The Bell Jar.* Generally, her practice seems to have been to try one longhand version and one typescript (often heavily marked with additions and deletions) of each poem before moving to unused paper for additional typescripts. Evidently the fresh typed versions were efforts to produce clean copy for submitting the manuscripts to her favorite publishers, most often *The New Yorker.* Rather than further substantive revisions, these show changes in line divisions, corrections of small typos or spelling errors, some care for the placement of the poem on the page. This stage usually includes her name and address in the upper right corner and a handwritten reminder of the date of composition.

What prompted Plath to compose on the back of *The Bell Jar*? The novel itself was typed on the reverse of Smith College memorandum paper. During her year of teaching, she'd appropriated enough of the high-quality pink bond memo pads for several drafts of her anticipated novel. It could be that she still hoarded her stock of good paper. I'm prone to believe the gesture is also tinged with a desire for sympathetic magic. The novel was safely in the hands of the printer in October; it would be published the next January. Nothing gave Plath such a sense of security and conviction of her own generativity as the tangible evidence of past success. The impressive stack of novel manuscript was at once satisfying proof of her productivity and a familiar stimulus to feelings of creativity. The determination with which Plath apparently used each page in sequence may indicate too that she felt a challenge to match her earlier prose output with her current poetic creativity. I'm inclined to think her choice was more likely emotionally over-determined than accidental. As much as Plath pretended to dismiss her novel as a potboiler, she's chosen to re-use in composing the bee poems some of its most memorable sections: Esther Greenwood's near fatal attack of food poisoning while at *Ladies' Day*, her horrified witnessing of a baby being born and cadavers being dissected on a visit to her medical student boyfriend, and finally her accidental discovery of Buddy Willard's sexual history that foils his attempted seduction of Esther.

It seems too neat to be coincidence that Plath should begin drafting these poems that respond so immediately to the break-up of her marriage with Hughes on the reverse of the chapter that marks Esther Greenwood's discovery of Buddy Willard's deception. I think Plath knew these chapters contained some of her best material. It also seems likely she was re-reading the novel while she was composing the poems, whether to reassure herself of her proven talent or because this earlier narrative touched similar feelings of vulnerability, revulsion, and betrayal. Chapter 6 contains Esther's devastating comment that Buddy's proud display of male flesh reminded her of a "turkey neck and turkey gizzards." In drafting "The Bee Meeting" on the reverse of Chapter 6, Plath's indelible image seems to have penetrated the paper to reappear again in the speaker's sense of her exposure in the second stanza: "I am nude as a chicken neck, does nobody love me?"

Although the three *Bell Jar* chapters make up the bulk of the material Plath composed on during this week, she drafts smaller sections on equally significant scraps borrowed from other sources. The Collection includes an earlier aborted attempt at "Stings" begun two months earlier. The four versions of the fragment each appear on the reverse of several poems Hughes wrote marking Frieda's birth. At the very end of this cycle of composition, on October 9, Plath types the final poem on another Hughes manuscript, this time a handwritten scene from his play *The Calm*. Both Hughes manuscripts date from the spring of 1960. These remnants of Hughes' work, which Plath had often typed for him, must have recalled the significant event of that spring two years before, when their personal and professional lives seemed symbiotically and auspiciously fused in the birth of their first child, the acceptance of Plath's first book, *The Colossus*, and excellent reviews of Hughes' second book, *Lupercal*. Again, the themes of these pages may have prompted Plath's re-use of the manuscript.

Among her present needs in these poems was to re-examine her authority in producing babies and in producing poems. She also needed to sever her identification with Hughes as her alter ego and to will herself to survive the rupture. The summer after her marriage to Hughes and completing her study at Cambridge, she was inspired by reading Virginia Woolf to vow "*No children until I have done it. My health is making stories, poems, novels, of experience.*" She hoped maternity and poetry were productively related: "I will write until I begin to speak my deep self, and then have children, and speak still deeper. The life of the creative mind first, then the creative body. For the latter is nothing to me without the first, and the first thrives on the rich earth roots of the latter."[4]

Would her faith in this optimistic analogy hold up under the test of her adult experience? Pragmatically, she questioned daily whether the birth of her babies would mean the death of her career as a writer without Ted to share the work and without sufficient income from her own publications to hire a nanny. Metaphorically, Plath attempts through these poems to deliver a reborn self who is defined independent of relationships. My guess is that by the time she typed the concluding poem in the sequence, she felt she'd done so. "Wintering" now overlies *The Calm*. The scene Plath borrows from Ted's play for scrap is, significantly, a deadly quarrel in which a wife accuses a husband of fraudulent artistic ambitions. Hughes' greater fame and financial promise as a writer, which had always caused Plath anxiety even while she pretended to admire her husband's successful headstart, must have deeply rankled the poet now alone with her infants far from the literary London scene. Material included in the worksheets of the bee poems suggests that anger rather than nostalgia led her to inscribe her own poetic autobiography on the leftovers of Hughes' literary past.

My point in describing the underside of Plath's worksheets in such detail is to restore an awareness the poet must have had during the process of composition: the story she tells about the experience of the summer and fall of 1962 is inscribed over earlier stories, her own and Hughes' past literary histories that she carefully preserved and now consciously returned to, whether for inspiration, reassurance, or vengeance. Plath's layered worksheets provide a literal realization of what Gilbert and Gubar have taught us to recognize as the palimpsestic nature of women's writing.[5] Reading the published version of the bee poems against the worksheets brings to light a covert text, vital in arriving at the later meanings but intentionally suppressed because the poet could not allow herself or, what I believe was more frequently the case for Plath, because she no longer needed to say it. From Plath's habit of beginning new work on used paper, we recover a densely figured backdrop for the poems. Even more striking, Plath's deletions from early drafts emerge in a revealing pattern.

The manuscript of "Stings," the third poem and the stunning centerpiece of the sequence, shows the most dramatic signs of revision. In August she began and abandoned an early fragment about an incident in June. Writing her mother on June 15, Sylvia describes the bees getting into Ted's hair because he neglected to wear a hat while they were setting up a hive and moving a queen.[6] Most of the afternoon's events are transmuted into the first poem in the sequence, "The Bee Meeting." However, the fragment contains several lines that survive into the final version of "Stings," most notably. "They think death is worth it." Most of the speaker's attention in the fragment is focused on the folly of the bees' suicidal attack; their end is an inglorious military defeat: "Gelded and wingless. Not heroes. Not heroes."

When Plath returned to the poem in October she used the incident to tell another story: the wounding of the male figure by the bees takes second place to the speaker's recovery of the queen. The final text is clearly an empowering fiction in which the speaker identifies with the queen who makes her mark indelibly on the heavens. Plath would rejoice in a letter to her mother just ten days later: "To make a new life. I am a writer . . . I am a genius of a writer; I have it in me. I am writing the best poems of my life; they will make my name." (Letters, p. 468) As in each of the other poems in the series, the speaker of "Stings" broods about her ability to control or order generation, the bees' as well as her own.

Her choice of the queen as alter ego is profoundly ambivalent. The queen's special status is uncontested inside and outside the hive. Without her, the hive dies, production ceases. Yet her distinguishing characteristic is her excessive generativity: her queenly estate is, in fact, perpetual confinement. In lines edged with self-irony, Plath admits in "Stings" that her own recent history already resembles the queen's biological destiny: "Here is my honey-machine, / It will work without thinking." On the other hand, to own the queen, to think for the honey-machine means to control vicariously her life force. And of course, her hive's honey devolves to the bee-keeper.

To take up bee-keeping and even more to write about it, was deeply resonant for Plath. She was self-consciously imitating her father's authority, a mastery she both desires and disdains in the earlier poem "The Beekeeper's Daughter." Keeping bees also served apparently to validate and extend her sense of her own reproductive health. Plath enjoyed the neat parallel that the same woman who taught her bee-keeping served as midwife at the birth of Nicholas. Written out of the matrix of this layered experience, the bee poems represent not only an implied meditation on the roles of daughter, wife, and mother, but a simultaneous search for an adequate shape in which to conceive of herself as a generative and powerful poet.

Just as the keeper manipulates the queen's productivity, the poet sought to exploit the queen as metaphor for her troubled questions about authorship. Repeatedly in the sequence, the powers of creation represented by the bees threaten to become agents of destruction. The speaker's conscious control over this transformation is alternately asserted and denied. Could identification with the queen confirm her self-image as naturally fertile and yet command for her the authority and liberty of independent self-expression? Could keeping the queen be consonant with releasing her from within? Remarkably, although the poet's correspondence with the queen is felt in the entire sequence, in all but one poem the queen's power is exercised obliquely. She governs the action but, except for "Stings," never appears.

In "Stings" the question of ownership, and of access to power, is initially posed with deceptive tranquility. The poem opens with a delicate and dangerous image of barter as the bare-handed speaker and an unnamed male transfer the honeycombs. The male and female figures appear innocently exposed ("Our cheesecloth gauntlets neat and sweet. / The throats of our wrists brave lilies"); the man smiles at the transaction. Yet the cleanly domesticity of setting up the hive and the honeyed sweetness of these images barely hint at the antagonism that is acknowledged in the drafts.

The anger Plath allows herself to express in the drafts clarifies the tension of "Stings." The earlier versions show the speaker engaged in a definition of herself that is primarily vengeful. She is the wronged wife and deserted mother whose verbal assault disfigures, emasculates, and finally destroys a male opponent. During the process of revision, Plath redirects her energy toward imagining an autonomous creative self in the queen. The scapegoat, who mysteriously appears in the eighth stanza and vanishes punished by the avenging bees in the ninth, has troubled many critics. He troubled Plath even more. In the first handwritten draft, he looms larger and much uglier. He also enters the poem a stanza earlier:

> It is almost over
> I am in control, I am in control.
> [Who is this third, this extra
> Who watches & helps not at all?]

The speaker's questions are meant to be rhetorical; she's identified him as an expendable, hindering force. Yet his appearance here threatens the control the speaker attempts, rather unconvincingly, to assert in her nervous, repetitive phrases. The amount of space and the intensity of affective response devoted to the scapegoat in the drafts is an unmistakable clue to the power this figure held for Plath. The scapegoat is aptly named; he's undoubtedly a composite of male authority figures whose role in the poet's generativity she would like, at this moment, to deny. "The sweat of his efforts a rain / Tugging the world to fruit" recalls father Otto Plath, the "maestro of the bees" (*CP*, p. 118), as much as Hughes, who fathered her children and, not incidentally, sometimes fathered her poems by suggesting subjects. That the speaker now feels the scapegoat is a jealous spy on her creative process is evident in his extended description which follows and which would remain in the poem until the penultimate version:

> Now he peers through a warped silver rain drop;
> Seven lumps on his head
> And a [great] big boss on his forehead.
>
> Black as the devil, & vengeful.

The name-calling and grotesque caricature in these lines make explicit the emotional projection that is underway throughout the poem. Feeling vengeful about her unexpected lack of control over her destiny, the poet sees the male figure as an evil spirit, a deformed troll who would block her rightful control of the queen bee's fertility. Her anger at the burdens of mothering, which Plath never expressed in her letters home, explodes in this burst of verbal vindictiveness; this devilish portrait of the male antagonist is one of the woman poet's monstrous offspring.

Plath labored even longer in the worksheets to give birth to a satisfying image of the terrible queen bee. She recognized in the first handwritten draft the authority of her claim "I / Have a self to recover, a queen." Nonetheless, she struggled through many variants in the next two drafts before bringing her into full view. She began this section over four separate times in her handwritten draft; she rewrites the concluding vision, beginning "more terrible than she ever was," another four times in the first typed draft. Having dispatched the male antagonist, the poet still had to envision an independent creativity for herself. Her first attempts remain largely reactive. The power Hughes has already exercised, Plath would restore in the poem to the queen. She is imagined "Rising this time, on wings of clear glass, / Over the deserted nurseries," or again. "Leaving the stiff wax, / The dead men at the lintel." She enacts the poet's unspeakable wishes to desert the nursery and to abandon "the stingless dead men." With each successive revision, the men are literally done to death: they are "stingless," then "rejected," then "old dead men," then simply, flatly "dead men." In the same line, the "deserted nurseries" remains constant and continues to appear as part of the closure in every draft until the last. Plath's instinctive first priority may have been to free her alter ego from the constraining definitions of wife and mother. Her process of recasting this vision, however, demonstrates vividly that the recovered self longs to leave her mark elsewhere than in the faces of her children. The queen's "more terrible" need is to inscribe her identity on the heavens.

I've concentrated so far on what the pattern of earlier alternatives, made visible through the worksheets, can reveal about Plath's process of self-definition. The drafts also provide further clues toward understanding a complex network of implied analogies through which the poet exploited the bees' story to tell her own. We can assume that Plath knew quite well the significant events in the queen's history, whether from her father's study, *Bumblebees and Their Ways*, or from the lore of her bee-keeping neighbors in Devon. Available to her for these poems were certain dramatic incidents: the virgins supplanting the aging queen, the bride-flight in which the males compete to mate with the queen, the mating itself which destroys the male partner and ever after confines the queen to the repetitive labor of reproducing the hive.

What the worksheets show is how the central feature of the queen bee's story — the elevation of one among many similar aspirants to the status of supreme authority — resembles other inherited cultural texts about female success. In a shadowy but insistent way, the manuscript for "Stings" reads like a subverted Cinderella story.[7] Just as the poems do not reproduce autobiography but rework it, the relationship I'm proposing between entomology and fairy tales is analogical rather than isomorphic. Finally what Plath changes in the stories she borrowed in order to tell her own is what continues to interest us in her poetic fabrication.

The protagonist, like Cinderella, is inwardly convinced of her specialness although she is bound in servitude with her unlovely sisters:

> [I think I am being cheated]
> I stand in a column
>
> Of winged, unmiraculous women.
> Honey-drudgers. [I am no drudge]
> I am no drudge
> Though for [seven] six years I have eaten dust
> And dried plates with my dense hair.
>
> And seen my strangeness evaporate.

In this version from the handwritten draft, the speaker's worry over whether a queen is hidden in the cells she's bought is linked more explictly with her own feelings of unrecognized worth. As in this passage, the worksheets frequently specify significant numbers reminiscent of fairy tales: there are eight combs of honey; the monstrous male figure has seven wens and vanishes in "eight great bounds"; the speaker's "dense hair" has been wasted in domestic drudgery for six years (the length of her marriage, although seven also exists as an alternate choice in the same draft). After this archetypal period of servitude, the heroine is ripe for a magical transformation. It occurs in her imaginative identification with the queen:

> [The new queen sings over the old queen.
> I am unstung.
> Now we are one.]

Surely the change from honey-drudger to queen bee resembles the alteration from scullery-maid to royalty. Yet in superimposing her narrative on the fairy tale motif, Plath has transformed other familiar elements. Her greatest necessity in borrowing either the queen bee's story or Cinderella's was to rewrite the ending since, in both, queenly authority is inevitably linked with producing biological heirs. Plath's female speaker gains her power not by marrying the prince but by appropriating his phallic dimensions. The queen undergoes a bodily metamorphosis that links her to masculine singularity and autonomy and leaves behind feminine dependence and derivative status.

The worksheets reinforce my conviction that throughout the poems, Plath subtly subverts the gender associations of the major figures. The mysterious male departs in haste leaving his slippers and a white handkerchief, but without leaving his name. The hidden queen meanwhile is becoming distinctly unfeminine: ". . . her long body / Rubbed of its plush — / Poor & bare, (poor & bare) unqueenly & even shameful." A specifically female identification of the queen who "dreams of a second bride-flight" is discarded in the handwritten draft and replaced with a male association, "her lion-red body." This phallic expressive queen is a rare alternative to Plath's images for the singular woman writer. More frequently these are pale, bald, deathly muses, disquieting in their sterility.

The lion-red queen who scars the sky in her flight is clearly a blood relative of the lioness in "Ariel" who flies like an arrow into the "red / Eye, the cauldron of morning" and the red-haired Lady Lazarus who devours and, I'd assume, incorporates men in her own resurrection. Plath was preoccupied with imagining a psychic rebirth for herself as she approached her thirtieth birthday. "Lady Lazarus" came two weeks after she completed the bee sequence; "Ariel" was composed on her birthday, October 27. In the endings of each of these poems, the speaker experiences her new beginning as access to power that was violent, wounding, potentially consuming. Like so many women writers before her, Plath felt her poetic authority was destructive of personal relationships; similarly, the imagery of these conclusions confesses a familiar female ambivalence about whether the self can survive once these relational bonds have been burnt, peeled off, or abandoned.

And yet the end of this power in "Stings," I believe, is distinct from the other two poems. In "Lady Lazarus," the speaker's eye is always on her audience. The energy that drives the poem is her desire to avenge, to exact a price for her pain. Lady Lazarus is originally evoked from the grave with the same epithet that brought forth the queen: "I rise with my red hair [terrible, feathery hair]." However, the rest of the handwritten draft reinforces the conclusion that her rebirth is achieved only through furious opposition to a male partner:

> [You age, & I am new]
> I am the baby
> On your anvil.
> [I eat fire.]

Truly, as the speaker confesses in the sixth handwritten version of the poem, "We are not done with each other!" At the other extreme, the speaker of "Ariel" is heedless, oblivious in her ecstatic fusion with the larger eye that brings extinction of the self. In the drafts for "Stings" we can observe the poet consciously checking her urge for retaliation and avoiding as well the temptation to self-immolation. Rather than destruction of the hostile crowd or combustion of the alienated self, what the poet requires in "Stings" is uninhibited self-expression.

I read the entire bee sequence as Plath's struggle to bring forth an articulate, intelligible self from the death-box of the hive. Significantly, one of the most terrifying words in these poems is "dumb"; it calls up the balled black "intractable mind" in "The Swarm" and "Wintering" that is inarticulate without being insensate. In "The Bee Meeting" the virginal speaker is uncertain whether her initiation into the community's secrets will spell her salvation or her death. The most extensive change the poet introduced in the drafts was to recast her initial assertions about the identity and purpose of the villagers into wondering questions. While the finished poem emphasizes the speaker's feelings of vulnerability and estrangement, the drafts reveal Plath exploring the moral power and purity enjoyed by the victim. The pattern of her revisions stresses the speaker's ignorance and thus innocence of the community's intention to confine her to the hive. Imagining herself without power or knowledge, she is also without responsibility for her speechless incarceration. Her premature burial in the queen's long box (explicitly identified in the draft as "that coffin, so white and silent"), she hints, is only the first stage of a transformation: "I am the magician's girl who does not flinch."

As Plath's speaker learns the secrets of bee-keeping, her oppression gives way to gestation. In "The Arrival of the Bee Box" she experiences frightening, uneasy intuitions of a poetic pregnancy.[8] This second poem in the sequence is worth comparing to Plath's optimistic riddle about natural childbirth, "You're" (written several months before Frieda's birth), in which the inverted baby is bound to come out "Right, like a well-done sum" (CP, p. 141). Plath uses riddles again here to give the unknown interior an articulate shape: "I would say it was the coffin of a midget / Or a square baby / Were there not such a din in it." But these are darker mysteries that require translation into intelligible language. What demands expression is perceived as alien, angry, and potentially mutinous. The grasping, teeming life within would overthrow the conventional, hierarchical authority she has allegedly acquired:

> How can I let them out!
> It is the noise that [terrifies] [appals] [alarms] [dismays] appals me
>   most of all.
> The unintelligible syllables.
> It is like a Roman mob.
> Small, taken one by one, but my god! together!
>
> I [put] lay my ear to furious Latin.
> I am not a Caesar, I am not a Caesar.

As the long list of alternate terms for the untranslated, terrible noise suggests, Plath is struck by the fundamental paradox of her creativity: owning her power to allow previously repressed material access to consciousness and to embodiment in words will destroy the temporary box of self-control. How much would she be willing to risk? Given her urge to discipline, order, and to perfect, could she accommodate a poetic birth that was monstrous? Earlier Plath had recorded in her journals her belief that "the writing lasts: it goes about on its own in the world. People read it: react to it as a person, a philosophy, a religion, a flower: they like it, or do not. It helps them, or it does not. It feels to intensify living: you give more, probe, ask, look, learn, and shape this: you get more: monsters, answers, color and form, knowledge." (*Journals*, p. 272) Her descriptions of her poetic offspring innocently minimizes the dark threat of deformity and destructiveness she confronts now.

Much as she is worried about mothering in this poem, Plath is also wittily experimenting with fathering. She re-enacts, with a subversive difference, the role her father played in "The Beekeeper's Daughter." In the earlier poem, the opulent, engulfing sexuality of the female bees exceeds the aging father's capacity to match it. He is an inadequate bridegroom for the queen bee; still he dominates. In "The Arrival of the Bee Box," the female owner anxiously asserts and retreats from her mastery. When she chooses to claim control, her tone is comically imperious: "They can be sent back. / They can die, I need feed them nothing, I am the owner." Her gestures are self-consciously unmaternal; she can starve or reject these dependent beings rather than teach them speech. This elaborate little dance around the bee box suggests to me not only Plath's ambivalence about following in her father's footsteps, but her hesitation about authoring the queen who would be born in "Stings." When she finally decides to play "sweet God" and set the bees free, her act speaks less of feminine Christ-like mercy than what she associated with male unconstrained exercise of power.

In "The Swarm," the speaker's power resides in the derisive emotional distance she keeps from her subject. She withholds her sympathy and imaginative identification from the male bee-keeper, who is a constantly smiling oppressor, as well as from the bees who are his ignorant victims. "The Swarm" has two apparent goals: venting dangerous emotions ("Jealousy can open the blood, / It can make black roses") and seeking a historical analogue for her own case. These may have been incompatible needs in the present poem. Plath's fusion of the smug, manipulative bee-keeper with the figure of Napoleon to serve as a surrogate for the absent Hughes is another complex projection. Throughout the poem, the imagery surrounding the bees and the hive is associated with Russia, while the "immensely practical" "man of business" who plunders their honey is linked with Napoleon. Systematically the poet's comparisons expose the keeper-conqueror's grandiose delusions of glory and authority.

Plath's identification of Hughes with Napoleon and the emotional landscape of the poem with Russia may have indeed been prompted by the bloodjet of jealousy. Hughes' lover, Assia, had Russian ancestry. When Plath discovered their affair she told a friend. "Ted lies to me, he lies all the time, he has become a *little* man."[9] Diminished in her eyes by his emotional deception, Hughes is shrunken by the poet's ire to a misshapen victim who is reminiscent of the troll in "Stings":

> It is you the knives are out for
> At Waterloo, Waterloo, my Napoleon,
> The hump of Elba on your short back.

Feeling Hughes' literary fame has preceded her own both in England and America, Plath may now wish to exile him to an island of unintelligibility:

> A red tatter, Napoleon! [You fatten. You're forty.]

> The last badge of victory.
> The swarm is knocked into a cocked straw hat,
> Elba, Elba, a bleb on the sea!

As clearly as these parallels seem suggested by biography, the poem's imagery is also noticeably informed by literary echoes, especially Tolstoy's *War and Peace*. Napoleon's calculating arrangement of human destiny as if it were a chess game, the slightly ludicrous representation of gunfire ("Pom, pom!"), and perhaps even a link between the unconscious life of the hive and the ineluctable forces of history were available to the poet in Tolstoy's characterization of Napoleon's Russian campaign.

Primarily, however, the figure of Napoleon functions as the key to a pattern of inversions in the poem. Just as Napoleon inverted the fleur-de-lis to form his personal symbol in the bee, the bee-keeper has inverted the significance of the outward signs of royalty ("[wifely] Mother France's upholstery") to serve, instead, as a disguise for death. The queen's "ivory palace" is, in fact, merely a "new mausoleum." The speaker seems powerless to prevent a re-enactment of her domestic history. Just as Napoleon plunders Europe, the smiling keeper repossesses the swarm, leads a new queen into servitude, and claims a "ton of honey." What the speaker wins, by contrast, is freedom from deception. She views the scene with bitter double vision:

> How instructive this is!
> The dumb, banded bodies
> Walking the plank draped with [wifely] Mother France's upholstery
> Into a new [coffin] mausoleum [with a new number,]
> An ivory palace, a crotch pine.

Again the poet trusts words, even this outburst of jealous scorn, to defend herself against such speechless wifely submission. Hughes excluded "The Swarm" from the English edition of *Ariel*, whether because he judged it inferior to the other poems of this period or because he found the portrait too unflattering is not clear.

Plath intended "Wintering," the last poem in the bee sequence, to close her second collection of poems. Like "The Arrival of the Bee Box," this poem is an attempt to give verbal shape to her inner resources. This poem lacks the manic metaphor-making wit used by the earlier speaker to defend her control over the dangerous contents of the bee box. Here, the speaker dares to descend herself to the interior. This time, rather than inchoate life clamoring for expression, she confronts a death-like stupor. Remembering that this poem was typed on the reverse of one of Hughes' plays (their shared earlier hopes for wealth) gives poignance to the speaker's hoarded reserves:

> I have whirled the midwife's extractor, I have my honey,
> [Half a dozen] Six jars of it,
> Six [gold, clear] corn nubs, six gold teeth,
> Six cat's eyes in [my] the wine cellar.

What did she have to show for this summer? This, her thirtieth year? These six years of marriage? Her stores are counted and recounted in the draft as a charm against "the black bunched in there like a bat." On the eighth of October, the distillation of experience into vision, her "six cat's eyes" that see in the dark, seemed uncertain protection against a winter alone. Whatever authority she claimed in the earlier poems as owner of the hive or as its ascending queen, she surrenders in this final identification with the bees' minimal, wordless survival:

> Now they ball in a mass.
> [Black ball]
> Black mind against all that white—
> . . . .
> [It is for] The woman still at her knitting,
> At the cradle of Spanish walnut,
> Her body a bulb in the cold and too dumb to think.

What the poet's interior promised or threatened changes throughout the sequence, the bee box delivers noisy, unruly maniacs who demand from their owner adequate translation. The wormy mahogany of "Stings" divulges a self-anointed queen. Finally, from the black hole of the cellar, the speaker utters a desperate prayer. Her difficulty with the conclusion of "Wintering" suggests her persistent uncertainty about the subject of her poetry, whether she must digest and express, in the terms of this poem, corpses or spring. The final questions are far from rhetorical in the first handwritten draft.

> Will the hive survive, will the gladiolas
> Succeed in banking their fires
> to enter another year?
> What will they taste [like] of the Christmas roses?
> Snow water? Corpses? [Thin, sweet Spring.]
>   [A sweet Spring?] Spring?
>   [Impossible spring?]
>   [What sort of spring?]
>   [O God, let them taste of spring.]

Later, in the typed draft, the poet appears more certain of "Snow water" and "Corpses" than of "Spring," which is crossed out and replaced by a tentative echo of the queen's ascent, "A glass wing?" Even through the third full draft of the poem, when all her other choices of image and phrase had been conclusively established, Plath had trouble believing in the certainty of spring as the end of her wintering. Her final revision, when it comes, moves in the opposite direction from her changes in "The Bee Meeting." Rather than introducing more questions, she wills herself to assert a compelling prophecy, continuing to hope, as she has throughout the rest of the sequence, that saying it would make it so: "The bees are flying. They taste the spring."

In her journals and letters, Plath indicates her deeply felt analogical connection between writing poems and having babies. The poems were always the more difficult birth: "I have even longed for that most fearsome first woman's ordeal: having a baby — to elude my demanding demons and have a constant excuse for my lack of production in writing. I must first conquer my writing and experience, and then will deserve to conquer childbirth." [*Journals*, p. 241] Yet she hoped the violent naturalness of her home deliveries of both Frieda and Nicholas might free the emergence of the poems. Whether consciously or intuitively, Plath seemed to discover in the autumn of 1962 that her analogies were false. Only in the heat of her anger and fear that the coming of the babies might have blocked her access to her creative powers did the poems begin to arrive as rapidly, as cleanly, and at the same pre-dawn hour.

Notes

1. Quotations from the poetry in this essay will be from the manuscripts in the Sylvia Plath Collection of Smith College. [ ] brackets in these quotations enclose material deleted by the poet during her revision of a particular draft. Citations of published poems will be identified within the text as they appear in *The Collected Poems of Sylvia Plath*, edited by Ted Hughes (New York: Harper and Row, 1981), hereafter, *CP*.

2. Ted Hughes quotes this observation in his introduction to *The Collected Poems*, p. 14.

3. This tabulation for the full sequence of five poems, made sometime after the composition of "Wintering" on October 8 and 9, suggests that "Stings" included thirteen stanzas for a total of 65 lines for some time. Thus the final revision that produces the published version (12 stanzas / 60 lines) was probably made later than October 9. The reverse of this typescript was used later for the first handwritten draft of "Winter Trees." The date on the carbon of the final typescript for "Stings" indicates a possibility as late as October 16.

4. Plath's journal entry was made in July, 1957, during a writing vacation on Cape Cod before her year of teaching at Smith. *The Journals of Sylvia Plath, 1950–1962,* edited by Frances McCullough and Ted Hughes (New York: Dial Press, 1982), pp. 164–65, hereafter cited in the text as *Journals.* The original journals are at Smith College. For convenience, page references are given to the published texts.

5. As if their stories were written on old parchment over earlier inscriptions, women writers produce "works whose surface designs conceal or obscure deeper, less accessible (and less socially acceptable) levels of meaning." Sandra M. Gilbert and Susan Gubar, *The Madwoman in the Attic: The Woman Writer and the Nineteenth-Century Literary Imagination* (New Haven: Yale University Press, 1979), p. 73.

6. *Letters Home,* edited by Aurelia Plath (New York: Harper & Row, 1975), p. 457, hereafter cited in the text as *Letters.*

7. I am indebted to Ellen Moers, *Literary Women* (New York: Doubleday, 1976) and Sandra Gilbert. "A Fine, White Flying Myth: The Life / Work of Sylvia Plath," in *Shakespeare's Sisters,* edited by Gilbert and Gubar (Bloomington: Indiana University Press, 1979), for making available the fairy tale structure, implicit in much female writing, as a useful framework for viewing these poems.

8. Sandra Gilbert persuasively establishes a series of connections between poetry and pregnancy in Plath's poems in "A Fine, White Flying Myth," pp. 253–57.

9. Quoted by Elizabeth Sigmund in "Sylvia in Devon: 1962," collected in *Sylvia Plath: The Woman and The Work,* edited by Edward Butscher (New York: Dodd Mead & Co., 1977], p. 104.

Sylvia Plath's Narrative Strategies   Margaret Dickie*

The narrative quality of Sylvia Plath's poetry has been identified with the family romance, the confessional mode, the myth of the white goddess — in short with structures that isolate the role of the individual. Such a view forces us to read in peculiar ways the number of poems, many written late in her life, which concern social situations, village life, bonds of kinship or friendship. Here the speaker must be seen as paranoid, sick, weakened, if she is to fit the lyric pressures of Plath as abandoned daughter or wife, mad queen, or mythic spirit. But the fact that this poet devoted a major portion of her creative energies to writing realistic fiction opens up the possibility that the acknowledged narrative bent in her poetry may derive from her experience as a fiction writer, and, if so, that her poetry should be read in

*Reprinted with permission from the *Iowa Review,* 13, No. 2 (1983).

that context as social commentary rather than as the rantings of an isolated victim.

Plath herself has acknowledged the cross-fertilization of the two genres. Claiming to envy the novelist, she complains that in a poem, "There is so little room! So little time! The poet becomes an expert packer of suitcases."[1] The obvious distinction between the long novel and the short poem would not bear citation if the poet did not want, in some way, to imitate the novelist. Hughes quotes Plath as saying "For me, poetry is an evasion from the real job of writing prose!"[2] And in the introduction to *Johnny Panic and the Bible of Dreams*, Hughes has remarked on the use, in her poetry, of her exercises in social observation: "poems which seem often to be constructed of arbitrary surreal symbols are really impassioned reorganizations of relevant fact."[3] According to Hughes, Plath set herself tests of observation in Flaubertian style. After visiting neighbors in Devon, she would return home and enter in her journal details such as the furnishings of the house, the clothes of the people, which often found their way into her poems. Along with the details, I want to argue, came a commentary on the life of the village which she observed so carefully.

Plath's intermingling of narrative and lyric modes may own something to Hughes' influence—since his early poems comment on social types, explore communal life, and narrate village incidents. However, whereas Hughes' poems conform to an English tradition of poetic realism and common sense, Plath's narrating lyrics are tightly-packed structures in which rapid shifts in point of view, highly selective characterizing gestures or external details, and compressed time sequences obscure the realistic base. Social commentary in Plath's poems is, thus, often read as neurotic self-revelation. It is only by attending to the narrative strategies of her poems that we can unravel their social knots and reveal the unique ways in which Plath has expanded the lyric poem. Like Robert Lowell's documentary autobiographical mode, Plath's social lyric may be regarded as one more means by which the poet has recouped the ground lost to poetry when Poe insisted on the brevity and Mallarme on the autonomy of the poem.

"Lesbos" illustrates some of the problems of Plath's way with narrative. What has struck readers of this and so many other poems by Plath is the intensity of its emotions. Plath's habitual opening of a poem with the designation of a state of mind has special force here: "Viciousness in the kitchen!" This scream, we imagine, details the speaker's own mood. In fact, the chief problem in understanding the poem is this way it starts with the announcement of an emotion unattached to a person. The reader is moved immediately to attribute it to someone. At first it seems to fit everyone: the woman whom the speaker visits who cannot stand the speaker's daughter or her kittens, the speaker herself who resents the woman's reactions, the interchange between them where distasteful confidences and advice are exchanged, the domestic life of the couple in the house. As the poem develops, however, viciousness begins to attach itself wholly to the woman visited where its roots are revealed as sexual. The speaker says, "You say your husband is just no good for you. / His Jew-Mama guards his sweet sex like a pearl." But, as the speaker realizes, he is actually quite good for this woman since he serves to deflect her spite and malice: "An old pole for the lightning, / The acid baths, the skyfuls off of you." In slumping out for coffee, lumping it down the plastic cobbled hill, this man leaves the speaker exposed to his wife's venom. Then we realize that perhaps it is not the Jew-Mama but the wife herself who has rendered this man impotent, and, reading back, we see that the poem itself provides evidence of her disgust with life, vitality, sexuality.

The artificiality of her enclosed kitchen, "all Hollywood, windowless," perfectly reflects this woman's attitudes. She not only hates children and kittens that "crap and puke," but she resists all life: the sun gives her ulcers, the wind gives her T.B. For her, sex is an act, "acted for the thrill," and the men she knew when she was beautiful said, " 'Through? / Gee baby, you are rare.' " It is a strange sexual comment actually although it is delivered here as a boast. For her the act is now over, but she recommends that the speaker take on an act, assume the siren's pose: "I should sit on a rock off Cornwall and comb my hair. / I should wear tiger pants, I should have an affair." This kind of advice must appear totally irrelevant to the speaker's situation which seems far removed from the sexually enticing. To someone "doped and thick from my last sleeping pill" and permeated with the "stink of fat and baby crap," the woman's comments might hit like "acid baths," not words of support, but caustic criticism. And eventually the speaker identifies herself and this woman as "venomous opposites."

But as the third stanza points out, the women are not just opposites; they are also linked in some way by their sexual frustration. It is this fact that irritates the speaker most thoroughly. The two women sit together on the sand, looking at the moon which "Dragged its blood bag, sick / Animal / Up over the harbor lights." The moon, that double symbol for Plath of sickness and normality, death and life, witch and protector, encloses both women — the woman visited who is later associated with its "blood-bag" and its evil qualities as a "blood-loving bat," and the speaker who is scared "to death" by this possibility, repelled by this woman and the stands she takes against procreation and life. At this point, however, the women are united, playing with the sand, "picking up handfuls, / loving it," until their playfulness turns into a manifestation of their sexual frustrations, as they are "working it like dough, a mulatto body."

Repelled by this realization, the speaker decides to leave, and packing up, she says of her hostess, "O vase of acid, / It is love you are full of. You know who you hate. / He is hugging his ball and chain down by the gate." Full of self-love or love without an object which has turned acid, this woman justifies her own marital situation as well as her advice to the speaker by flinging out at the end, " 'Every woman's a whore. / I can't communicate.' " It is another strange sexual commentary. Whores communicate, but, for this woman, being a whore cuts off communication with women. And the speaker's last view folds this woman back into her setting: "I see your cute décor / Close on you like the fist of a baby." This visit is no idle gossip, but a painful exchange between women who have not only made different sexual choices (one, procreation; the other, performance), but who are exposed at some very basic level. "I am still raw," the speaker concludes. The title of this poem is ironic: these two women cannot communicate, there is no bond between them, they cannot console or counsel each other. The rage of the speaker stems from her helplessness, from her real need for companionship, and from her sense of betrayal by this woman-actor-whore, as well as from her contempt for her.

Here, as in a number of Plath's late poems, the narrative embedded in the poem offers an explanation for the intense emotions it engenders. The poems are often hard to plot nonetheless because it is not always clear who is speaking, from what perspective, in what tone of voice. Nor is it easy to attach references to terms such as the opening viciousness or later on the isolated phrases, "O jewel! O valuable!" where nothing in the situation seems to fit the attributes. Nor are the time span and cause-effect sequence always simple to discern. Here the time seems laid out carefully ("Meanwhile," "That night," "Now"), but even in this sequence it is difficult to jump from the scene on the sand to the shift in mood announced by "Now I am silent, hate / Up to my neck." The change is only clear if we look at the images in this stanza that are carried over from the opening. Here the speaker is packing "the hard potatoes like good clothes," "the babies," "the sick cats," and in this act she is accepting all the elements that the woman visited had rejected. The "hate / Up to my neck" is directed righteously against the woman visited who herself hates every aspect of domesticity. And, it is clear, the visitor is also submerged in the hatred inside that household. The narrative strategies of this poem are designed to explain this reaction and the rejection of this hated and hateful woman.

Here Plath seems to be defending or at the least deploring the lack of the traditional values of motherhood, full adulthood for women, even the community of woman. It is thus puzzling to read critical responses to the poem that claim it is a poem about lesbianism "as an escape from the grubby details of motherhood, but always in terms of sardonic satire."[4] Or again, it is difficult to accept such an acute critic as Joyce Carol Oates when she argues that "the intensity of 'Lesbos' grows out of an adult woman denying her adulthood, her motherhood, lashing out spitefully at all objects — babies or husbands or sick kittens — with a strident, self-mocking energy." Oates claims that "a woman who despises herself as a woman obviously cannot feel sympathy with any other woman; her passionate love / hate is for the aggressors, the absent husband or the dead fathers who have absorbed all evil."[5] Oates' diagnosis of the problem is not entirely incorrect, but, in attributing it to the speaker of the poem, Oates has failed to follow the shifts in point of view. Plath is indeed describing someone who denies motherhood, but the rage of her speaker is directed *against* that woman, not in support of her.

Plath wrote a number of poems about women confronting each other, and the stories they tell involve affronts, disappointments, hurts, all stemming from the emotional inadequacies of the presumed stronger partner. A common confrontation in Plath's poems is between a controlled, life-denying, mechanistic woman, somewhat like the woman visited in "Lesbos," and a more tormented, messy, frequently lonely woman who disdains the comfort that she desperately needs but seldom receives from her organized opposite. Weak and vulnerable, she still triumphs in her misery, assured that hers is the preferable fate. This split in Plath's conception of women goes way back to her earliest "Two Sisters of Persephone" with its barren mathematical sister and the nature-loving sister who opens herself to danger, bears a king; but, while the early poem had simply named the two types, implying their opposition, the later poems set up domestic dramas, fill out the social context somewhat, characterize and specify the women. However, this realistic setting and what looks like a simple narrative frame are rendered more complex by the peculiar details that crop up: hissing potatoes, for example, children called schizophrenics, exploding ice boxes. The speed with which dreary domestic realism slips into fantasy is disturbing, and readers, wanting to fix the poems, tend to attribute this shift to a presumably deranged speaker. And of course the speaker's tone of voice which is often frenzied, clipped, assertive, as well as her fine sense of rhyming and hypnotic rhythms, all these attributes combine to characterize her as having a suspicious, even hysterical, command of the situation. If she is as beleaguered as she claims to be, how can she be so witty, so nasty, so verbally controlled, we wonder.

These interpretative problems present themselves with particular force in "The Tour," a poem like "Lesbos" about a visit, but this time the speaker herself is visited. It is a simple domestic situation: the young housewife with a messy house and messy life of migraines and retching is invaded by her "maiden aunt" with her neat and mechanical life and her artificially decorated house. The aunt has "come to call," to "be shown about," to poke into the mess, not to help or console or comfort, rather to judge and condemn, we may assume. But, since she does not get a chance to talk herself and we see her only through the speaker's eyes or we hear her only through the speaker's voice, we have no real way of knowing why the aunt has come. We must judge her by the details the speaker gives us, and they do characterize a particularly unattractive person. The speaker notes the aunt's jewelled "Gecko, the little flick!" a detail that seems to reflect the aunt's insinuating ways. We learn that the aunt's "place" is decorated with "Javanese / Geese and the monkey trees," another "cute décor" against which the speaker's real life troubles seem more human. The aunt with her "specs" and her purse and her "flat hat" seems to be a caricature of a meddlesome old maid; but some of the sympathy that we might feel for the speaker subjected to this person is deflected by her cleverly rhymed monologue which seems too much in control, too severe a judgement on the simple aunt. The tone of the poem makes it difficult to remember that the narrative situation details a real invasion of privacy, an inspection of psychic turmoil which appears to be motivated only by idle curiosity. The aunt's only reaction is to consider the speaker "bitter," "averse."

"The Tour" is interesting because it shows how Plath's narrative interests clashed with her prosodic ingenuity, or perhaps it could be argued that certain stories she wanted to tell forced from her a rhythmic and rhyming intensity. She simply could not tell them calmly at a low pitch. The situation itself in which she is made to be polite, to let in the maiden aunt, to show her about, may create the stylization of language which the speaker uses. The insistent form, the incessantly repeated phrases, sounds, rhymes, serve to distance the actual situation, to control verbally what seems like an invasion over which the speaker has no control.

"Eavesdropper" is a poem that seems to substantiate the claim that certain rather common situations elicited from Plath extremely elaborate verbal responses. While "The Tour" has exploited Plath's genius for rhyming and rhythm, "Eavesdropper" tells its story through metaphors of startling particularity and power. It is a poem of intense feeling, this time of resentment, against a nosey neighbor who seems to live off the speaker's domestic miseries. The poem opens with the straightforward exclamation, "Your brother will trim my hedges!" And what might have been a kindly offer is quickly revealed for the self-serving gesture it is, "They darken your house." The person who finally gets attacked as "Toad-stone! Sister bitch! Sweet neighbor!" in the last line is called "Nosey grower," in the opening. At first it is just a reference to her gardening skills and her neighborly interference, but the term soon suggests another kind of growth, and the neighbor becomes "Mole on my shoulder, / To be scratched absently, / To bleed, if it comes to that."

The parasitic process is almost instantly reversed, and the loathesome growth on the speaker's body now becomes the deadly addiction of her neighbor. The speaker says, "Your body one / Long nicotine-finger / On which I, / White cigarette, / Burn for your inhalation, / Driving the dull cells wild." The speaker goes on to develop the weird metaphor of cancer-causing addiction in the third stanza:

> Let me roost in you!
> My distractions, my pallors.
> Let them start the queer alchemy
> That melts the skin
> Grey tallow, from bone and bone.
> So I saw your much sicker
> Predecessor wrapped up,
> A six and a half foot wedding cake.
> And he was not even malicious.

In the context of the metaphor, we learn that the eavesdropper is a new neighbor, replacing the one who has died of cancer, and, as the poem develops we find out that the new neighbor is a native of the small isolated town, "a desert of cow people / Trundling their udders home / To the electric milkers, the wifey," in which the poem's speaker is a stranger. The neighbor is a gossip, "Tarting with the drafts that pass, / Little whore tongue," a meddler, insinuating her way into every opening: "Levering letter flaps, / Scrutinizing the fly / Of the man's pants / Dead on the chair back, / Opening the fat smiles, the eyes / Of two babies / Just to make sure." We learn that the speaker herself is sleepless, harassed by "distractions," critical of her fellow townspeople, alone with two babies.

Wishing cancer on her neighbor may seem too severe a reaction to simple inquisitiveness, and the speaker may be accused of projecting some of the rage that her domestic situation generates onto her neighbor, that hapless "Chenille beckoner." But the violence of the metaphors is in some way mitigated by the narrative situation. If the neighbor is an eavesdropper whose life revolves around the miseries she can uncover in the speaker's life, then rage may be a justified response to such a heartless invasion of privacy, such a perversion of charity. Alone, abandoned, a stranger, the speaker desperately needs a "sweet neighbor," and thus she is doubly vulnerable to this woman's prying habits. Her only protection against such an unwelcomed invasion is words, the exclamatory attack.

In addition to its name-calling defensiveness, "Eavesdropper" relinquishes itself to a kind of wild metaphorical energy, which seems typical of Plath's poetry. Plath has commented on how this process worked. In her comparison of novels and poems, she writes,

> I do not like to think of all the things, familiar, useful and worthy things, I have never put into a poem. I did, once, put a yew tree in. And that yew tree began, with astounding egotism, to manage and order the whole affair. It was not a yew tree by a church on a road past a house in a town where a certain woman lived . . . and so on, as it might have been in a novel. Oh, no. It stood squarely in the middle of the poem, manipulating its dark shades, the voices in the churchyard, the clouds, the birds, the tender melancholy with which I contemplated it—everything! I couldn't subdue it. And, in the end, my poem was a poem about a yew tree. The yew tree was just too proud to be a passing black mark in a novel.[6]

Thus, it is possible to see how the actual woman next door, a gardener and a gossip, could develop by association from "Nosey grower," to a mole to cancer, one metaphor calling up another in rapid succession. In this particular poem, however, the metaphorical development works in the context of certain social facts. First of all, it is not a yew tree but a human being who is being described, and this woman does retain some of the qualities of a character in a novel: she does live in a house next to the house of the speaker in the poem and she does certain things. The speaker's metaphorical elaboration of her may take over the poem, but it never frees itself entirely from the real life situation. So, if reading the poem, we look mainly at the social context, we may find the speaker herself malicious. On the other hand, if we attend only to the metaphors, we see how the speaker has revealed the "queer alchemy" of gossiping. It is difficult to accommodate in any single reading both the narrative situation and the metaphorical development because they undercut each other in their mutual inappropriateness. Emphasizing one, we distort the other and make wrong-headed judgments of the poem. Yet, both elements demand attention. Together, they articulate the disparity we saw in "The Tour" between verbal control and actual powerlessness. The speaker can fix her neighbor all right in a deadly epithet, but she is in turn squirming under the unrelenting attention of this "Sister bitch." They are locked in deadly combat: the speaker, imaginative and quick witted, and the neighbor, who derives her power from the sanctions of the community, "the ciphers" who need to be filled. The lyric voice in this novelistic situation is shrill, it must be admitted, but its shrillness is not without motivation. Combining modes here, Plath seeks to broaden the range of the lyric voice. The poetic patterns of rhyme and rhythm, of metaphors, may be insistent, but she attempts to pack into them as much narrative life as she can.

Indeed, in some poems, Plath seems to be experimenting with the way in which patterns erupt from narrative details, depend upon them even as they develop along what appears to be an autonomous course. Plath's speakers can turn every contingency into a discrete image, and that image into another one, until a pattern forms. It is not Plath's "lithic impulse," as Richard Howard has termed it, her desire "to reduce the demands of life to the unquestioning acceptance of a stone," that is at work here; it is rather her incredible imaginative energy, her ability to capture a whole situation or character in a single image, to open a door on a life, shut the door, and in the interval reveal the entire drama.[7] The poem which Plath entitled "Medusa" (although it might be better titled "Medea") is a good example of the way Plath's image-making works. Packing into the strict patterns of poetry some messy autobiographical incidents, Plath offers a revealing insight on motherly concern.

"Medusa" is curiously a poem about connections, those between a mother and her daughter and particularly between Mrs. Plath and Sylvia, we may assume from the biographical information of the letters. Thus, this poem is important to keep in mind when we are tempted to think of Plath as a visionary whose poetic self is isolated, unconnected with the social world, projected outward by objectifying emotions. The poem develops by a basic image pattern of bonds, ties, "barnacled umbilicus, Atlantic cable," "Tremulous breath at the end of my line," "eely tentacle." Although this imagery is more surrealistic than some in Plath's more realistic poems, in fact certain narrative details emerge in the poem. It is addressed to a mother who lives on the other side of the Atlantic, who came for a visit, intruded on some domestic fight, and whose solicitations and stifling concern cannot at this point help the speaker. The number of peculiar religious references to this mother suggests that she wants to establish strange connections, to play God or to offer herself as a sacrifice or intercessor for her child. But such interference only intensifies the speaker's misery. "Green as eunuchs, your wishes / Hiss at my sins," she says. Whatever the daughter's sin is, and the mention of "eunchs" and "kicking lovers" suggest that the daughter's sin has been to grow up to full sexuality, the mother's desire to protect her, to maintain close bonds, is really a desire to keep her forever as a dependent, to stifle her life. "I could draw no breath," the daughter complains, and her only wish is to escape the clutches of her mother's tentacles. Whether she does in fact escape is rendered ambiguous by the last line. "There is nothing between us" could indicate the daughter's wrenching free from this maternal solicitation or it could also suggest that the mother has narrowed the distance between herself and her daughter and has indeed become identified with her.

A mother who comes even when not called, who is always there "upleaping / To my water rod, dazzling and grateful, / Touching and sucking," "Squeezing the breath from the blood bells," nurtures destructive connections. She is indeed the dangerous, engulfing mother who would go on providing her children with life supports long after they have developed such systems of their own. The auntie and the eavesdropper seem to be variations on such a mother, intrusive people who would sustain themselves on other's tragedies. To frame them in rhyme or metaphor or image patterns is to contain their evil doing, to reduce them to images before they suck the life from their victims.

The four poems discussed here, all dealing with bonds between women, are not among Plath's best known work, but I think that their peculiar combination of narrative details within an intricate poetic pattern is typical of her poetry. She does tell stories, frequently complicated ones, and their point is usually to justify an intense emotion — viciousness, resentment, love — which stems from some social circumstance. There is always a central figure in her poems, but she is surrounded by a cast of characters, and the interchange between the characters is essential to the meaning of the poem. The lyric voice tells the stories by manipulating point of view — sometimes repeating what she has been told, sometimes commenting on other persons, sometimes articulating her own thoughts or emotions — and this manipulation gives the poems a narrative density which is often difficult to plot. Characters are developed by a skilled and economic use of external detail (the aunt's "Gecko" jewelry, the eavesdropper's whore tongue, the mother's "Bottle in which I live") in much the same way, although in more condensed form, that character is defined in the short story. But these poems make few concessions to prose as do the poems of Robert Frost, for example, which attempt to play down the poetic line by accommodating it to colloquial phrasing and natural speech rhythms. Plath's poems toy with their musical qualities, heighten them, even flaunt them. "You do not do, you do not do" is one famous example. In this respect, her true progenitor is probably Edgar Allan Poe although even he might have sacrificed a few narrative twists for some of those "Nevermores." Plath never does. Her point is to tell all the truth and to tell it, not slant, but straight out.

Plath's tendencies toward this narrating lyric emerged early in her work—"Two Lovers and a Beachcomber by the Sea" from her Smith College days, for example, or the equally early "Circus in Three Rings." The habits of her fiction writing, as Hughes has explained, spilled over into her poetry, and the archive of details, so like a novelist's notebook, which she was collecting not only at Devon but certainly as early as her Fulbright year in Cambridge, was a valuable source for her poetry as well as her prose. Specific accounts of Cambridge activities form the basis of "All the Dead Dears," "The Eye Mote," and "Watercolour of Granchester Meadows," among others. But the narrative strategies intensified in her late work, especially in the harrowing last months of her life when everything that happened to her seemed to have a heightened quality as if it were already in a fictional frame, and even more than that where Plath's need to explain and justify and blame and exonerate was sharpened.

The narrative element in Plath's poetry is instructive, however. When we look closely at it in her late poetry, we discover that it expresses conservative social views that seem at odds with the vituperative tone and iconoclastic attitude of the speaker. For example, the speaker in "Lesbos" is violent in her attack on the "Stage curtain" housewife in her "cute decor" who denies life. Despite her own emotional difficulties, this speaker presents herself as a responsible mother, a life nurturer, identified strongly with the domesticity that the woman she visits scorns. Again in "The Tour," the speaker contracts her own domesticity, however disruptive, with the aunt's ordered but sterile life. Here too, it is domesticity, even the survival of what appears to be a domestic holocaust, that is acclaimed. And by domesticity I mean the house and hearth (even if it is a biting "frost box" or exploding furnace or even the bald nurse) rather than the pairing of husband and wife since in most of these poems the husband is absent. "Eavesdropper" and "Medusa" are similar narratives of the invasion of domestic privacy where the sanctity of the home is the point of contention.

Although the speaker in all four poems feels estranged from the people around her, she sees herself as part of a community or family and even more she presents herself as a housewife and mother. While she admits to being beleaguered and harried in these roles, she never abandons them and they give her at the same time a kind of privilege. Thus, we see it as heartless for the neighbor to scrutinize "the fly / Of the man's pants"; but it is downright perverse for her to go "Opening the fat smiles, the eyes / Of two babies / Just to make sure." This mother whose problems may have led her to "mad soft / Mirror talk" or the "zoo yowl" has managed nonetheless to keep her children safe and happy in their "fat smiles," managed presumably against the great odds of her own unhappiness, and yet she cannot protect them from this unspeakable invader. If it is hard to reconcile someone who calls her neighbor "Sister bitch" and her mother "God-ball" with the champion of domestic virtue, it must be remembered nonetheless that such a champion might have expected to find support for her social position in the small town community and the family, and thus would be doubly hurt by gossip and inquisitiveness.

The speaker of these Plath poems shares her criticism with early twentieth-century chronicles of small-town American life such as Sherwood Anderson, Edwin Arlington Robinson, Edith Wharton, but most important of all, her position here is close to views expressed by Hughes both in his poetry and fiction. Like Plath, these writers too harbored hopes for a community of values and meaning where they discovered only pettiness, destructive gossip, even viciousness. In Plath's poetry, of course, this slightly old-fashioned point of view of the sanctity of domesticity is wedded to a tormented modern consciousness. Unlike the puzzled and confused narrator of an Anderson story or the eccentric but hidden character of a Robinson poem, the speaker in Plath's poetry is forthright in her attacks on the community which she imagines as itself predatory. She does call names as old Eben Flood does not, but these names are prompted by the same despair and loneliness and estrangement that drove Flood to drink. There is this difference between a Plath speaker and a Tilbury town man, however: Flood's misery can be attributed to changing times, to worlds overpassed; but Plath's woman seems to have suffered some private disaster, some violent emotional upheaval totally unconnected with the sociology of the small town. It is this fact, of course, that attracts neighbors or family members as Ted Hughes said in "The Casualty": "Sympathies / Fasten to the blood like flies." In "a desert of cow people," her miseries would have the fascination of a side show attraction, and understandably she resents this fact.

Since *The Bell Jar* offers ample evidence of Plath's scorn for domesticity and procreation, the question remains whether the narratives discussed here are some aberrant sub-plot in her life's larger story or if indeed the conservative social position these narratives relay is central to her best work. It is true that her poems generally lack the acerbic force of her attack in *The Bell Jar* on male-dominated marriage and cow-like pregnancy, but they can jab at the lust of the empty-headed man for a mechanical doll-wife ("The Applicant") or reduce the pregnant woman to a comic "melon strolling on two tendrils" ("Metaphors"). Still these particular poems reveal not so much a scorn for domesticity or pregnancy as an attack on the conventions or a playful regard for the grotesque quality of pregnancy. When she treats these subjects directly in her poems, Plath displays a kind of knowing humor.

It is when Plath sets domesticity and children in a social situation that her attitudes become more conservative. From "The Manor Garden" on, she fears for her children's safety, longs to protect them in a family whose heritage is "Hours of blackness" ("The Manor Garden") and in a world that "will kill and eat" ("Mary's Song"). Behind these fears may be her own longing for a father to protect her, as we can see from the narrative details in "Daddy" which recite a life-long effort to find such a father, a loving search for roots and for a language with which to address him. When she realizes that she will be forever frustrated in this search, she grows spiteful, attacks the father, and rejoices when the villagers join her in stamping on him. Beneath the malice and vindictiveness of the speaker's tone is a narrative that recounts conservative, not to say regressive, efforts to restore the lost father, to reconstitute the conventional family disrupted by his death. When she kills him at the end, she does so by aligning herself with a new family, the community which supports her rage. The Plath speaker here hates her father not for what he was (although she tries to castigate him as a Fascist) but for what he was not (the conventional, ever-present, protective father). He was too little the dominant figure in her life, not Fascistic enough, as it turns out.

It is true that Plath's late poetry is dominated by a rising figure who seeks to escape domesticity, children, contingency itself: the figure flying into the "cauldron of morning" ("Ariel"), rising with "red hair" to "eat men like air" ("Lady Lazarus"), dissolving into "a pure acetylene / Virgin" ("Fever 103°"). She seems to be a figure of radical energy. But balancing her is a socially conservative figure. She is the survivor of "Little Fugue" "Arranging my morning. / These are my fingers, this my baby," "The woman, still at her knitting, / At the cradle of Spanish walnut, / Her body a bulb in the cold" of "Wintering", the mother "cow-heavy and floral / In my Victorian nightgown" of "Morning Song," the woman who "would like to believe in tenderness" in "The Moon and the Yew Tree." She is finally the woman in "Edge" who folds her children "back into her body as petals / Of a rose close." For her, the blood jet may be poetry, but the children are "two roses." It is this woman whose outbursts at the community stem not from her own derangement or psychic turmoil but from the inadequacies of the larger social circle in supporting the smaller domestic circle of mother and child. This woman embodies the virtues of survival, or nurturing, or protection, against a community that would destroy, intrude, and condemn. She may be witty and nasty but underneath is a tone of self-righteousness. She is right, and her narrative strategies are designed to explain and justify her rage against those who are wrong.

Notes

1. Sylvia Plath, "A Comparison," *Johnny Panic and the Bible of Dreams* (New York: Harper Row, 1979), p. 62.

2. Ted Hughes, "Introduction," *Johnny Panic*, p. 3.

3. Hughes, ibid., p. 2.

4. Edward Butscher, *Sylvia Plath: Method and Madness* (New York: Seabury Press, 1976), p. 323.

5. Joyce Carol Oates, "The Death Throes of Romanticism: The Poems of Sylvia Plath," *The Southern Review*, IX (July 1973), p. 517.

6. Plath, "A Comparison," *Johnny Panic*, pp. 62–63.

7. Richard Howard, "Sylvia Plath: 'And I have No Face, I have Wanted to Efface My-self;'" in Charles Newman, ed., *The Art of Sylvia Plath* (London: Faber and Faber, 1970), p. 79.

Apprenticed in a Bible of Dreams:
Sylvia Plath's Short Stories

Melody Zajdel*

Although Sylvia Plath wrote approximately 70 short stories, only 10 were published in her lifetime. Since her death, three appeared in popular magazines and an additional seven stories were printed in the recently published volume *Johnny Panic and the Bible of Dreams*. What is interesting to the reader of these twenty stories is the consistency with which Plath dealt with the same materials and themes throughout her fiction. Although her prose works span over ten years, much of that time seems spent in writing and rewriting the same story, the story which reaches its fruition in *The Bell Jar*. This is particularly obvious in several of the short stories published after her death ("Tongues of Stone," "Sweetie Pie and the Gutter Men," and "Johnny Panic and the Bible of Dreams"). These stories, along with "In the Mountains," (published in the *Smith Review*, 1954), serve almost as apprentice pieces for key scenes in *The Bell Jar*, containing episodes with the same actions, characters, images, sometimes even the same words. Beyond these apprentice pieces, however, a reader discovers that not only do Plath's stories stylistically show her direct movement into the writing of *The Bell Jar*, but they also mirror her continued thematic concern with two interrelated ideas: first, the idea of living and sustaining a life of the imagination, and second, the socio-mythic form of this theme, what Josephine Donovan has called "the sexual politics of Sylvia Plath."[1] Although Plath's short stories will probably not change her reputation from poet to proficient popular fiction writer (an epithet that Hughes suggests she desired[2]), they are markers to understanding Plath's skill in her finished fictional effort, *The Bell Jar*, just as *The Colossus* stands as a necessary apprenticeship to the final poems of *Ariel*.

Hughes indicates that Plath "launched herself into *The Bell Jar* in 1960."[3] But at least the four stories mentioned above, written between 1954 and 1959, deal with some of the same material. One in particular, "Tongues of Stone" (1955), uses the experience of a young girl's nervous breakdown much as Plath uses it in *The Bell Jar*. At least six key incidents appear first in this story, before being transformed and interpolated into the novel. The start of the breakdown is the same in both pieces. The main character is suffering from extreme apathy, anxiety and insomnia. In *The Bell Jar*, Esther enters the first clinic, Walton, after three weeks of not sleeping; in

*This essay was written specifically for this volume, and appears here for the first time by permission of the author.

"Tongues of Stone," the character is at the end of two months of sleeplessness. In setting the scene, the "Tongues of Stone" narrator explains "It was sometime in October; she had long ago lost track of all the days and it really didn't matter because one was like another and there were no nights to separate them because she never slept anymore."[4] Both young women try to forestall their depression by looking for intellectual occupations to, literally, kill time. Each tries particularly hard to read, only to find the print on the pages of their books indecipherable, "dead black hieroglyphs" (JP, 263) and "fantastic, untranslatable shapes, like Arabic and Chinese".[5] Both are denied solace by their alienation from the dead intellectual world represented by the printed books. But more obvious in their similarities than these parallels of general circumstances are the active steps in their attempted suicides and their subsequent treatments. Looking at these steps, the reader can see Plath's movement from a rather flat narrative to the evocative and powerful personal voice of the novel. The apprentice piece has all the isolated units but doesn't have the developed style, theme or political focus of *The Bell Jar*.

First, in both "Tongues of Stone" and *The Bell Jar*, each of the girls visits her sleeping mother and comes to an important realization: there is neither parental security nor any meaningful reason to continue being in either the present or the future. In "Tongues of Stone," the main character slips into her mother's bed and, lying beside her, "listen[s] to the thin thread of her mother's breathing, wanting to get up and twist the life out of the fragile throat, to end at once the process of slow disintegration which grinned at her like a death's head everywhere she turned" (JP, 265). The girl (who remains nameless throughout the story), has sought out her mother. By getting close to her, the girl hopes to stave off the fears and despair she feels. But the mother can neither solace nor protect her daughter. Asleep, she is even unaware of the girl's presence. She is perceived by her daughter as fragile and disintegrating, not a possible haven or shelter against the death her daughter sees everywhere, even in her. This same incident occurs in *The Bell Jar*, but some of the narrator's feelings have changed. In the novel, the mother is less mutual victim, another fragile throat which can be stopped, and more a despised perpetrator of circumstances, a guardian of the world's values and actions. The main character, Esther, looks at her sleeping mother, listens to her piggish snores, and explains ". . . for a while it seemed to me that the only way to stop it [the sound in her mother's throat] would be to take the column of skin and sinew from which it rose and twist it to silence between my hands" (BJ, 101). Not only is the mother more unattractive in this version (being piggish and irritating), but the action of strangling her is not done to stop a mutual disintegration, a slow and painful change, but more to assuage Esther's aggressive dislike of what her mother represents. She and her mother are struggling against one another, tussling between them expectations for Esther's future and Esther's own inchoate desires. Neither is totally passive. Esther views the strangling not as euthanasia, but as a means of effectively changing her own world.

Where in "Tongues of Stone" the girl creeps into her mother's bed for solace, in *The Bell Jar* Esther merely looks at her mother from the bedroom door, not seeking communion with a source of safety so much as observing the enemy.

After this scene, both stories show the female protagonist trying to escape the world around her by hiding under the mattress of her bed. In each case, she hopes to be crushed, to never reawaken to the oppressive world of sleepless, meaningless, comfortless living. In "Tongues of Stone," the girl leaves her mother's bed, "Creeping back to her own bed, then, she had lifted up the mattress, wedging herself in the crevices between mattress and bedsprings, longing to be crushed beneath the heavy slab" (JP, 265). More immediately, the same scene is enacted in *The Bell Jar:* "I crawled between the mattress and the padded bedstead and let the mattress fall across me like a tombstone. It felt dark and safe under there, but the mattress was not heavy enough. It needed about a ton more weight to make me sleep" (BJ, 101). In the second scene, the tone is sharper. The slab has been defined as a tombstone, the oppression and death imagery are more overt. Plath's character recognizes consciously what she is seeking (the safe dark of death) and what it would take to achieve it (about a ton more).

Both girls then attempt suicide (actually reach out to take hold of the darkness), but are discovered at the last moment and saved. Upon first awakening from their drugged state, each believes herself blind. In "Tongues of Stone," the narrator explains that

> At first they thought she would be blind in that eye. She had lain awake the night of her second birth into the world of flesh, talking to a nurse who was sitting up with her, turning her sightless face toward the gentle voice and saying over and over again, "But I can't see, I can't see."
>
> The nurse, who had also believed that she was blind, tried to comfort her, saying, "There are a lot of other blind people in the world. You'll meet a nice blind man and marry him someday."
>
> (JP, 266)

In this scene the nurse is an acknowledged presence, someone known and staying *with* the girl, not just beside her. She is described as gentle and comforting, albeit not well-informed. This same scene is recreated in *The Bell Jar*, only this time the nurse's presence is not so immediately felt as sympathetic.

> I opened my eyes.
> It was completely dark.
> Somebody was breathing beside me.
> "I can't see," I said.
> A cheery voice spoke out of the dark. "There are lots of blind people in the world. You'll marry a nice blind man someday."
>
> (BJ, 140)

Although the changes are slight, they do match up with the more sinister and detached feelings of Esther in the novel. The nurse in the second presentation is not known immediately, she is somebody. She is not with the girl, she is beside her. Although she is cheery, unlike the original image of comforting presence, we have no reason to assume her intentions are personal; rather, they smack of habitual, professional cheeriness.

Each girl also tries to strangle herself, although the timing of the attempt varies. In "Tongues of Stone," the girl is in the sanatorium, frustrated and depressed that the insulin treatment is not working. She considers strangulation as a means to end the continuing depression and self-disgust.

> One night she hid the pink cotton scarf from her raincoat in the pillowcase when the nurse came around to lock up her drawers and closet for the night. In the dark she had made a loop and tried to pull it tight around her throat. But always just as the air stopped coming and she felt the rushing grow louder in her ears, her hands would slacken and let go, and she would lie there panting for breath, cursing the dumb instinct in her body that fought to go on living.
>
> (JP, 266)

In *The Bell Jar*, Esther considers and experiments with strangulation as one possible form of suicide, trying a number before the final attempt with sleeping pills. At first, in her version of the scene, she hopes to hang herself, but finding no adequate beam in the house, she explains,

> . . . I sat on the edge of my mother's bed and tried pulling the cord tight.
>
> But each time I would get the cord so tight I could feel a rushing in my ears and a flush of blood in my face, my hands would weaken and let go, and I would be all right again.
>
> Then I saw that my body had all sorts of little tricks, such as making my hands go limp at the crucial second, which would save it, time and again, whereas if I had the whole say, I would be dead in a flash.
>
> (BJ, 130)

In this revised scene, the body's instinctual response is more malevolent; it is not simply "dumb," but it has "all sorts of little tricks." In *The Bell Jar* the character's paranoia and mind-body split is strongly felt. The world is active in its oppression, the body active in its rebellion to the will.

Finally, both stories describe the insulin treatment used to combat the character's suicidal depressions. Each story starts with the appearance of a nurse to administer the insulin injection. In "Tongues of Stone,"

> At seven the nurse came in to give the evening insulin shot. "What side?" she asked, as the girl bent mechanically over the bed and bared her flank.
>
> "It doesn't matter," the girl said. "I can't feel them any more."
>
> The nurse gave an expert jab. "My, you certainly *are* black and blue," she said.
>
> (JP, 267)

In *The Bell Jar*, the characters are both detached as well. The section is a little less calm, however, since we are at least aware of what Esther sees when she views herself.

> The nurse gave a little clucking noise. Then she said, "Which side?" It was an old joke.
>   I raised my head and glanced back at my bare buttocks. They were bruised purple and green and blue from past injections. The left side looked darker than the right.
>   "The right."
>   "You name it." The nurse jabbed the needle in, and I winced, savoring the tiny hurt.
>
> (BJ, 157)

It is also useful to note that Esther does feel something in this episode: Pain. And that is welcomed, for it is something instead of the dull apathy of the first scene.

The final movement in each story is the breakthrough caused by the girls' reactions to the insulin treatment. In each case, the reaction signals the momentary lifting of the oppressive atmosphere, the depression, and bell jar which each of the characters is laboring under. After what has seemed a fruitless waiting in "Tongues of Stone," a period where even the sun's warmth is absent from the day, the girl's reaction occurs, accompanied by a proliferation of growth and light images.

> In the blackness that was stupor, that was sleep, a voice spoke to her, sprouting like a green plant in the dark.
>   "Mrs. *Pat*terson, Mrs. *Pat*terson, Mrs. *Pat*terson!" the voice said more and more loudly, rising, shouting. Light broke on seas of blindness. Air thinned.
>   The nurse Mrs. Patterson came running out from behind the girl's eyes. "Fine," she was saying, "fine, let me just take off your watch so you won't bang it on the bed."
>   . . . .
> The dark air had thinned and now it lived. There had been the knocking at the gate, the banging on the bed, and now she was saying to Mrs. Patterson words that could begin a world: "I feel different. I feel quite different."
>   "We have been waiting for this a long time," Mrs. Patterson said, leaning over the bed to take the cup, and her words were warm and round, like apples in the sun. "Will you have some hot milk? I think you'll sleep tonight."
>   And in the dark the girl lay listening to the voice of dawn and felt flare through every fiber of her mind and body the everlasting rising of the sun.
>
> (JP, 267–68)

As the ending of the short story, this scene optimistically portends a healing conclusion. The sun has returned; in fact, it is speaking directly to the girl. Both the blackness she emerges from and the real world (represented by the nurse) are positive; the first is a plant; the second, warm and round as an apple. The air is clear, the light quite literally and figuratively dawns. The girl herself speaks words and listens to a voice which apparently signals the start of a new world. In *The Bell Jar*, the parallel scene follows the same progression, but has a slightly different tone.

> I had fallen asleep after the evening meal.
>
> I was awakened by a loud voice, *Mrs. Bannister, Mrs. Bannister, Mrs. Bannister, Mrs. Bannister.* As I pulled out of sleep, I found I was beating on the bedpost with my hands and calling. The sharp, wry figure of Mrs. Bannister, the night nurse, scurried into view.
>
> "Here, we don't want you to break this."
>
> She unfastened the band of my watch.
>
> "What's the matter? What happened?"
>
> Mrs. Bannister's face twisted into a quick smile. "You've had a reaction."
>
> "A reaction?"
>
> "Yes, how do you feel?"
>
> "Funny. Sort of light and airy."
>
> Mrs. Bannister helped me sit up.
>
> "You'll be better now. You'll be better in no time. Would you like some hot milk?"
>
> "Yes."
>
> And when Mrs. Bannister held the cup to my lips, I fanned the hot milk out on my tongue as it went down, tasting it luxuriously, the way a baby tastes its mother.
>
> (BJ, 164)

In this version of the scene, several things have changed. In "Tongues of Stone," the girl is the first one to focus on the change in both herself and her surroundings. She feels "different" and it is not just her, but the atmosphere, the world, which is light and airy. In *The Bell Jar*, Esther feels "funny," "light and airy." But we have no sense of whether the external world is in accord. In "Tongues of Stone," the girl seems to have become attuned again to the physical, natural world. In *The Bell Jar*, the natural world referred to is that of mother and child, not the most hopeful image when taken in the context of the heavily negative connotations given to that relationship throughout the rest of the novel, both before and after this scene. (Consider, in particular, Esther's own relationship with her mother, her sense of all mothers — hers and Buddy's — as circumscribing her opportunities, the notion that becoming a mother herself would kill her chances to be a writer, a complete person in her own right.)

Obviously, Plath is using the same material, even some of the same phrases and images, in this early story and *The Bell Jar*. Equally obviously, there are some significant differences in her presentations, many of which seem caused by an increased thematic awareness on Plath's part in the novel. In "Tongues of Stone," we have a description more than a clearly delineated conflict. The causes of the breakdown, the fears for the future, the active resistance of the girl to both medical help and her surroundings, are never presented. It seems doubtful that the girl herself is aware of all the factors surrounding her previous actions. We are given a third-person, limited view of the events. All conflicts and conditions leading to the suicide attempt are cloaked. In the expanded scope of *The Bell Jar*, on the other hand, the older Esther, the narrator, has moved to a recognition, frequently frustrated and angry, of the social and familial forces which lead to her breakdown. Her mother is seen in sharply critical relief. Her male doctor is at best indifferent to Esther's struggle; at worst he denies its value. It is a world of stultified options and intellectual sterility which places Esther under the bell jar. It is this thematic awareness even more than a stylistic change which gives *The Bell Jar* a power lacking in the earlier story. This same factor accounts for much of the difference between the other apprentice pieces and the novel.

"In the Mountains" also rehearses a scene for *The Bell Jar*. Isobel, a young college woman, goes to visit her boyfriend, Austin, who has been in a TB sanatorium for six months. (This parallels Esther Greenwood's later visit to Buddy Willard under the same constraints.) Isobel comes to visit, to find an unchanged Austin, "Still strong, she thought, and sure of himself . . ." (JP, 277). But she comes also with the awareness that "everything was changed for her," (JP, 277), and it is this awareness that she needs to articulate to Austin. In a discussion about marriage in general, their differences are highlighted. Austin implies his desire for a commitment, a marriage, while Isobel, in her newly changed persona, explains that she is not ready to consider such a step. " 'Affairs are one thing,' she said. 'But signing your life away because you're lonely, because you're afraid of being lonely, that's something else again. . . . That's the way I figure it now anyway.' " (JP, 278). For the first time in their relationship, Austin is vulnerable and expresses his need for Isobel. But part of his attraction to her is still the result of seeing her as appropriate to be his wife. Austin notes she is attractive, just as his doctor's wife is attractive, just as a doctor's wife should be. He sees her as fitting a role, a role which he needs filled, not necessarily one she *wants* to fill. He recalls all the things they've "been through together," but where they serve to be fond memories for him, Isobel recalls "how it was all so lovely and hurting then. How everything he said had hurt her" (JP, 282). Where he is now able to proclaim his need for her, she is no longer as needing of him, nor does he offer her anything beyond his need. In the end, when he reaches out for her, thinking to claim her, she is stricken, immobilized and feels them surrounded by a landscape "hushed and still" (JP, 284), frozen and deathlike. In the story, the reader is made aware of the change in Isobel, as we are similarly made aware in *The Bell Jar* of the change in Esther. However, in "In the Mountains," there is less overt understanding of the cause of Isobel's change. The novel form allows Plath to finally put all the isolated scenarios together, to juxtapose them until the common conflicts become clear. Esther's rejection of Buddy is more clearly a rejection of not just the individual, but also the prescribed role which her relationship to Buddy (as his future wife) threatens to lock her into. Likewise, the almost malicious pleasure that Buddy feels when Esther breaks her leg (and thus becomes less threatening, less independent) is missing from the short story. In the story, the reader can still pity Austin, if only slightly; in the novel, Plath gives us little option to disliking Buddy almost as much as Esther does because we see the large issues capitulation to his vulnerability and vision would represent.

In "Sweetie Pie and the Gutter Men," Myra Wardle, a young, childless, married woman who has lately "started wondering about babies," (and simultaneously has taken to "tearing off low-hanging leaves or tall grass heads with a kind of wanton energy"), (JP, 140), tells of viewing a birth with her medical school boyfriend while she was in college. The details she remembers and the horror she feels at the process are reiterated almost word for word by Esther Greenwood. Myra remembers walking in the hospital, past "blind, mushroom-colored embryos in the jars" and "four leather-skinned cadavers, black as burnt turkey . . ." (JP, 138). Esther, too, sees four cadavers with "leathery, purple-black skin," and big glass jars of fetuses (BJ, 51). But what lingers with both women most strongly is the memory of the drugging of the patient and her subsequent forgetfulness of the pain of childbirth. Both blame the invention of the drug, which doesn't stop the pain, just induces later forgetfulness, a "twilight sleep" (JP, 139; BJ, 53), on the sinister intents of men. Both view men as acting for their own good without a concern for women's experience. Myra first describes her horror at the false security induced by the drug.

> Although erased from the mind's surface, the pain was there, somewhere, cut indelibly into one's quick — an empty, doorless, windowless corridor of pain. And then to be deceived by the waters of Lethe into coming back again, in all innocence, to conceive child after child! It was barbarous. It was a fraud dreamed up by men to continue the human race; reason enough for a woman to refuse childbearing altogether.
>
> (JP, 139)

Esther later recalls the same scene, using even the image of "that long, blind, doorless and windowless corridor of pain" (BJ, 53) and noting that if women knew or remembered the pain they would forget about having children altogether (BJ, 53). More than "Tongues of Stone," written in 1955, "Sweetie Pie and the Gutter Men," written in May of 1959, shows not just the same incident but Plath's increased thematic awareness. Myra has begun to focus on her discontent — more importantly, finding its source in the negative implications of her role as wife / mother. She finds herself having to bite back her views concerning being "just" a mother. She is depressed at the thought of joining the rest of women in this reproductive role and blames men for devising means to keep women unconscious of the pain involved. For Myra, this pain extends beyond the labor process and stretches into the rest of her potential lifetime as a mother. Myra's depression is presented less as a result of a personality defect and more as an understandable disgust with an undesired, unfulfilling expectation. She has begun to move into a clearer awareness of gender delineation and the politics of sexuality.

The fourth short story, "Johnny Panic and the Bible of Dreams," contains two shorter images rather than major events that move into *The Bell Jar.* The first is simply the description of a woman who enters the psychiatric clinic and whose dream the narrator seeks to record. The woman was brought to the Emergency Room because her tongue was stuck out and she couldn't return it to her mouth. This occurred during a party for her French-Canadian mother-in-law, whom she hated "worse than pigs" (JP, 156). This same character appears equally briefly in the novel, in the state psychiatric ward, as Mrs. Tomolillo. Again, she has a hated French-Canadian mother-in-law, and again her symptom is the uncontrollable tongue which sticks out until it's swollen. The second image is more powerful, for it is crucial to both the story and the novel: the narrator's experience of electroshock treatment. In "Johnny Panic and the Bible of Dreams," the final scene is the administration of the shock treatment. In the misapplied shock, the narrator sees her first direct sight of Johnny Panic himself. He comes into view as she is "shaken like a leaf in the teeth of glory," while "the air crackled with blue-tongued lightning-haloed angels" (JP, 166). The treatment is likewise described in *The Bell Jar,* when Dr. Gordon fails to properly administer the shock. "Then something bent down and took hold of me and shook me like the end of the world. Whee-ee-ee-ee-ee, it shrilled, through an air crackling with blue light" (BJ, 117).

What distinguishes this story from the three previously discussed is that for the first time the story is as strong a narrative as the novel. In part, this is because of the stylistic change to first-person. For the first time we have a conscious persona dealing with the experience of the breakdown. There is no additional narrator-filter to feeling and understanding the character. Further, "Johnny Panic and the Bible of Dreams" is a short story which contains a very central theme of Plath's, one which she is building up to in *The Bell Jar* and one which has appeared in other stories throughout the '50's not related to the breakdown: the need to validate the realm of imagination and possibility against the "real world," the world of limited and stereotyped roles. In "Johnny Panic," for the first time in the stories relating the story of her breakdown, Plath's narrator is not becoming aware of the conflict, she already understands it and has begun to act in response to it. She has taken up a battle that the other three narrators are just discovering might exist. It is this recognition and choice of action which thematically is the focus to almost all of Plath's fiction, even those stories which stand apart from the drafting of *The Bell Jar.*

Given the centrality of this theme, it is not totally coincidental that the two strongest characters in Plath's fiction, Esther Greenwood and the narrator of "Johnny Panic," are writers. Plath's major fictional characters, from Elizabeth Minton (in "Sunday at the Mintons'," 1952) forward, are all incipient artists. That is not to say that all, or most, are professional artists. Rather, they are, as so many characters in feminist fictions, engaged in creating themselves, reshaping the world around them to give significance to the actions and places in which they spiritually and actually reside. They come to see themselves as the creation of an imagination at odds with the culture and people around them. They are constantly striving to keep at bay the deadening, self-invalidating, oppressive sterility of the "real world," a world which devalues their experience and prohibits new patterns of thought and self awareness. Their true world is the realm of imagination, even if this imagination leads to socially defined madness. When not so extremely labeled, the characters are at least alienated from the technical, coldly rational world they exist in. They escape from this real world to the one of imagination, for none can accept a world which denies the power of fantasy, denies the right of each individual — regardless of gender — to be fully developed and fulfilled, denies (then electrically and chemically obliterates) the fears and thoughts of adults without replacing them with stronger beliefs and dreams.

Thematically, the feared death of the imagination runs throughout all of Plath's fiction in the decade preceding publication of *The Bell Jar*. Plath's characters reverse Hamlet's cry: they wish to dream, not sleep, much less just exist. As Plath explains in the "Cambridge Notes" excerpt from her journals:

> What I fear most, I think, is the death of the imagination. When the sky outside is merely pink, and the rooftops merely black; that photographic mind which paradoxically tells the truth, but the worthless truth, about the world. It is that synthesizing spirit, that "shaping" force, which prolifically sprouts and makes up its own worlds with more inventiveness than God which I desire. If I sit still and don't do anything, the world goes on beating like a slack drum, without meaning. We must be moving, working, making dreams to run toward; the poverty of life without dreams is too horrible to imagine; it is that kind of madness which is worst: the kind with fancies and hallucinations would be a Bosch-ish relief.
>
> (JP, 260)

The main characters in "Sunday at the Mintons' " (1952), "Superman and Paula Brown's New Snowsuit" (1955), "The Wishing Box" (1956), "All the Dead Dears" (1956 / 57), "Stone Boy with Dolphin" (1957 / 58), and "Johnny Panic and the Bible of Dreams" (1958) all express a need and determination to foster and live in a world governed more by that "synthesizing spirit," that God-like personal inventiveness, than the social strictures of the people around them. For example, Elizabeth Minton's fanciful daydreams are continually interrupted by her brother Henry, a demanding but practical man. Elizabeth's image for their differences is summed in her imagined view of the interior of their minds. Henry's mind would be "flat and level, laid out with measured instruments in the broad, even sunlight. . . . The air would be thick with their accurate ticking." (JP, 301). Conversely, her mind would be "a dark, warm room, with colored lights swinging and wavering . . . and pictures . . . [and] from somewhere sweetly coming, the sound of violins and bells" (JP, 301). Clearly her preference (and the author's) is for the vague impressionist world of her mind.

Likewise, in "The Wishing Box," Agnes Higgins despairs of her loss of dreams. She can remember "her infinitely more creative childhood days" (JP, 206), but she seems doomed to be unable to recapture them in the adult world in which she now lives. Suicide finally releases her from her empty reality to another world, "some far country unattainable to mortal men . . . [where she is] waltzing with the dark, red-caped prince of her early dreams," (JP, 210). More importantly, Agnes' death is a triumph, not a defeat, for she *does* reenter the world of the imagination.

Similarly, in "Stone Boy with Dolphin" Dody Ventura longs for something to happen, for something to match the intensity of her dreams. Her dreams are peopled by visionaries:

> In her third-floor attic room she listened, catching the pitch of last shrieks: listened: to witches on the rack, to Joan of Arc crackling at the stake, to anonymous ladies flaring like torches in the rending metal of Rivera roadsters, to Zelda enlightened, burning behind the bars of her madness. What visions were to be had come under thumbscrews, not in the mortal comfort of a hot-water-bottle-cozy cot. Unwincing, in her minds' eye, she bared her flesh.
>
> (JP, 175)

Although all the characters mentioned (witches, Joan of Arc, Zelda) are "mad," their madness is the "Bosch-ish relief" that Dody (and her creator) craves. This same craving is most graphically presented in "Johnny Panic and The Bible of Dreams," where the narrator's entire life's goal is to be the recorder of dreams, the treasurer of the imaginative world which both underlies and runs counter to the pragmatic world we recognize as "reality."

Plath's short stories show her development as a fiction writer. Stylistically and thematically they prefigure and serve as her apprenticeship for *The Bell Jar*. Without them as test grounds, *The Bell Jar* could not have been so rapidly produced, so strongly presented. After all the pre-tellings and thinking, in *The Bell Jar* Plath is able to move into her own narrative voice and pace. Her well-wrought and hard wrung apprenticeship yielded to a haunting powerful craftsmanship.

Notes

1. Josephine Donovan, "Sexual Politics in Sylvia Plath's Short Stories," *Minnesota Review* (Spring, 1973), pp. 150–57.

2. Ted Hughes, "Introduction," in *Johnny Panic and The Bible of Dreams* by Sylvia Plath (New York: Harper Colophon, 1980), p. 3.

3. Ibid., p. 6.

4. Sylvia Plath, "Tongues of Stone," in *Johnny Panic and The Bible of Dreams* (New

York: Harper Colophon, 1980), p. 262. Hereafter, all page references to short stories are from this edition and noted in the text (JP).

5. Sylvia Plath, *The Bell Jar* (New York: Bantam Books, 1972), p. 102. Hereafter, all references to the novel refer to this edition and are noted in the text (BJ).

Plath in Italy   Roberta Mazzanti*

I. THE ITALIAN PUBLICATION OF PLATH'S WORKS

In February, 1968, exactly five years after Sylvia Plath's suicide, the first Italian translation of *The Bell Jar* (by Daria Menicanti) was published. In 1979 the novel was reprinted, with a preface by Claudio Gorlier, in view of the interest in Plath occasioned by the Italian publication of *Letters Home* and a television program about Plath.[1] From 1979 on, Plath's name began to be known in Italy, even among readers who were neither feminists nor readers of contemporary poetry. The diffusion of her name and the circulation of *The Bell Jar* among a non-academic readership was encouraged by the feminist movement, which had discovered in her novel a "revelation-and-liberation-book,"[2] inciting many women to investigate Plath's artistic and existential interests. Fascination with Plath has assumed the proportions of what Sandra Gilbert calls the "Plath myth."[3]

Ironically, by 1974, only three of Plath's poems — "Stings," "Lady Lazarus," and "Daddy" — were available in Italian (those in an anthology of feminist poetry).[4] The inaccessibility of her poems gave a privileged position to the few readers who had access to the original British editions, or to the collections edited by A. Alvarez or the writing of M. L. Rosenthal. Until the mid-1970s, Plath was best known as the author of *The Bell Jar*, and Bianca Maria Frabotta described the sense of Plath as "sort of godmother of fire but also of an underground nightmare." The knowledge of her fragmented biography "made Plath a romantic ensemble of depressive neurosis, high poetry, and suicidal intention."[5]

In 1975 the poetess Amelia Rosselli translated fourteen poems, among them the least autobiographical. She also translated "Ariel" and "The Moon and The Yew Tree," which were to appear later in other translations. In 1976 another poet, Giovanni Giudici, presented a collection of Plath's poetry, emphasizing the later work, and concentrating on its remarkable formal achievement rather than its biographical connections. Giudici saw the Plath poems as "a poetic work destined to uphold itself splendidly on its own without the need for anecdotic supports." In 1977 Carlo Majer translated "Last Words," "Lady Lazarus," and some of "Three Women" to accompany

*This essay was written specifically for this volume, and appears here for the first time by permission of the author.

his short essay in *Gong*, a musical review. Majer coupled Plath with Diane Arbus, the photographer, because each, said Majer, had the capacity to express the "(un)reality of the contemporary world," focusing in part on the "new tragic beauty of humanity after surviving the Nazi extermination camps."[6]

Another poet, Marta Fabiani, translated and edited *Letters Home*, stressing that the collection was important as a "privileged conversation" with Plath's mother, rather than as a diary. Unfortunately, in this edition of the collection, Aurelia Plath's preface to the original was omitted, and many reviewers criticized the loss of the mother's point of view.[7]

From 1979 on, Plath's name recurs more and more frequently on the Italian cultural scene — both in academic circles and beyond. Several radio programs were broadcast (as was the poem "Three Women"), and the second television program ("In the Life of Sylvia Plath," directed by Alessandro Cane) was aired. Nearly 30,000 copies of *The Bell Jar* were sold by mid-1980, and over 8,000 copies of *Lady Lazarus and Other Poems* by January 1, 1982. A new collection of poems is in the process of being translated, as is a collection of Plath's short stories and prose from *Johnny Panic and the Bible of Dreams*.

II. ITALIAN CRITICISM, 1969–1983

The survey of the past fifteen years of criticism on Plath must distinguish between that of the poetry and that of the fiction. Critics of the poetry insist on dividing the poetic self from the biographical self, while those who have examined *The Bell Jar* (and, at times, the letters) have found greater difficulty in separating the tangled personae of Plath in her various roles — the "creature of paper," as Bianca Maria Pisapia defined her.[8]

Renato Oliva has been among the first in Italy to write perceptively about Plath's poetry. He based much of his criticism on the earlier work of Robert Lowell, M. L. Rosenthal, George Steiner, and Giuseppe Sertoli, denying that Plath is a prisoner of "the iron circle of disease" which Sertoli described. Oliva contends that "Plath as a writer, is not a prisoner of disease but a voluntary explorer of the hidden folds of the psyche." Vertigo and metamorphosis are the metaphors Plath uses to explore reality as she tries to create her own personal mythology. Oliva points out that Plath draws on sources as different as modern painting, African folklore, history, mythology, religion, and psychoanalysis. He finds that her will to achieve a "voice which has freed itself from the chains of the confessional tone" is one of her most important contributions to contemporary poetry.[9]

Pisapia's "Sylvia Plath's Art" was the first essay to consider prose and poetry together, and to supply biographical information in a systematic and relevant way. One of the essay's greatest merits is its willingness to correlate Plath's early fiction with her later, better-known works. She thereby provides paradigmatic psychological situations that service the reader through Plath's oeuvre:

> "Plath's rare pieces of prose, in fact constitute the transposition of a repertoire of memories, of 'facts' of her life around which her poetic visions and troubling metaphysical questions are concentrated. Emblematical knots that end by ordering themselves in a sort of spiritual autobiography that often creates the illusion, as in *The Bell Jar*, that the Author and the literary mask almost coincide. Prose, therefore, almost acts as a comment on poetry, in which, on the contrary, real data seems to gradually fall apart."

Pisapia divides Plath's production into two phases — the first, 1952 to 1960, shows the poet building upon the opposition between real and imaginary worlds; the second, the late, shows Plath relinquishing her belief in the power of the word to change anything.[10]

Also in 1974, Bianca Tarozzi's fine essay "The Birth of the Monster" appeared in *Per la Critica*. Here, Tarozzi identifies not only Lowell's influence but also that of Anne Sexton, "who at the time was writing her best things, shamelessly feminine, and who, despite her vexing narcissism, had found her own form."[11] Tarozzi points out that Plath's use of the gothic, eventually within domestic situations, is one continuing practice throughout her poetry. In the gothic "we recognize our daily terrors. In the house presided over by the ghosts of grandmothers, mothers and terrible fathers Plath finds her monsters. Here the leap from narrative to myth takes place and the housewife becomes Medea, witch, whore and suicidal stripper."

Ginevra Bompiani, in another important critical piece, discovers "a system of figures and landscapes, connected with each other, that form a sort of grid or hidden structure." Imagery that recurs tends to reveal Plath's vision of the world, and create for the Plath reader a mythic experience. As Bompiani insists, the task of criticism is to discover the writer's "code" and then to interpret the work in terms of that system. She emphasizes, in Plath, the contrast between appearance and being, health and sickness, and painful knowledge and peaceful ignorance.

She views Plath as a perpetual outsider, an exile figure, and therefore finds "the nostalgia and the regret which one feels for the law or the country one will end up by betraying." There is, consequently, a deep ambiguity, rendered dramatically through the figures of mother and father — the passive, yea-saying mother and the elegant, public father. She notes the pervasiveness of the image of marriage — of the two opposing figures as well as literal marriage — and, in the late poems, the importance of the figure of the child, product of the ultimate fusion.[12]

Marta Fabiani, in her introduction to *Letters Home*, sees Plath being greatly influenced by Melville, Poe, and Hart Crane, as well as Dickinson. She thinks Plath's return to the States in 1958, and her subsequent participation in Robert Lowell's workshop, crucial; Lowell's *Life Studies* offer Plath "a lesson of freedom and the authorization to proceed" which she had been searching for. Both Fabiani and Bompiani consider Plath's marriage to Hughes of great importance, particularly as a liberating factor in the development of her art. Fabiani also sees Plath's learning about magic, through Hughes' interests, of great significance; and ties the titles of Plath's major collections to that kind of knowledge: her evolution from "*The Colossus* (the Giant) to *Ariel* (the Dwarf) is the passage from the reign of the 'tout possible' to the rarified void of a reduction to lowest terms."[13]

Other important essays are "Analysis of a Poem: Survey of Poetic Language" by Maria Vittoria Tessitore, 1973, and "Sylvia Plath, The Mirror, Metaphor of Poetry in the Making" by Paola Russo, 1981. Tessitore works through textual analysis of "Morning Song," using linguistic practices that determine the "load-bearing structures." She finds these to be, in part, the myths of Narcissus, Oedipus and Ophelia — "three modalities through which the perception of the world and of its truth does (or does not) occur" as well as being "three faces of the poetic text."[14] The three myths converge, within the structure of the poem, in the image of the mirror (an image Russo sees as central to much of Plath's poetry). Narcissus is the first form of self-perception, "the act of mirroring oneself is therefore the act of creating and speaking to oneself as a self."

Russo finds Plath's poems "Mirror," "Words," "Face Lift," "Insomniac" and others are poems about birth through a confrontation with duplicity (narcissus-like). She continues, the two fundamental elements of the Narcissus myth — reflection and water — recall what Bachelard named "the complex of Ophelia," the immersion in another element which gradually annuls one's own being. The Ophelia figure suggests several of Plath's creatures, among them the "Lorelei."

Russo also determines Plath's creation of "metapoetry," the intention which "constitutes itself beyond connotative meaning, and often conceals itself behind it, but which is easily unmasked once the constitutive process of writing has been learnt." Here, the mirror becomes the most meaningful metaphor for Plath's poetic act (and her poems become a mirror in which the poetic self is too closely connected with the self of the writer). This relation is called, by Russo, the "specular imprisonment of the text" for the latter is denied its necessary autonomy.

In the Oedipic dimension, "the text is a blind mirror, a sick eye that cannot see itself." Blindness and silence come together here in a dimension of castration, and reality is disabled, dismembered. It is not by chance that the operation of castration is connected with the father figure, in various mythical representations, among them the Colossus "cut to pieces by the voice in the text."

Her feverish effort to recompose the self pushes Plath toward the illusion of the mirror, and "the text tries to be the mirror of the narrative voice where all divisions, conflicts and incapacities are eliminated and recomposed in the compact and ordered surface of the written page." The threat of castration, however, mars Narcissus' contemplation, "insinuating the doubt that writing may not be the mirror in which everything is perfect and complete, but the medium in which all betrayals and anguish concentrate . . . writing, in as much as it is language, can only be symbolic and castrating in regards to the poet's imaginary world, and doubly castrating if one considers that the poet is a woman."[15]

In Italy, too, there is a strong strain in Plath criticism that begins with her suicide and works through the poetry and fiction from that death-oriented perspective. These critics tend to read Plath's work as an urgent statement about the need for a recomposition of the self, struggling constantly against the poet's own personal schizophrenia and the schizoid society which surrounds her.

The possible error in critical perspective which this stance occasions may be that of not being able to understand the complex dialectics of adhesion / refusal which connects Plath to her world, and to see her only as victim or as avenger, either defeated or triumphant. Many critics have fallen into error because they are attempting to explain not so much Plath's artistic production as her death. Suicide occurred, *because of* art or *despite* art? The question in itself is wrong, because it forces the reader to try to find some existential destiny in Plath's work. The solution to such an endeavor seems to lie, at least in part, not in removing biographical and historical material — which is absolutely necessary for any real understanding of Plath's work — nor in "desexualizing" her writing, in the hope of universalizing it. Marisa Bulgheroni justly emphasizes the fact that Plath's death is still today an unsettling event, even if men are inclined to "sell it off as a private fact" while women are "more attentive in perceiving the theatrical connections between it and the great funereal and hallucinated poems of the end, in evaluating the political meaning of her act and in understanding the voluntary scandal of the final option for silence."[16]

Even the beginning reader comes to understand that the excessive attention of criticism for the biographical dimension has often led to mystifications and errors on both the literary level and the social / political one. What we might speak of as "the Plath case" bears important ramifications for the study of most women writers.

When dealing with the prose, critics have made the most outright concessions to autobiographical consideration. B. Pisapia, in her comments on *The Bell Jar*, begins, "it is really difficult not to consider the novel as a sort of autobiography." She warns, however, that it is not adequate to analyze Plath's narrative method by subtracting "those events to the dimension of the diary or of a personal venting of feelings." Plath's use of verb tense — present alternated with past forms — from the very first paragraph of the novel, permits the alternation of two points of view: that of the adolescent and that of the more mature woman, who is already herself a mother. Using this perspective, Plath is able to obtain an ironic, detached tone, even during the most dramatic moments, and to follow, moreover, the path of the protagonist's maturity which permits her to remember in a more objective fashion the events of her own past. Both Pisapia and Gorlier[17] find that *The Bell Jar* is part of the tradition of the "novel of initiation" (*Huckleberry Finn, The Great Gatsby, The Catcher in the Rye*), but whereas these novels were constructed on the archetype that "journey equals knowledge," in *The Bell Jar* "the structure repeats the typical outline of puberty rites that include the Trial, the Death and the Rebirth of the novice . . . the fundamental outline of the book repeats itself for each single episode with a continuous pattern."[18]

Pisapia concludes that the novel is a success because finally, "the two points of view — the very involved point of view of 'Esther — the girl' and the more critical one of 'Esther — the woman' — gradually coincide. The change is underlined by the change in style: "with the disappearance of the frivolous and bizarre tone and of the use of student jargon, with the reduction of the number of images which expressed the restlessness and hallucinations of folly, language becomes more relaxed, more adherent to facts and precise."

Even Gorlier wants to clarify the idea of the biographical dimension of the novel, which "is in no way and at no level, a simple confession or even less, a private story. . . . Even a rapid reading of the novel . . . permits one to understand that *The Bell Jar*, in whose suffocating atmosphere the protagonist lives, symbolizes the alienated world, the conditioning which institutions and precise and concrete behavioural codes subject the individual and private self to." In Gorlier's opinion, it is evident from both the fiction and the poems that suicide is for Plath "a point of passage." In contrast to the kind of death inflicted on the Rosenbergs — by institutions — or to electroshock — about which Plath has no choice, the very volition possible in suicide is positive.

In 1981, Giovanna Covi's essay on *The Bell Jar* appeared in a collection of essays on women's literature. Covi calls for a reading of the novel in the perspective of other women's autobiographical work. Covi finds Plath's novel less successful than do the other critics mentioned here, seeing the shifts in point of view and tense as indications of Plath's naive abilities. She also sees Plath's use of symbolic names as evidence of her failure to come to grips with the life quest, whereas it could easily be argued that Plath's satirical intention, evident in many of these names, belies Covi's feeling that these are forms of deep personal disguise.

Covi sees the novel operating under a misleading identification between Esther and the Plath persona, whereas this identification could be understood as an ambiguous but controlled game, on a literary level, between the positive and the negative elements within the imaginary universe of the novel. For example, the apparent confusion that slowly is established in the symbology of colours, by which the meaning of black and white changes and interchanges throughout the book to the point where "it is no longer possible to attribute a constant meaning to the two colours that had previously been authentic" does not seem to me "a warning light" of Plath's inability to adhere to the symbolic function of the images but, on the contrary, a sign of Plath's conscious choice. By shifting meanings here, it could be that Plath wants to stress the fact that Esther's maturation leads to overcoming the manichaean and schematic vision of the world, divided into positive vs. negative, white vs. black, success vs. failure.[19]

Anna Brawer's perspective on Plath's use of autobiography in *The Bell Jar* seems inherently more useful than some approaches surveyed. In "With Sylvia, born Plath," Brawer sees Plath's writing and personal history as a ball of knotted threads that must be unravelled and then connected with one's own threads and those of other women. Brawer's perspective is accordingly both stylistic and personal, as well as cultural.

Her analysis is carried out according to three different linguistic and thematic models: the first, the most traditional, is essentially sociologic and psychoanalytical. The second is a direct conversation between Brawer and Plath, an imaginary dialogue in which the latter speaks with pieces and quotations from her works. The third is Brawer's addressing Sylvia, as an interlocuter, during a consciousness-raising experience, and this flow of consciousness is emphasized graphically because the passages are printed in italics. Brawer is obviously searching for a form in which she may express different levels of experience, rationality, sensitivity, body, and sexuality, in this way reducing the gap between conscious knowing and unconscious perception. "For this reason, of Sylvia I want to express not so much a literary judgment on the product of writing but rather say something about the product in the making, a woman's writing experience."[20] Brawer's ball of threads becomes even larger when to all this one adds the experiences of each individual reader: "in the relationship writing-reading, modification of myself, rereading . . . the interweaving of the relations between writer and writing and the intertwining of these with the relationships between writing, reader and re-reading becomes a political relation."

Brawer believes that Plath's journey is moving to reduce the gap between existential experience and writing, toward the destruction of the defenses between "self" and "non-self," even in literature. In *The Colossus*, says Brawer, "with such an effort you wrote gothic images of a language which was not yet your own . . . you did not sing your mother, you sang the colossus." After marriage and maternity, Plath progressively changes her writing as well, "a change which begins with the passage from self-expression in poetry to self-expression in the form of a novel." Brawer finds it significant that Plath chose not to write autobiography, but instead fiction; thereby she is able to "reinvent reality," which she then "shows" through a "subjective order: that is, the order of she who writes, or more explicitly, the unconscious of she who writes." But the moment of full acceptance of her unconscious has not yet come." That is to occur through the process of writing *The Bell Jar*.

Once Plath has realized the centrality of the maternal, according to Brawer, she creates "an aggressive cry against the world, a cry in harmony with herself, a cry that creates poetry," and "the rupture between rational and emotional, mind and body is reduced to a minimum." Plath chooses, then, to write poems that are to be read aloud, as if she wished to bring her body, her voice with its tonality, its sounds and its rhythm, into "poetry." Poems such as "Daddy," "Purdah," "The Applicant," and "The Moon and the Yew Tree" show this need to become aware of the self, as a woman-daughter, wife and mother. In this respect, Plath's bee poems are particularly crucial. For example, in the final poem of that sequence, "Wintering," poetic imagery allows the creation of a world of women, in which a mother serenely awaits Spring and the birth of the being which she holds like a bulb.

Maternity is the theme that connects the cycle of bees to the drama "Three Women," works which Brawer believes reveal Plath's fundamental problem, her inability to be mother and daughter simultaneously, to live as an adult woman: "to be a mother that feels like a daughter in constant search of a mother, means being mother and daughter, in terrible division and in search of unity." The recomposition of the division seems to come from the poetic word, and "Edge" is its best expression: however, poetry is not sufficient to save life because, finally, the poetic word does not influence reality. With "Words," Plath is finally and fully aware that "those words, already written, are no longer sufficient, because those words no longer express her. They are 'dry' and 'riderless' words; that is, words without a subject, without her to speak them . . . the crisis of the word is the final crisis."

Brawer's essay is among the best work being produced in Italy today, even if, as Bianca Maria Frabotta writes: "in a worthwhile effort to shorten critical distance, she does not avoid a sort of emotional rhetoric which, let us not forget, greatly irked Plath."[21]

In this rhetoric, other critics of Plath inexorably fall, or, in more extreme cases, drown. Teresa Campi, writing about *The Bell Jar*, finds in it an "experience of absolute negativeness . . . a life of depression," giving a truly reductive interpretation of Esther Greenwood's crisis. Campi also confuses Plath's life with the plot of the novel.[22] More convincing are the remarks appearing in the feminist review *Effe* by Maria Pia Fusco. Fusco charts the experience of a group of women reading and discussing Plath's novel, but in her discussion, she misleadingly suggests attitudes that I doubt Plath ever held. For example, Fusco writes, "Sylvia profoundly hated America and all that such words as efficiency and consumerism entailed," while Plath's own work suggests a much greater ambivalence on her part toward those attitudes (and her biography suggests that she was in good part the product of some of those attitudes).[23]

Rosetta Loy's essay on the novel records its reception in Italy when it was first published ("almost unobserved"), and suggests that its present high critical position stemmed from "the new generation that turning to the old and searching for someone who best represented that obscure and nebulous period, made of Sylvia Plath a symbol and reproposed her as one of the greatest writers of the English language."[24]

Many women reopened the debate on the "Plath case" when *Letters*

Home appeared in Italian; undoubtedly the gap between "Sylvia as Esther" and "Sylvia as Sivvy" stimulated new ideas. *Il Manifesto* dedicated an entire page to "the surprising poetess, idol and fetish of feminism" with articles by Frabotta, Russo and Pia Candinas. The work of the latter described the *Letters* as evidence of the "senseless game of two women," Sylvia and Aurelia, and accused Plath of building her image, for her mother, of the ideal daughter.[25]

In 1980 Roberta Piazza published one of the best non-specialized essays on Plath to appear in Italy, stressing the reasons Plath had become so important to the feminist movement. Piazza found the constant and anguished search for identity, the weak relationship with the mother, and the "competition-identification" with the men in her life "suggest typically feminist themes." Even though there is no "underlying base of political commitment" and "little feminist consciousness" in Plath's work, readers found important values in both the fiction and the poetry. But because, as Piazza recognizes, Plath's work was being read by people other than her intended audience, by readers searching for political sustenance, some distortion in her achievement was bound to occur.[26]

Brawer's and Piazza's ideas about Plath as feminist differ somewhat from other views, however. In 1981 a group of women produced a sort of document-diary of an experience of collective research centered on the texts of a number of women writers — Gertrude Stein, Jane Austen, Ivy Compton-Burnett, Elsa Morante, Emily Bronte, and, among others, Sylvia Plath. The portion dedicated to a reading and discussion of Plath was mingled with a series of reflections on mother-daughter relationships, and on relationships among women more generally. It seemed clear from this discussion that women in the late 1970s and 1980s were looking for more affirmation instead of complaint, that they failed to see suicide as in any way positive — unlike some of their colleagues a decade earlier.[27]

Plath seems, then, to be the object of a sort of rejection syndrome, a rejection which unfortunately has more to do with her personal history than with any serious knowledge of her work. But even worse, many women readers find any consideration of her work difficult because of the shadow of her suicide. The result of this obsession is that Plath's literary production is always examined in the ghastly light of her tragic end, and examined in a dimension of the negative which does justice neither to the writer nor, in the last analysis, to the woman and her courageous and desperate struggles with the contradictions of her times.

The sometimes morbid curiosity of the public was unquestionably stimulated by the publication of *Letters Home*. In a period like the present, when interest in letters, biographies and autobiographies runs high, the "letters to the mother" naturally received a great deal of attention from the press and contributed to a wider knowledge of at least her novel. It is a shame that her short stories, which are just now being translated, have not been accessible; and it also seems necessary to acquaint the Italian public with her *Journals*, recently published in the United States, because they represent the very last piece of the literary and existential mosaic which Plath created, and which we are still attempting to reconstruct.

Of the many reviews of the *Letters* to appear, one of the harshest toward Aurelia was Rossana Rossanda's in *L'Espresso*. After describing Plath's story in a manner reminiscent of the story of *The Bell Jar*, she sketched in the figure of Plath's mother, an ambitious woman who had sacrificed her ambition to her husband's career and therefore attempted to live a life of success and literary brilliance through her daughter. According to Rossanda, Aurelia repressed each of Sylvia's crises, and closed her eyes to the cracks in the image of the exemplary daughter-wife-mother-artist that Sylvia built up for her because "on the whole Sylvia was going strong and in her Aurelia was able to cash in on the moral dividends for all of her sacrifices." Rossanda saw Plath's suicide as escape from the retribution she knew would be hers once her mother had read the novel, in which she allowed herself to portray her mother as she has always viewed her. Aurelia, to defend her own image and the fictional image of Sylvia which she wanted to keep up, was thus forced to "call Sylvia to stand witness in her, Aurelia's, favor and against her very own self"[28] by publishing the letters.

An opposing opinion is that of Osvaldo Guerrieri's, which appeared in a special page on Plath in *Tuttolibri* (March, 1979). In "The Last Dare," Guerrieri too confuses Plath's life with her fiction, but he contradictorily accepts Aurelia's analysis of Plath's suicide ("a sudden, enormous weakness") and does little to explain to any reader some of the complexity of that act.[29]

Several months later, when the television screenplay was about to be shown and the *Letters* put on the market, Bianca Pisapia wrote a brief but intense review attacking those critics who "as a ploy to seduce the reader, could find nothing better to do than to offer them up the *Letters* as a sort of epistolary *feuilleton* narrating the everlastingly pathetic kitsch melodrama of the lovely young suicide, and favoring a romantic type of identification." Plath should be viewed not as a "love-story character" but rather as "a creature of paper existing only in the lines of the text," an artist who aspires with every bone of her body to the complete realization of her vocation as writer. The *Letters* can help us to better understand the difficult itinerary she covered in her conquest of form, just as they can provide us with "some referential supports for the enigmatic complexity and dense symbolism of Plath's poetry. . . . Thus, the letters cannot be taken as an immediate and direct expression of feelings, but must be read as a calculated biography, a self-portrait composed for her friends, her family and her mother."[30]

Pisapia's view is shared by Gigliola Nocera, who considers Plath's *Letters* from the perspective of the epistolary genre. In the context of Jane Austen, the Brontes, Virginia Woolf and Lytton Strachey, Nocera places Plath as both fiction writer and letter writer, and points to the possible confusion between the two. The letters often slide over into fiction, just as the epistolary novel might become a mirror of truth. In Plath's case, "we are the ones who must unmask the lie . . . the bright and shiny face free of the shadows cast by doubt and contradiction which Sylvia Plath showed to others, especially to her mother." Nocera points to the contradiction between what Plath's poetry was showing about her feelings, and the placid surface of the letters being written simultaneously.[31]

Perhaps the most interesting focus of further study will be this interplay among the various surfaces of Plath's writing — fiction, poetry, journal, letter, and journalism — this final "play of mirrors" that its own creator is seldom able to understand. Hopefully, when Plath's *Journals* are accessible in Italy, critics will benefit from the addition of that surface to those already available.

Notes

1. Sylvia Plath, *La campana di vetro*, tr. D. Menicanti (Milano: Mondadori, 1968). Plath, *Lettere alla madre*, tr. M. Fabiani (Milano: Guanda, 1979).

2. M. P. Fusco, "Il bikini bianco. Note parlate su S. Plath, nate da una conversazione tra donne," *Effe*, 7 (July-Aug., 1979), 41.

3. Sandra Gilbert, "A white, fine, flying myth," in *Shakespeare's Sisters, Feminist Essays on Women's Poetry*, ed. Sandra Gilbert and Susan Gubar (Bloomington: Indiana Univ. Press, 1979).

4. N. Fusini and M. Gramaglia, ed. *La poesia femminista. Antologia di testi poetici del Movement* (Roma: Savelli, 1974), pp. 178–91.

5. B. Frabotta, "Nei suoi versi mi accade spesso di udire il sussurro del serpente," *Il Manifesto*, 12 (1980), 4.

6. A Rosselli, "14 Poesie," *Nuovi Argomenti*, no. 45–46 (Maggio-Agosto, 1975), pp. 95–110; Sylvia Plath, *Lady Lazarus e altre poesie*, tr. with intro. by G. Giudici (Milano: Mondadori, 1974); C. Majer, "Ultime parole nel buio," *Gong*, Nov., 1977, pp. 23–25.

7. M. Fabiani, intro. *Lettere alla madre*, p. 7.

8. B. Pisapia, "S. Plath essere di carta," *Rinascita*, 21 (Dec., 1979), 19.

9. R. Oliva, "La poesia di Sylvia Plath," *Studi Americani*, No. 15 (Roma: Edizioni di Storia e Letteratura, 1969), pp. 341–81.

10. B. M. Pisapia, *L'arte di Sylvia Plath* (Roma: Bulzoni, 1974), pp. 15, 10, 85, 62, 64, 29, 77–78, 81.

11. B. Tarozzi, "La nascita del mostro," *Per la critica*, No. 7 / 8 (July-Dec., 1974), pp. 75, 76, 78, 80–81, 84.

12. G. Bompiani, "Le figure del mito" in *Lo spazio narrante* (Milano: La Tartarugo, 1978), pp. 124–39, 145, 152–63, 177–79.

13. M. Fabiani, intro. *Lettere alla madre*, pp. 14–16, 18.

14. M. V. Tessitore, "Analisi di una poesia: indagine sul linguaggio poetico," *Annali della Libera Universitá* della Tuscia, a.a. 1973–1974, Anno V. Fasc. III-IV, p. 2.

15. P. Russo, "Sylvia Plath. Lo specchio, metafora del farsi poetico," *Nuova Corrente*, 28 (1981), 552–54, 564, 568–69, 571–76, 578.

16. M. Bulgheroni, "S. Plath, un giorno piú cupo del solito," *L'Unitá*, (Gennaio 5, 1980), 3.

17. C. Gorlier, intro. to *La campana di vetro*, pp. v–viii.

18. B. Pisapia, pp. 48–49, 53.

19. G. Covi, "*The Bell Jar* di S. Plath, tra romanzo e autobiografia" in *Come nello specchio, Saggi sulla figurazione del femminile*, pp. 75–89.

20. A. Brawer, *Con Sylvia, Nata Plath* (Milano: La Salamandra, 1979).

21. B. M. Frabotta, *Il Manifesto* essay.

22. T. Campi,

23. M. P. Fusco, *Effe* essay, p. 41.

24. R. Loy, "Sylvia e nessun 'altra,' " *Noidonne*, Aprile 20, 1979, p. 49.

25. B. M. Frabotta, op. cit.; P. Russo, "Uno nota biografica," *Il Manifesto* (Jan. 12, 1980), p. 4; P. Candinas, "Sylvia piccola, Sylvia sorridente, Sylvia scrittrice, Sylvia suicida. Sylvia e Aurelia. Senza tregua, senza tenerreza, il gioco dissennato di due donne," Ibid.

26. R. Piazza, "Una riappropriazione culturale; il caso Plath," *Sintesi*, IV (July-Dec., 1980), 2.

27. *Catalogo No. 2*, "Le Madri di tutte noi," (Milano: Libreria delle donne, 1982), pp. 12–16.

28. R. Rossanda, "Felice da morire," *L'Espresso*, no. 44 (Nov. 4, 1979), pp. 86–92.

29. O. Guerrieri, "L'ultima sfida," *Tuttolibri*, v (March 3, 1979), 12.

30. B. M. Pisapia, "Sylvia Plath, essere di carta," *Rinascita*, Dec. 21, 1979, p. 19.

31. G. Nocera, "Il genere lettera," *Alfabeta*, no. 23 (April, 1981), pp. 25–26.

In Yeats' House: The Death and Resurrection of Sylvia Plath

Sandra M. Gilbert*

By an absolute *fluke* I walked by *the* street and *the* house . . . where I've always wanted to live. . . . And guess that, *it is W.B. Yeats' house* — with a blue plaque over the door, saying he lived there!
— Sylvia Plath to Aurelia Plath, Nov. 7, 1962†

That crazed girl improvising her music,
Her poetry, dancing upon the shore,
Her soul in division from itself
. . . . that girl I declare
A beautiful lofty thing, or a thing
Heroically lost, heroically found . . . .
— W.B. Yeats, "A Crazed Girl"

As the thunder rolled bumping and snarling away across the sky, they saw the figure of a man appear from the darkness. . . . A brilliant flash lit up the white face and its frame of heavy hair. . . .
 Yeats: and he lived here . . . all the time his presence would cast its light upon their frontage.
— Dorothy Richardson, *The Trap*

---

*This essay is published here for the first time, by permission of the author.

. . . in the house of a famous poet . . . my work should be blessed.
— Sylvia Plath to Aurelia Plath, Nov. 7, 1962

Climb to your chamber full of books and wait,
No books upon the knee . . .
— W.B. Yeats, "To Dorothy Wellesley"

The panther's tread is on the stairs,
Coming up and up the stairs.
— Sylvia Plath, "Pursuit"

What climbs the stair?
Nothing that common women ponder on
If you are worth my hope! Neither Content
Nor satisfied Conscience, but that great family
Some ancient famous authors misrepresent,
The Proud Furies each with her torch on high.
— W.B. Yeats, "To Dorothy Wellesley"

Well, here I am! Safely in Yeats' house!
— Sylvia Plath to Aurelia Plath, Dec. 14, 1962

In the evening, *Yeats.* Far away from the tumult; hidden, untroubled
in his green room.
— Dorothy Richardson, *The Trap*

. . . I saw the wildness in her and I thought
A vision of terror that it must live through
Had shattered her soul. . . .
— W.B. Yeats, "A Bronze Head"

. . . I feel Yeats' spirit blessing me.
— Sylvia Plath, to Aurelia Plath, December 14, 1962

"I am afraid of getting older," wrote the seventeen-year-old Sylvia
Plath in 1949, "I am afraid of getting married. Spare me from cooking three
meals a day — spare me from the relentless cage of routine and rote. I want
to be free. . . . I want, I think, to be omniscient. . . . I think I would like to
call myself 'The girl who wanted to be God.' Yet if I were not in this body,
where *would* I be — perhaps I am *destined* to be classified and qualified.
But, oh, I cry out against it. I am I — I am powerful — but to what extent? I
am I." (*LH*, 40) "I am I": oddly, prophetically, that somewhat theatrical
adolescent phrase echoes the words of a poet whose works even a precocious
teenager might not yet have read — William Butler Yeats, who was to become Sylvia Plath's "beloved Yeats" and in whose house, some thirteen and
a half year later, she was to die in a suicide that, as most critics see it, might
have been either a cry for help or a crying out against being "classified and
qualified" or, more simply, a cry of pain. For in a late verse called "He and

She" Yeats had used just the phrase the young Plath used in her journal — "I am I" — and used it explicitly to examine what I will argue she was herself exploring: the relationship between male authority and female identity, or, to be more specific, between male creation and female creativity.

> As the moon sidles up [writes Yeats]
> Must she sidle up,
> As trips the sacred moon
> Away must she trip:
> 'His light had struck me blind
> Dared I stop.'
>
> She sings as the moon sings:
> 'I am I, am I;
> The greater grows my light
> The further that I fly.'
> All creation shivers
> With that sweet cry.

Tentatively, provisionally, I want in this essay to discuss the ways in which the life, the death, and ultimately the poetic resurrection of "the girl who wanted to be God" were affected by her increasingly intense consciousness that the very scene of writing is now, as never before, shared and shaped by the dialogue between a literary "He and She." I want, in other words, to explore Plath's sometimes exuberant, sometimes anxious awareness that she was born at a moment in history when her "I am I, am I" might for the first time "shiver" all creation. In addition, taking Plath as a paradigmatic precursor of "women writing poetry in America" today, I want to think about what might be some important implications of that historical awareness (as it influenced both her death and her resurrection) for those of us who share Plath's literary desire, if not her destiny.

Criticism of Plath's poetry has, of course, proliferated in recent years; in fact, her reputation, or, perhaps more accurately, her *image*, seems never to have undergone the "eclipse" that so often causes readers to forget a major writer in the first decades after her or his death. On the contrary, as I noted when I reviewed the 1979 criticism of contemporary poetry for the 1981 edition of *American Literary Scholarship*, Plath in that year got more attention than any other poet treated in my section of the book, a significant phenomenon, since my section surveyed writings on such major artists as Lowell, Roethke, Levertov, Rich, Ginsberg, and Ashbery. Plath's work, as I pointed out, is "still controversial. Yet even those who dislike it find it absorbing, even mesmerizing, as if this thirty-one-year-old woman who died in 1963 were in some troubling sense what Keats might call a 'figure of allegory.' "[1]

But in what sense, specifically, does Plath become allegorical for critics? Here I think that writers and reviewers like Denis Donoghue, Gary Lane, David Holbrook, Hugh Kenner, Margaret Dickie Uroff, and Marjorie

Perloff would speak to very different issues. Rather extravagantly, one set —
probably the majority — would praise or blame Plath's suicidal intensity,
tracing an allegorical, psychodramatic, even melodramatic relationship between life and art. More conservatively, the second set would explain or analyze Plath's stylistic influences, tracing a somewhat less problematic
though still allegorical relationship between art and art. To give a few examples of what the first group would say: Denis Donoghue might elaborate on
his idea that Sylvia Plath was "a girl who lived mostly and terribly on her
nerves," explaining in particular how "she showed what self-absorption
makes possible in art"; David Holbrook might explain why he thinks Plath's
"poetry seduces us to taste of its poisoned chalice"; Hugh Kenner might support his assertion that *Ariel* offers us "insidious nausea" and "bogus spirituality" fashioned "with the gleeful craft of a mad child"; and Marjorie
Perloff might explain her contention that Plath "had really only one subject:
her own anguish and consequent longing for death."[2] To give fewer examples of what the second set would say: Gary Lane, Margaret Dickie Uroff,
and Marjorie Perloff (who is versatile enough to belong in both sets of critics) might show how Plath's poetic evolution was helped or hindered by
powerful male precursors like Yeats, Thomas, Stevens, Roethke, Lowell and
Hughes, and, to a lesser extent, by powerful female precursors like Dickinson, Bishop, and Moore.[3]

The first set of critics, in other words, would moralize; the second set
would analyze. Few, however, would try to consider whether there is a connection between, on the one hand, the poetic influences that shaped Plath's
style and, on the other, the personal dilemma that became her subject.
More specifically, few would speculate on what it meant to be a woman,
born in America in 1932, reading major poetry and trying to write major
poetry in the years from, say, 1952 to 1963 — what it meant, that is, to be a
"girl who wanted to be God" setting out, like a female Stephen Daedalus, to
"forge" an identity, an "I am I," in Wellesley, Mass., at Smith College, at
Mademoiselle, at Cambridge University, in Spain, in Boston, in London, in
Devonshire, and finally in Yeats' house.

But almost by itself the list of places I've just offered should suggest how
new, if not unique, Plath's historical situation was. It hardly seems necessary to remind ourselves that, born a century earlier, neither Emily Dickinson nor Christina Rossetti, two of Plath's major literary foremothers, could
ever have journeyed from continent to continent, college to college, city to
city that way. When their precursor, Elizabeth Barrett Browning, started
her dramatic travels, after all, she had to tiptoe like a thief out of that infa-
mous house on Wimpole Street, and even so her father never spoke to her
again. As for the literary constraints of which such geographic constrictions
were emblematic, moreover, it hardly seems necessary to remind ourselves
that those were equally severe. Elizabeth Barrett Browning looked "everywhere for [poetic] grandmothers and found none"; while Emily Dickinson,
feeling "shut up . . . in prose," fell in love with "that foreign lady" Elizabeth

Barrett Browning precisely because she constituted in her own person (and created in Aurora Leigh) a unique precursor.[4] By the time the seventeen-year-old Sylvia Plath took up her pen in 1949 and wrote "I want to be free . . . I want to be omniscient," however, the world had radically changed, for an event had long since taken place that, as Virginia Woolf says in *A Room of One's Own*, "if I were rewriting history I should think of greater importance than the Crusades or the Wars of the Roses. The middle-class woman began to write."[5] Beginning to write, moreover, that symbolic woman began to travel — into the universities, into the professions, into a series of surprisingly various rooms of her own all over the world. What Barrett Browning, Rossetti, and Dickinson had struggled to start became a living female tradition that was handed down to women like Virginia Woolf, H. D., Marianne Moore — and Sylvia Plath. It became a tradition, too, that had to be confronted by men like W. B. Yeats, D. H. Lawrence, James Joyce, T. S. Eliot, and Ted Hughes.

When Virginia Woolf implies in "Professions for Women," therefore, that writing is in some way the most "harmless occupation" a woman can pursue, she oversimplifies the case. It is true that, as she says, "the road was cut many years ago . . . many famous women, and many more unknown and forgotten have been before me, making the path smooth, and regulating my steps."[6] But it is also true that the new (female) road, whether it parallels or intersects the old (male) one, complicates our literary geography, for every new road makes the landscape more intricate, more problematic, even while it elaborates possibilities. Thus when Plath writes in "The Disquieting Muses" about "the kingdom you bore me to, / Mother, mother,"[7] she is hinting at an anxiety Woolf does not really explore. For the world to which Plath's mother bore her was complex indeed, as we can instantly perceive if we stop for a moment to consider who was writing half a century ago, in the year when Aurelia Plath produced her *Wunderkind*. On the one hand, Yeats, Joyce, Pound, Eliot, Faulkner, Hemingway — many of the major male (and mostly masculinist) modernists were publishing, though a few would soon be perishing. On the other hand, Stein, H.D., Millay, Moore, Barnes, and Woolf — many of the major female (and mostly feminist) modernists were publishing, and (except for Woolf) none would soon be perishing. Among them, these representatives of both sexes created a dialectic that became an inheritance which may well have been "disquieting" to an ambitious young woman poet, a "girl who wanted to be God."

Because Plath is usually seen as either a sort of neurasthenic sorceress of syntax — a witty, wily, willful witch of words — or a diligent devotee of Roget's *Thesaurus* — a docile and decorous ephebe of 'fifties elegance — she isn't often understood to be what she really was: an extraordinarily conscious and at least semi-*self*-conscious student of the peculiarly new literary tradition in which she quite pivotally participated. Yet from the first, of course, as her early flirtation with her Thesaurus should indicate, she was a voracious reader, and a reader who surely understood the implications of the literary history that she imbibed, she tells us, almost as if it were her mother's milk. "I recall my mother . . . reading to me . . . from Matthew Arnold's 'Forsaken Merman,' " she writes, recounting her personal myth of origins in "Ocean 1212-W," adding that "A spark flew off Arnold and shook me like a chill. . . . I had fallen into a new way of being happy."[8] If not from the first, too, at least quite early she must have understood the implications of her gender for the genre she had chosen. At Cambridge, for instance, she played the part of Phoebe Clinkett, Pope's parodic portrait of the 18th-century poet Anne Finch as, in Plath's own words, a "mad poetess," (*LH*, 190), a "verbose niece who has high flown and very funny ambitions to write plays and poetry." Mouthing the absurdities of this savagely satirized woman artist, she gave what her director told her was an "excruciatingly funny" performance, but of course it was also a performance whose deeper meaning, had she allowed herself to confront it, might have been merely excruciating, because of the message it gave to a "girl who wanted to be God" about literary men's attitudes toward literary women's aspirations. By the time she was well established at Cambridge, moreover, Plath was exactly what many of her most expert readers are: a sophisticated student of a twentieth-century literary tradition that was constituted out of an implicit if not explicit battle between highly cultured intellectual men (Pound, Eliot, Joyce, Lawrence) and their female counterparts, literary ladies who seemed either to be part of a less cultivated group like the one that Hawthorne called a "damned mob of scribbling women" (Teasdale, Millay, Olive Higgins Prouty) or part of a more cultured but also more dangerous, even presumptuous group that we might call a Black Mass of scrivening women (H.D., Stein, Woolf, Moore).

That Plath saw herself as oscillating between these two, or rather three, unprecedented male and female / female poles, becomes clear when we read the countless letters home she wrote from Smith and Cambridge. Articulating her loyalty to the male tradition out of whose figurative rib she had been born like a new Eve, for instance, she expressed her worship of her "beloved Yeats," her admiration for Lawrence, her reverence for Joyce, her respect for Thomas. At the same time, she hinted at her feelings of rivalry towards these men and, by implication, her powerful sense of her own power in comparison to theirs: "I am learning and mastering new words each day, and drunker than Dylan, harder than Hopkins, younger than Yeats in my saying" (*LH*, 243). Simultaneously, however, she indicated her anxiety about being a "scribbling woman": her poems, she said, are "not quailing and whining like Teasdale or simple lyrics like Millay" (*LH*, 277). Again, at the same time, she expressed her admiration for what she considered serious female precursors, noting when she sent her mother poems from college that "any resemblance to Emily Dickinson is purely intentional," praising the brilliance of Dorothy Krook ("a woman on the Cambridge faculty for whom I would sweat my brains out"), and observing that "I get courage by reading Virginia Woolf's Diary," that she felt "very akin to Woolf," that she found Woolf's novels "excellent stimulation for my own writing" (*LH*, 305, 324), and that, indeed, "Her novels make mine possible."[9] Thus, even while Plath repudiated what she saw as the bitterness, sentimentality or oversimplification of one part of the female literary tradition she had inherited, or excoriated most of the women dons at Cambridge as "bluestocking grotesques," she deliberately defined herself as "a woman poet like [*sic*] the world will gape at. . . . One of the few women poets in the world who is a rejoicing woman . . . a woman singer" (*LH*, 248, 256), and insisted that she wanted to be "a woman famous among women" (*J*, 260).

What were the implications of such a self-definition, rising, as it did, out of divided loyalties, ambivalences, ambiguities? A casual but crucial sentence Plath tossed off in another letter suggests that one central implication was an extraordinary sense of guilt and consequent terror: guilt over her own power; terror that she might be, should be, punished for that power. Complaining about the burden of domesticity in England, a country that had not yet at that point discovered "the Cookie-sheet, Central Heating, and Frozen Orange Juice," she commented that "if I want to keep on being a triple-threat woman: wife, writer and teacher . . . I can't be a drudge."[10]

A *triple-threat woman:* the phrase is telling, for it both explains her early fascination with "The Forsaken Merman" and foreshadows her later fascination with images of herself as an arrow, an acetylene virgin, a runaway, a queen bee, a crackling moon, a murderess, a deadly interloper, a ferocious transgressor. Arnold's poem, after all, tells a tale of the way a poetically pathetic merman is seduced and abandoned by a "cruel" earthwoman who, claiming her own place in the sun, leaves "lonely forever / The kings of the sea." As for Plath's later images of her own threatening self, they record similar cruelties, from "the upflight of the murderess into a heaven that loves her" described in "Stings," to the violently "dancing and stamping" villagers let loose in "Daddy," to the "face / So murderous in its strangle of branches" encountered in "Elm," to the man-eating heroine resurrected in "Lady Lazarus," to "the lioness, / The shriek in the bath, / The cloak of holes" imagined by the Clytemnestra-like speaker of "Purdah."[11]

Even while most women "fight for the father, for the son," wrote Plath in her Cambridge notebook, as if proleptically explaining such later images, most have also the power to "believe in [men] and make them invincible," along with the complementary, more terrible power of "the vampire," who expresses "the old primal hate. That desire to go around castrating the arrogant ones who become such children at the moment of passion" (*JP*, 250–51). Significantly, moreover, a moment after she made this confession, she implicitly alluded to Yeats: "How the circling steps in the spiral tower bring us back to where we were!" (*JP*, 250–51) — alluded to him as if she knew how he might refer to her — as a "thing heroically lost, heroically found," as a Helen for whom there was "no second Troy" to burn, as an adept of "the Proud Furies," as a creature full of "wildness," as one of Herodias's desirous and demented daughters, blasting through "the labyrinth of the wind."[12]

For if Pope reacted with comic rage against Anne Finch's poetic presumption by satirizing her as Phoebe Clinkett, Plath's more recent masters, male modernists like Yeats, Joyce, and Lawrence, had responded even more censoriously to what they perceived as "the old primal hate" of the "vampire" women who seemed to want to usurp not only (like Olive Higgins Prouty) the literary marketplace, but even (like H.D., Woolf, and Plath) the scene of writing itself. Portraying the vulgarly virginal Gerty MacDowell in the Nausicaa section of *Ulysses*, for instance, Joyce satirized the "namby-pamby jammy marmalady drawersy" style of "scribbling women" like Maria Cummins, the author of *The Lamplighter*, at least as savagely as Pope, in his depiction of poor Phoebe Clinkett, had parodied what he took to be Anne Finch's style while in one of his Notebooks he exulted that in his misogynistic *Waste Land* "T. S. Eliot ends idea of poetry for ladies."[13] Similarly, in a ferocious verse called "The Lady Poets with Footnotes," Ernest Hemingway had attacked literary women as fat or sterile or drunk or nymphomaniac or all those reprehensible things together, while in *Miss Lonely-hearts* Nathanael West's reporters had fulminated against lady writers with three names—"Mary Roberts Wilcox, Ella Wheeler Catheter, Ford Mary Rinehard—what they all needed was a good rape," and in "Portrait d'Une Femme" Ezra Pound had told a chaotically cultured woman that "Your mind and you are our Sargasso Sea."[14] If the messages conveyed by the life / work of Plath's "beloved" Yeats were more complicated, they must have sometimes been equally daunting, for even as Maude Gonne's erstwhile lover praised strong women like Lady Gregory, Dorothy Wellesley, and Maude herself, he deplored the way Con Markiewicz's mind had become "a bitter, an abstract thing," denounced the "vague Utopia" of feminism dreamed by Eva Gore-Booth, observing that "she seems / When withered old and skeleton-gaunt, / An image of such politics," praised "woman / That gives up all her mind," and prayed that his own daughter might "become a flourishing hidden tree."[15] When we read her anxious insistence that she is "not a bitter or frustrated or warped man-imitator" (*LH*, 256), therefore, we can see that Plath must have intuited and internalized the misogyny implicit or explicit in all these masculinist modernist statements.

Internalizing such misogyny, however, she did not respond as women poets from Anne Bradstreet and Anne Finch to Christina Rossetti and Elizabeth Barrett Browning did, by trying to renounce or repudiate, deny or disguise her own power. Rather, Plath's first response, like that of many other women artists who are her contemporaries or descendents, was to affirm her strength, to revel and rejoice in it: "I am making a self, in great pain, often, as for a birth, but it is right that it should be so" (*LH*, 223); "by reforging my soul, I am a woman now the like of which I could never have dreamed" (*LH*, 241).

To be sure, some of her precursors had made similar assertions, beginning perhaps with Anne Finch, who replied to Pope's criticisms by warning, "Alexander, have a care / And shock the sex no more, / We rule the world our life's whole race, / Men but assume that right."[16] But all too often such women, like Finch herself, succumbed to spleen or melancholy, and imagined flying only "with contracted wing."[17] Between Plath and those foremothers, however, a new age of literary equality had intervened, an age that made possible her sharing, as she put it, "her husband's dearest career" (*LH*, 276), an age that brought this couple up as a representative "He and She" to "romp through words" together (*LH*, 235), an age that let her live in Yeats's house.

It was, of course, an age that had been defined in the first part of this century, long before Plath was born — and it was defined by male historians like John Langdon-Davies as well as female prophets like Virginia Woolf. "Once both sexes use their reason equally," wrote Langdon-Davies in a passage Plath underlined in his 1927 *History of Women*, ". . . then women cannot fail to dominate. Theirs is the stronger sex once nature and art cease their cruel combination against them, because it possesses a greater singleness of purpose and a greater fund of imagination."[18] And a year later, in 1928, Virginia Woolf, to whom Plath felt so much akin, predicted, as we well know, the second coming of the mythic woman poet Judith Shakespeare: "The opportunity will come, and the dead poet who was Shakespeare's sister will put on the body which she has so often laid down. Drawing her life from the lives of the unknown who were her forerunners . . . she will be born" (*A Rm*, 118).

Was she born in Sylvia Plath? Was she born when, alone and (like Judith Shakespeare) abandoned in London, Plath finally in 1962 wrote her mother that "I am a writer . . . I am a genius of a writer . . . I am writing the best poems of my life; they will make my name. . . ."? (*LH*, 468) I would suggest that she was, but that she had to "lay down" her body again not because, like Woolf's Judith, she had been discouraged or denied, but precisely because, encouraged as she was by history and prophecy, she had to suffer in her own person the sexual battle that marked a turning point in time. I would suggest, in other words, that, to paraphrase Adrienne Rich's poem on Marie Curie, Plath died a famous (not an obscure) woman, and died not denying but knowing that "her wounds came from the same source as her power."[19]

The connection in Plath's career between the literary history her letters ambitiously review, the power her poems ambivalently renew or repress, and the wound her death ambiguously reveals, is made clearest in two short stories obstensibly about dreams but really about reading and writing, stories which enter vigorously, though very differently, into a dialogue with the twentieth-century male literary tradition represented in them by D. H. Lawrence and his north of England descendent Ted Hughes. The first, "The Wishing Box," was evidently written in 1956; the second, "Johnny Panic and the Bible of Dreams," dates from December 1958. The first, about suicide, is slight, blackly comic, barely successful. The second, about what we might call femicide, is longer, bleakly sardonic, brilliantly successful. But despite these distinctions the two constitute in some sense a single narrative which dramatically summarizes the sense of transgression or usurpation that seems to have haunted their author when she considered the possibility (or the reality) of female creative power.

To be sure, "The Wishing Box" is at least on the surface a comic tale of female powerlessness. Harold and Agnes, a young married couple — clearly surrogates of Ted and Sylvia — meet at breakfast to discuss *his* dreams, which are always vivid, richly formulated, funny visions of aesthetic triumph. In one, he discusses manuscripts with William Blake, in another he plays the Emperor Concerto, in a third he is introduced to a gathering of American poets in the Library of Congress, and in two others (the ones that most comically and definitively relate him to Hughes) he encounters, respectively, a red fox (who presents him with a bottle of permanent black Quink) and a giant pike. Listening with pretended admiration to his accounts of these nighttime events, Agnes, who has only a few dreams herself (and those are nightmares), finds herself "wrestling with the strange jealousy which had been growing on her like some dark malignant cancer ever since their wedding night" (*JP*, 204) and thinks that "It was as if Harold were spending one third of his life among celebrities and fabulous legendary creatures in an exhilarating world from which [she] found herself perpetually exiled, except by hearsay" (*JP*, 205).

At first, in an attempt to compete, she plans to study Freud on the sly and fortify "herself with a vicarious dream tale by which to hold Harold's interest each morning" (*JP*, 207), a strategy that recalls both the literary seductions of Scheherezade and the occult wiles of George Yeats. But finally she gives up and confesses her inadequacy to her husband, who sets her a series of dream exercises not unlike the group of poetic exercises Hughes set Plath. Even these don't work, however, and though Agnes tries to restore her "shaping imaginative powers" (*JP*, 209) by reading novels, cookbooks, "home appliance circulars . . . anything to keep from facing the gaping void in her own head of which Harold had made her so painfully conscious," the very letters she looks at writhe "like malevolent little black snakes across the page in a kind of hissing, untranslatable jargon" so that finally, insomniac as Esther Greenwood in *The Bell Jar*, and hysterical at the "intolerable prospect of wakeful visionless days and nights stretching unbroken ahead of her" (*JP*, 210), she consumes a "wishing box" full of sleeping pills and dies into the only country of dreams accessible to her.

What is frightening and crucial about this tale, it seems to me, is its obsession with the dream competition between husband and wife, and, more specifically, its emphasis on both the sense of creative, even sexual inadequacy and the "dark malignant cancer of jealousy" Agnes feels when facing the fertility of Harold's imagination. Indeed, considering that Plath wrote the story at just the time when she was boasting to her mother that she and Hughes "romp through words together," that he "is my best critic as I am his," and that she was "glad his book is taken first," proud that he is "always just that many steps ahead of me intellectually and creatively so that I feel very feminine and admiring" (*LH*, 270), "The Wishing Box" comes as something of a surprise, for it suggests that its author had, on the one hand, a deeply traditional female anxiety that she could not keep up with the élan of the male imagination, and, on the other hand, a deep, *Ladies Home Journal* conviction that she *should* not keep up. Better death than the expression of (female) desire, the story seems to say. Or, more accurately, death is the most appropriate expression of female desire, the best dream a woman can have.

But of course Plath knew, in the truest part of herself, that she could and did keep up with Hughes's, and many other men's, imaginative élan. Thus, "Johnny Panic and the Bible of Dreams" offers, as it were, the other term of the painful puzzle the two tales together articulate. For in "Johnny Panic," a story Hughes himself saw as "moving straight toward *The Bell Jar* and the more direct poems of *Ariel*" (*JP*, 6), the female narrator—"Assistant Secretary in [an] Adult Psychiatric Clinic"—becomes "a dream connoisseur" (*JP*, 153), a dedicated transcriber of the horrendous nightmares inspired by the god "Johnny Panic," and "this," she says with the sardonic pride of a Lady Lazarus, "is my real calling." By comparison with the comically ambitious or innocently poetic dreams recounted in "The Wishing Box," however, the nightmares of "Johnny Panic" are intricate, metaphysical poems; more, they are exactly the Plathian nightmares—"dark glowing landscapes peopled with ominous unrecognizable figures" (*JP*, 205)—that Agnes had rejected as inadequate in that story.

In some sense, then, the narrator of "Johnny Panic" is a prophetically visionary version of the poet herself, an impassioned imaginative woman whose powerful ambition is to record all the dreams contained in the old books of the clinic, books that were begun when "the clinic started thirty three years ago—the year of my birth, oddly enough." But when finally, after much plotting and scheming, she does undertake that task, contriving to spend all night in the hospital copying the contents of the "dream book [that] was spanking new the day I was born" (*JP*, 164), she quickly and traumatically learns that her inspired transcription is an awful transgression. Finding her among the files at dawn (Plath's own regular writing time), the clinic director marches her off to a sado-masochistic place of punishment where a terrible nurse and "five false priests in white surgical gowns and masks" ritually strip her, annoint her, robe her in "sheets virginal as the first snow," extend her full-length on a white cot, and place a "crown of wire" on her head, a "wafer of forgetfulness" on her tongue" (*JP*, 166). The shock of the sacrificial shock treatment she then undergoes elicits a vision that does indeed influence and, in a searing blue light, illuminate both *The Bell Jar* and *Ariel:*

At the moment when I think I am most lost the face of Johnny Panic appears in a nimbus of arc lights on the ceiling overhead. I am shaken like a leaf in the teeth of glory. His beard is lightning. Lightning is in his eye. His Word charges and illumines the universe.

The air crackles with his blue-tongued lightning-haloed angels.

Coupled with "The Wishing Box," in fact, this story also illuminates the problem that Suzanne Juhasz has called (and that Plath must have seen as) the "double bind" of the woman poet: if she empties her head of her own dreams, she dies into (as Forster put it) "panic and emptiness"; but if she ambitiously studies and records what are, symbolically speaking, her own dreams, she is shaken and shocked by a panic that also, inevitably, produces emptiness. Worse still, her panic is energized not only by her Pandora-like curiosity about the secret facts of her own history that are recorded in the clinic's musty dream books, it is also activated by her consciousness that her identification of *her* history with these sacred tomes constitutes a fearful usurpation of literary history itself. In other words, Plath is aware that when the clinic director shocks her transgressive dream connoisseur out of her mind he is doing so because this scribbling woman's appropriation of the dream books offers a challenge to his authority over them, his mastery of the mystery of their material.

Plath's awareness of this specific point is most dramatically revealed, I would suggest, by the fact that "Johnny Panic" is very clearly a revision of one of D. H. Lawrence's most ferociously misogynist tales, "The Woman Who Rode Away," a story which recounts the miserable misadventure of a *thirty three year* old, nerve-worn, white woman who escapes from her boringly bourgeois marriage only to be seized by a band of male Indians, ritually annointed, stripped, splayed out on a flat rock by *five* priests, and offered as a sacrifice to their sun god so that they can recapture "the mastery that man must hold, and that passes from race to race"[20] For, says Lawrence in a concise statement of the story's central theme and a statement which would surely have proffered Plath a terrifying summary of male modernist reactions to the transgression implicit in the dream transcriptions of her poems, his heroine knew that "Her kind of womanhood, intensely personal and individual, was to be obliterated again, and the great primeval symbols were to tower once more over the fallen individual independence of woman. . . . Strangely as if clairvoyant, she saw the immense sacrifice prepared" (569). And why must such an immense sacrifice be prepared? Precisely because it is the white woman's power — the power, let us say, of feminist-modernists like Lawrence's rival Katherine Mansfield and his patroness Mabel Dodge Luhan — that has debilitated not only the white men but the Indian men and the traditionally dutiful Indian women. The moon, says one of Lawrence's noble savages, must be told that "*the wicked white woman can't harm you any more.*"

As we saw, Hughes noted that Plath's revision in "Johnny Panic" of Lawrence's fiction of female sacrifice leads directly to *The Bell Jar* and *Ariel*, a point that he seems to have intended as a comment on the exuberantly colloquial style of this early tale. But it is worth remembering that, like the narrator of "Johnny Panic" and the speaker of many of the *Ariel* poems, Esther Greenwood in *The Bell Jar* defines herself as a "wicked" — that is, a wickedly ambitious — woman, a woman who wants to "shoot off in all directions" herself instead of being the passive "place the arrows shoot off from."[21] Not surprisingly, then, Esther's emotional crisis is directly precipitated by a confrontation with male modernism (and ultimately, through it, male literary history) like the one to which "Johnny Panic" indirectly alludes. As you may recall, home for the summer and shut out of a creative writing course she hoped to take, this fashion magazine prize-winner plans to write her Honors Thesis on *Finnegans Wake*. But when she opens Joyce's *magnum opus* — a "thick book [which] made an unpleasant dent in my stomach" — Esther is overwhelmed by the horror of interpretation and, implicitly, by the horror of what she must interpret. "My eyes sank through an alphabet soup of letters to the long word in the middle of the page," she says, describing her encounter with the fatal fall of HCE. "Why should there be a hundred letters? . . . Haltingly I tried the word aloud. It sounded like a heavy wooden object falling downstairs." (102) Then, when she tries to read on, as in "The Wishing Box" the alphabet itself becomes alien and alarming: "The letters grew barbs and ram's horns [and] associated themselves in fantastic, untranslated shapes. . . ." (102) Finally, therefore, she decides to "junk" her thesis, the Honors program, and even (because it would require her to take a course in the eighteenth century) her college English major. For, says this surrogate self of the Cambridge student who claimed to have so much fun playing the part of Pope's Phoebe Clinkett, "I hated the very idea of the eighteenth century, with all those smug men writing tight little couplets, and being so dead keen on reason" (102).

Given the ferocious alphabet in which she seems to have felt ensnared, what way out could there have been for Plath? Certainly everything I have said so far about the literary battle of the sexes that she internalized as a war in her own mind would seem to have precluded her writing at all. Yet, as we know, write she did, and, as I have hardly had time to note, she wrote great poems. How? Why? I want in an attempt to come to some sort of conclusion to suggest that, for her, paradigms of poetic (if not personal) survival came from a woman novelist — Virginia Woolf — who did not herself personally survive, and, paradoxically, from one of the male poets — W. B. Yeats — whose awe of female power facilitated Plath's art even while, as we saw, his anger at female intellectual energy repressed and depressed her ambitions. As early as 1956, after all, Plath was telling her mother proudly that "all the scholarly boys [At Cambridge] think of me as a second Virginia Woolf" and not much later she confided that "I get courage by reading [Woolf's *Diary*]" because "I feel very akin to her" (*LH*, 230, 305). By the time she wrote her radio play, "Three Voices," in 1962—a text that, like "Johnny Panic," Hughes sees as a crucial transition work from *The Colossus* to *Ariel*—that kinship was manifesting itself in the very texture and tempo of Plath's verse as well as in its increasingly brilliant illumination of the complex "I am I" that constitutes human consciousness. Specifically, I would argue that the cadences of the three introspective women speakers in Plath's verse play evolved out of the cadences that define the voices of the three introspective women speakers whose lives Woolf explored in what she called her "play-poem," *The Waves*.[22] In addition, the prototypical female personalities Plath's three women represent seem significantly analogous to the female paradigms represented by Woolf's Susan, her Rhoda, and her Jinny, for the first voice, like Susan's, is that of a fiercely nurturing mother; the second, like Rhoda's, that of a woman who feels herself almost metaphysically "lacking" in appropriate femaleness; and the third, like Jinny's, that of a woman who wills herself to live seductively but without attachments.

Significantly, as I discovered after I began to speculate along these lines, Plath's copy of *The Waves*, now held by the Smith College Rare Book Room, is the most heavily underlined of all her books, with the exception of a few texts in which she took notes when she was a student. Even without such documentary evidence of influence, however, we can see, if we juxtapose a few sample passages from *The Waves* with some representative lines from "Three Voices," how the reveries of Plath's women are not only substantively but stylistically shaped by the meditations of Woolf's heroines, for both Woolf's and Plath's "dramatic soliloquys"—the phrase is Woolf's but applies equally well to Plath's verses—rely heavily on self-defining metaphors, on incantatory incremental repetition, and on interpolated rhetorical questions, to characterize their speakers. Comparing school (where she is) to home (where she wants to be), for example, Woolf's earth motherly Susan thinks that "something has grown in me . . . gradually I shall turn over the hard thing that has grown here in my side."[23] Similarly, Plath's first voice, as the speaker enters labor, thinks that "A power is growing in me, an old tenacity . . ." (53). Later, Susan declares that "I am the field, I am the barn" (242) and still later, become a mother, she defines her self as "spun to a fine thread round the cradle, wrapping in a cocoon made of my own blood the delicate limbs of my baby" (294). Similarly, Plath's first voice resolves to be "a wall and a roof protecting . . . a sky and a hill of good" (53) and, become a mother, she imagines herself as a "river of milk . . . a warm hill" (57). Guarding her children, Susan asks "Where can the shadow enter" (308), and similarly, resolving to guard, Plath's first voice wonders "How long can I be a wall keeping the wind off?" (60) The parallels between their lives and their words, their realities and their rhetoric, seem obvious.

In the same way, where Woolf's Susan and Plath's first voice are singleminded and even—as Woolf puts it—"fell" in their femaleness, Woolf's Rhoda and Plath's second voice are faint with the failure of identity, aching with emptiness. Rhoda imagines her defiance of life as "a thin dream

. . . a papery tree" (213), while the second voice—a secretary who has mis-carried—fears that "the streets may turn to paper suddenly" (64); Rhoda approaches a puddle and confesses that "I could not cross it. Identity failed me. We are nothing, I said, and fell" (219), while the second voice insists that "I am found wanting"; after the mythic Percival's demise in India, Rhoda broods on death, elaborating upon her male double Louis's assertion that "Death is woven in with the violets . . . Death and again death" (273), while the second voice, bleeding away her embryonic child, declares "This is a disease I carry home, this is a death. / Again, this is a death." (48)

To turn, finally, to Woolf's Jinny, a *femme fatale* who lives the purely passionate "life of the body," she is perhaps less akin to Plath's third voice than Susan is to the first and Rhoda to the second, but even between these last two figures there are significant resemblances. Jinny claims, for in-stance, that "I do not settle long anywhere; I do not attach myself to one person in particular" (296), while the third voice, a student who has given her illegitimate child up for adoption insists that "It is so beautiful to have no attachments! / I am solitary as grass" (62); again, Jinny sees "every blade of grass very clear" (206) and gives herself to "a tree . . . the river . . . after-noon" (351) while the third voice is haunted by "Hot noon in the meadows [where] the buttercups / Swelter and melt. . . ." (62) The options for women, say Woolf's novel and Plath's play in a kind of antiphonal chorus over time, are threefold: the qualified power of maternity, the absolute powerlessness of metaphysical consciousness, and the pseudo-power of se-ductive indifference. But when exploring those limited options, women can and should speak in a style marked by unlimited metaphorical energy, a style of liberated self-analysis that persistently and insistently explores the crucial "I am I" of female identity. The woman writer, or so Woolf taught Plath, may indeed be destined to "be classified and qualified" but she still has the imaginative power to articulate the tension between the self that "wants to be God" and the classifications which would constrain that self.

The explosion of *Ariel* is thus a breakthrough into further and even more powerful Woolfian self-analyses, a breakthrough accomplished when the poet remembers that "I have a self to recover, a queen." Not surprisingly, therefore, many of the *Ariel* poems continue to echo key passages from *The Waves*, including a few spoken by Woolf's male characters. Plath's confes-sion in "Tulips" that "I have no face. I have wanted to efface myself," for instance, recalls Rhoda's frightened, twice-repeated recognition that "I have no face" (203); Plath's "I think I am going up, / I think I may rise" in "Fever 103" echoes Rhoda's "I am above the earth now . . . I mount; I es-cape. . . ." (193); Plath's "I am dark-suited and still, a member of the party" in "Berck Plage" recalls Louis's "I become a figure in the procession, a spoke in the huge wheel" (198); Plath's "Now I break up in pieces that fly about like clubs" in "Elm" parallels Rhoda's "I am broken into separate pieces; I am no longer one" (248); Plath's "I / Am a pure acetylene / Virgin" echoes Rhoda's "I am unsealed, I am incandescent" (214); Plath's continual visions of smiling or sinister "hooks" recall Rhoda's "I feel myself grappled to one spot by these hooks [people] cast. . . ." (337); Plath's galloping words with their "indefatigable hoof-tapes" echoes Neville's "words and words and words, how they gallop. . . ." (232). Even the hard-won processes of composition through which both these women artists achieved such powerfully self-defining cadences are significantly similar, moreover. Woolf, who suspected she had "not yet mastered the speaking voice," rewrote *The Waves* by "reading much of it aloud, like poetry" (*WD*, 153) while, as Hughes reminds us, Plath began around the time she wrote "Three Voices" to "compose her poems more to be read aloud," and indeed to compose them, often, by reading aloud. The female voice, such a process of composition suggests, must not be silenced; it must and will be *heard*, even, in Plath's case, broadcast to an audience of thousands. Neither "Roget's trollop" nor the silent furtive transgressor of "Johnny Panic," the woman poet can speak out and up for herself.

Yet when Plath was speaking her last potent self analyses in that strong bitter late voice many of us have heard on records and tapes, she was speaking, of course, in and from Yeats' house. Given the censoriousness of the tradition this "beloved" poet must at least in part have represented for her, how, even with the help of Virginia Woolf, could she have achieved such acts of linguistic audacity? In answer to this question, I want finally to suggest that in the end Plath felt "Yeats's spirit blessing" her, as the apparition of Yeats blessed Dorothy Richardson's Miriam, because, despite his ambivalences, Yeats, among all the male modernists, had the most reverence for female power. Indeed, in plays like "Cathleen ni Houlihan" and "The Only Jealousy of Emer" and in sequences of "dramatic soliloquys" like "A Woman Young and Old" and the "Crazy Jane" poems, he himself tried to capture the unique inflections of the female voice, with its pride in sexuality, its ambivalence toward patriarchal authority, its impassioned assertion of identity, and its amused contempt for male pretensions. By dwelling on Yeats's writings, then, while literally dwelling in his house, Plath may have ultimately learned to resurrect rather than reject the subversive strength he predicted for the woman poet when he told Dorothy Wellesley to expect a visit from "that great family / Some ancient famous authors misrepresent, / The Proud Furies, each with her torch on high." Like Dorothy Wellesley, no "common" woman, Plath took on the revisionary role of such a Fury, rising ferocious as "God's lioness" from the earth in which those great and greatly misunderstood figures were shut up at the close of the *Oresteia*. In doing so with Yeats' implicit approval, moreover, she found a poetic father—a liberating male muse rather than an inhibiting male master—to match the poetic mother she had discovered in Virginia Woolf.

I am saying, in other words, that with what must have felt like the tacit encouragement of Yeats and Woolf, Plath gave herself up to *herself* and acknowledged her own ambition to be "a woman famous among women." To be sure, her engagement with such powerful precursors did at times involve her in a kind of Bloomian struggle for authority: not only did she boast (with some anxiety) that she was "younger than Yeats in [her] saying," she also claimed that she would find "images of life: like Woolf found. But . . . *I will be stronger*" (*J*, 165; ital. mine). Nevertheless, together these literary parents became not primarily antagonists but, rather, sacred facilitators; Plath felt Yeats' "spirit blessing" her and spoke with awe of Woolf's "blessed diary" (*J*, 152). Thus it was with what she perceived as the sacramental benedictions of Yeats and Woolf that she became the person she most feared and desired to be—most terribly, the lion-red queen with her wings of glass, the voraciously resurrected Lady Lazarus, the glamorously guilty murderess boasting that "If I've killed one man, I've killed two"; and most triumphantly, the fierce virgin whose fallen selves peel away from her as she ascends to a heaven of her own invention, shivering all creation with her purified "I am I, I am I." If her body could not sustain such a difficult flight out of "the mausoleum, the wax house" of a literary history that wanted to kill her, her spirit could and did, for she is, after all, resurrected every day as a crucial member of the visionary company who continue to inhabit the twentieth-century poetic tradition we might call "Yeats's house." Because (as her Pulitzer prize shows) she does victoriously inhabit that house; moreover, her unquiet ghost continues to haunt not just the women readers and writers who look to her words for strength but the male readers and writers who look at her work with mingled admiration and anxiety.

As the most peculiarly privileged of these readers, Ted Hughes—speaking in strikingly Plathian cadences in a poem called "Cadenza"—articulates the ambivalence all of them must feel, an ambivalence that may well explain the hostilities of critics like Denis Donoghue, Hugh Kenner, and David Holbrook:

> And I am the cargo
> Of a coffin attended by swallows.
>
> And I am the water
> Bearing the coffin that will not be silent.
> The clouds are full of surgery and collisions,
> But the coffin escapes—as a black diamond,
>
> A ruby brimming blood,
> An emerald bearing its shores.[24]

Even when she is dead, says Hughes' poem, this woman poet is irremediably alive: her coffin will not be silent; her voice has changed the field of our hearing forever. Past the "snow blitz," past the gas, past the cries of "Johnny Panic" and his armies of critics cursing the "poisoned chalice" of her poetry and the acclaim of disciples blessing her anguish, her coffin goes on singing its ambiguous messages to us—warning us to the perils of power even as it praises the possibilities of power. Half a century after her birth, we who are

Sylvia Plath's contemporaries and descendents must still listen to the questions she hammered out in such great pain: her askings are in the words of "Words." "Axes, / After whose stroke the wood rings," "indefatigable hooftaps" of a puzzled Pegasus let loose on a new road, prayers that "fixed stars" may not forever govern our lives.

Notes

In a slightly different form, this essay was first delivered as a keynote address at a conference on Women Writing Poetry in America that was held at Stanford University in April 1982; I am grateful to the organizers of the conference, especially to Marilyn Yalom and Diane Middlebrook, for advice and encouragement. In addition, I am grateful to Susan Gubar, to whose ideas I am indebted throughout the paper; ultimately, after much expansion, this piece will become a chapter in "No Man's Land: The Place of the Woman Writer in the Twentieth Century," a sequel to *The Madwoman in the Attic*, which Prof. Gubar and I are at present writing in collaboration.

†Epigraphs: All from Aurelia Schober Plath, ed., *Letters Home* by Sylvia Plath (New York: Harper, 1975); W. B. Yeats, *Collected Poems* (New York: Macmillan, 1955); Dorothy Richardson, *The Trap*, in *Pilgrimage*, Vol. II (New York: Knopf, 1938).__

1. James Woodress, ed., *American Literary Scholarship* 1979 (Durham: Duke, 1981).

2. *New York Times Book Review*, 22 November 1981, pp. 1, 30; David Holbrook, *Sylvia Plath: Poetry and Existence* (London: Athlone, 1976), p. 131; Hugh Kenner, "Sincerity Kills," in Gary Lane, ed., *Sylvia Plath: New Views on the Poetry* (Baltimore: Johns Hopkins, 1979), pp. 43, 44, 42; Marjorie Perloff, "Sylvia Plath's 'Sivvy' Poems: a portrait of the poet as daughter," in Lane, p. 173.

3. See Lane, "Influence and originality in Plath's poems," in Lane, *op. cit.*; Margaret Dickie Uroff, *Sylvia Plath and Ted Hughes* (Urbana: Illinois, 1979); Perloff, *op. cit.*

4. *The Letters of Elizabeth Barrett Browning*, ed. Frederick G. Kenyon (2 vols. in 1, New York: Macmillan, 1899), I, 230–32; Thomas Johnson, ed., *The Complete Poems of Emily Dickinson* (Boston: Little, Brown, 1960), #613.

5. *A Room of One's Own* (New York: Harcourt, 1928), p. 68. Further citations will be included in the text.

6. *The Death of the Moth* (New York: Harcourt, 1942), p. 235.

7. *The Colossus* (New York: Vintage, 1968).

8. Sylvia Plath, *Johnny Panic and the Bible of Dreams: Short Stories, Prose, and Diary Excerpts* (New York: Harper, 1980), p. 21. Further citations will be included in the text.

9. *The Journals of Sylvia Plath*, ed. Ted Hughes and Frances McCullough (New York: Dial, 1982), p. 168. Further citations will be included in the text.

10. Lois Ames, "Notes Toward a Biography," in Charles Newman, ed., *The Art of Sylvia Plath* (Bloomington: Indiana, 1971), p. 166.

11. All in *Ariel* (New York: Harper, 1966) except "Purdah," which is in *Winter Trees* (New York: Harper, 1972).

12. See Yeats, "To Dorothy Wellesley," "No Second Troy," "Nineteen Hundred and Nineteen," all in *CP*.

13. See Richard Ellmann, *James Joyce* (New York: Oxford, 1959), pp. 487 and 510.

14. See Hemingway, "The Lady Poets With Footnotes," in *88 Poems*, ed. Nicholas Gerogiannis (New York: Harcourt, 1979), p. 77; West, *Miss Lonelyhearts* (New York: New Directions, 1946), p. 14; *The Selected Poems of Ezra Pound* (New York: New Directions, 1957), pp. 16–17.

15. See "On a Political Prisoner," "In Memory of Eva Gore-Booth and Con Markiewicz," "On Woman," and "A Prayer for My Daughter," all in *CP.*

16. Katherine M. Rogers, ed., *The Selected Poems of Anne Finch, Countess of Winchilsea* (New York: Ungar, 1979), p. 82.

17. *Ibid.*, p. 7.

18. Quoted in Aurelia Plath, Introduction, *Letters Home*, pp. 32–33.

19. Adrienne Rich, "Power," in *The Dream of a Common Language* (New York: Norton, 1978), p. 3.

20. *The Complete Short Stories of D. H. Lawrence*, vol. II (New York: Viking, 1961), p. 581. Further citations will be included in the text.

21. *The Bell Jar* (New York: Bantam, 1972), p. 68. Further citations will be included in the text.

22. Woolf, *A Writer's Diary*, ed. Leonard Woolf (New York: Harcourt, 1953), pp. 107, 134. All references to "Three Voices" are to the poem as printed in *Winter Trees*, and further citations will be included in the text.

23. Virginia Woolf, *The Waves* (New York: Harcourt, 1931) in Woolf, *Jacob's Room and the Waves* (New York: Harvest, 1959), pp. 211–12; further citations will be included in the text. I am grateful to Ruth Mortimer of the Smith College Rare Book Room for facilitating my work with the collection there.

24. Ted Hughes, *Selected Poems* (New York: Harper, 1972), p. 58.

INDEX